GREAT MINDS® WIT & WISDOM

Grade 1 Module 1:
A World of Books

Teacher Edition

COPYRIGHT STATEMENT

Published by Great Minds®

Copyright © 2016 Great Minds®. All rights reserved. No part of this work may be reproduced or used in any form or by any means—graphic, electronic, or mechanical, including photocopying or information storage and retrieval systems—without written permission from the copyright holder.

ISBN: 978-1-63255-949-4

2 3 4 5 6 7 8 9 10   CCR   24 23 22 21

Table of Contents

MODULE OVERVIEW

Module Summary **2**

Module at a Glance **3**

Texts **3**

Module Learning Goals **4**

Module in Context **5**

Standards **6**

Major Assessments **7**

Module Map **10**

INSTRUCTIONAL LESSONS

Focusing Question: Lessons 1–6

How do library books change life for Tomás?

Lesson 1 .... **17**

- TEXTS: *Tomás and the Library Lady*, Pat Mora, Raul Colón • *Museum ABC*, The Metropolitan Museum of Art
  - Style and Conventions Deep Dive: Common Nouns

Lesson 2 .... **29**

- TEXTS: *Tomás and the Library Lady*, Pat Mora, Raul Colón • *Museum ABC*, The Metropolitan Museum of Art
  - Vocabulary Deep Dive: Ask and Answer Questions About Vocabulary

Lesson 3 .... **41**

- TEXTS: *Tomás and the Library Lady*, Pat Mora, Raul Colón • *Museum ABC*, The Metropolitan Museum of Art
  - Style and Conventions Deep Dive: Finding Common Nouns

Lesson 4 .... **53**

- TEXTS: *Tomás and the Library Lady*, Pat Mora, Raul Colón • *Museum ABC*, The Metropolitan Museum of Art
  - Style and Conventions Deep Dive: Finding Proper Nouns

Lesson 5 .... **67**

- TEXT: *Tomás and the Library Lady*, Pat Mora, Raul Colón
  - Vocabulary Deep Dive: Frayer Model for *Value*

Lesson 6 .... **77**

- TEXT: *Tomás and the Library Lady*, Pat Mora, Raul Colón
  - Vocabulary Deep Dive: Frayer Model for *Value*

iii

Focusing Question: Lessons 7–12

How does the Biblioburro change life for Ana?

Lesson 7... 91
- TEXT: *Waiting for the Biblioburro*, Monica Brown, John Parra
  - Style and Conventions Deep Dive: Finding Verbs

Lesson 8... 103
- TEXTS: *Waiting for the Biblioburro*, Monica Brown, John Parra • *Museum ABC*, The Metropolitan Museum of Art
  - Vocabulary Deep Dive: Ask and Answer Questions About Vocabulary

Lesson 9..115
- TEXT: *Waiting for the Biblioburro*, Monica Brown, John Parra
  - Style and Conventions Deep Dive: Verbs in the Past

Lesson 10... 127
- TEXT: *Waiting for the Biblioburro*, Monica Brown, John Parra
  - Vocabulary Deep Dive: Adding the Inflectional Ending –*ing* to Root Words

Lesson 11... 137
- TEXT: *Waiting for the Biblioburro*, Monica Brown, John Parra
  - Vocabulary Deep Dive: Frayer Model for *Inspire*

Lesson 12... 149
- TEXTS: CNN Heroes: Luis Soriano • *Waiting for the Biblioburro*, Monica Brown, John Parra
  - Vocabulary Deep Dive: Adding the Inflectional Ending –*ing* to Root Words

Focusing Question: Lessons 13–16

How do people around the world get books?

Lesson 13..161
- TEXTS: *My Librarian Is a Camel*, Margriet Ruurs • *Museum ABC*, The Metropolitan Museum of Art
  - Style and Conventions Deep Dive: Declarative Sentences

Lesson 14... 175
- TEXT: *My Librarian Is a Camel*, Margriet Ruurs
  - Vocabulary Deep Dive: Frayer Model for *Remote*

Lesson 15... 187
- TEXT: *My Librarian Is a Camel*, Margriet Ruurs
  - Vocabulary Deep Dive: Frayer Model for *Mobile*

Lesson 16... 197
- TEXT: *My Librarian Is a Camel*, Margriet Ruurs
  - Vocabulary Deep Dive: Direct Vocabulary Assessment

WIT & WISDOM™   G1 > Module 1

Focusing Question: Lessons 17–22

How does the packhorse librarian change life for Cal?

Lesson 17..**207**

- TEXTS: *That Book Woman*, Heather Henson, David Small • *Museum ABC*, The Metropolitan Museum of Art
  - Style and Conventions Deep Dive: Understanding Adjectives

Lesson 18..**219**

- TEXT: *That Book Woman*, Heather Henson, David Small
  - Style and Conventions Deep Dive: Declarative Sentences

Lesson 19..**231**

- TEXT: *That Book Woman*, Heather Henson, David Small
  - Vocabulary Deep Dive: Frayer Model for *Scholar*

Lesson 20..**241**

- TEXT: *That Book Woman*, Heather Henson, David Small
  - Style and Conventions Deep Dive: Adjectives Are Feeling Words

Lesson 21..**251**

- TEXTS: *That Book Woman*, Heather Henson, David Small • Pack Horse Librarians
  - Vocabulary Deep Dive: Multiple Meaning Words

Lesson 22..**263**

- TEXT: *That Book Woman*, Heather Henson, David Small
  - Style and Conventions Deep Dive: Adjectives Are Picture Words

Focusing Question: Lessons 23–27

How do books change my life?

Lesson 23..**273**

- TEXTS: *Museum ABC*, The Metropolitan Museum of Art • *Green Eggs and Ham*, Dr. Seuss
  - Style and Conventions Deep Dive: Interrogative Sentences

Lesson 24..**287**

- TEXTS: *Green Eggs and Ham*, Dr. Seuss • *Museum ABC*, The Metropolitan Museum of Art
  - Vocabulary Deep Dive: Words Around Text

Lesson 25..**301**

- TEXT: *Green Eggs and Ham*, Dr. Seuss
  - Style and Conventions Deep Dive: Imperative Sentences

Lesson 26..**313**

- TEXT: *Green Eggs and Ham*, Dr. Seuss
  - Style and Conventions Deep Dive: Time Order Words

Lesson 27..**323**

- TEXTS: *Green Eggs and Ham*, Dr. Seuss • *Museum ABC*, The Metropolitan Museum of Art
  - Style and Conventions Deep Dive: Excel at Sequencing Events

v

Copyright © 2016 Great Minds®

Focusing Question: Lessons 28–32

How do books change lives around the world?

Lesson 28.. **333**

- TEXTS: *My Librarian Is a Camel*, Margriet Ruurs • *Museum ABC*, The Metropolitan Museum of Art
  - Vocabulary Deep Dive: Direct Vocabulary Assessment

Lesson 29.. **345**

- TEXTS: All module texts
  - Style and Conventions Deep Dive: Editing and Revising Sentences

Lesson 30.. **355**

- TEXTS: All module texts
  - Style and Conventions Deep Dive: Editing and Revising Sentences

Lesson 31.. **363**

- TEXTS: All module texts
  - Style and Conventions Deep Dive: Editing and Revising Sentences

Lesson 32.. **371**

- TEXTS: All module texts

Appendices

Appendix A: Text Complexity... **379**

Appendix B: Vocabulary... **383**

Appendix C: Answer Keys, Rubrics, and Sample Responses................................. **389**

Appendix D: Volume of Reading.. **405**

Appendix E: Works Cited.. **407**

WIT & WISDOM™   G1 > Module 1

Teacher Edition

GRADE 1, MODULE 1

A World of Books

Copyright © 2016 Great Minds®

Module Summary

To read a book for the first time is to make an acquaintance with a new friend; to read it for a second time is to meet an old one.

—Chinese proverb

A *World of Books* harnesses Grade 1 students' inherent desire to read and learn. Through inspiring texts, students journey to new places, meeting diverse characters whose lives change positively and irrevocably because of books. With each new text, students construct more knowledge and collect more evidence about how and why children everywhere read in order to answer the Essential Question: *How do books change lives around the world?*

The module begins with an exploration of museum masterpieces through the lens of the alphabet in *Museum ABC*. These beautifully curated works of fine art offer students a rich opportunity to engage with an accessible text with increasing depth, mining the works of art for details and understanding. All the texts that follow paint a picture of the joy and power that books bring to children everywhere. The three narrative picture books, *Tomás and the Library Lady* (based on the experiences of a Mexican boy from a migrant family), *Waiting for the Biblioburro* (based on the experiences of Ana, a Colombian girl from a rural village), and *That Book Woman* (based on the stories of packhorse librarians in rural Applachia) show, in exquisite detail, how books transform each character's life. In *My Librarian Is a Camel*, students discover a world of ways that children access books and the heroic efforts of those who dedicate their lives to bringing the joy of reading to all. With the final book, *Green Eggs and Ham*, students experience the power of books for themselves as they delight in how this timeless classic with an inspiring message can impact their lives.

Students then share their knowledge and joy through the End-of-Module (EOM) Task: an original narrative story about a character that is changed in some way by books. Each student designs a cover page for this narrative inspired by *Museum ABC*, showing four characters reading joyfully—B is for Books! With this new perspective, the instruction that students encounter in subsequent modules and years of study will be richer because of their enduring understanding about the power of a book.

Module at a Glance

ESSENTIAL QUESTION

How do books change lives around the world?

SUGGESTED STUDENT UNDERSTANDINGS

- Reading books helps people everywhere build knowledge.
- Stories have messages that can change the way people think and feel.
- People all over the world enjoy books, though people living in different places get books in different ways.
- Some people, including all kinds of librarians from around the world, dedicate their lives to making sure others have access to books.
- Reading changes lives by helping people imagine things they haven't experienced.

Texts

CORE TEXTS

Picture Books, Literary

- *Tomás and the Library Lady*, Pat Mora and Raul Colón
- *Waiting for the Biblioburro*, Monica Brown and John Parra
- *That Book Woman*, Heather Henson and David Small
- *Green Eggs and Ham*, Dr. Seuss

Picture Books, Informational

- *Museum ABC*, The Metropolitan Museum of Art
- *My Librarian Is a Camel*, Margriet Ruurs

G1 > Module 1 WIT & WISDOM™

SUPPLEMENTARY TEXTS

Video

- "*CNN Heroes: Luis Soriano*," CNN
- "*Pack Horse Librarians*," SLIS Storytelling

Module Learning Goals

KNOWLEDGE GOALS

- Describe how books can change the lives of people around the world.
- Identify and describe how people in different places get books.
- Appreciate the people that dedicate their lives to helping others access books.
- Identify and explain the elements of a story and how those elements contribute to the joy of reading.

READING GOALS

- Ask and answer questions about key details in literary texts and informational texts on books and reading. (RL.1.1, RI.1.1)
- Retell and describe stories through the lenses of character, setting, and major events, using key details. (RL.1.2, RL.1.3)
- Use illustrations and details in a text to describe its key ideas. (RL.1.7)

WRITING GOALS

- Write short narrative summaries with increasing independence, using key details from stories. (W.1.3)
- Write an original narrative about how books changed the life of a character that recounts appropriately sequenced events with some detail. (W.1.3)
- Strengthen writing by adding details in response to questions and suggestions from teachers and peers. (W.1.5)

SPEAKING AND LISTENING GOALS

- Respond to what others say by listening carefully and building on their thoughts in collaborative conversations. (SL.1.1.b)
- Notice pauses in conversations, and use them to decide when to speak and when to listen. (SL.1.1.a)

4

Copyright © 2016 Great Minds®

LANGUAGE GOALS

- Produce and expand complete sentences including ending punctuation. (L.1.2.b)

- Use frequently occurring nouns and adjectives in speaking and writing. (L.1.1.c, L.1.1.f)

- Determine the meanings and deepen understanding of unknown words and phrases encountered in module texts. (L.1.4)

Module in Context

- **Knowledge:** No knowledge is more essential or foundational to a thoughtful English Language Arts (ELA) curriculum than the knowledge of what books can do to change lives. Module 1 launches this exploration with compelling stories about children who value reading and how this experience with books changes each of their lives. While students delight in the stories, they also build awareness of how books are universal and that literacy advocates like librarians dedicate their lives to making sure that people everywhere have access to books and knowledge. This understanding will serve students well as they themselves work hard to build their literacy skills and content knowledge, using books to change their own lives.

- **Reading:** In this first module of Grade 1, students slowly build their understanding of each of the Content Framing Questions as they use them to deepen their understanding of complex texts. Because few of the texts are independently accessible in this module, students focus strongly on asking and answering questions about both literary and informational texts, using illustrations and photographs as an important and accessible vehicle for understanding the texts more deeply. This deep questioning work, along with describing details of characters, settings, and events, drives their ability to recount stories in sequence and ultimately compose a structured narrative of their own during the EOM Task.

- **Writing:** In this first module of Grade 1, students build their understanding of literary texts alongside the skills they need to execute their own retellings of the stories. Through this work of using Sentence Frames for structure, practicing conventions that help them create complete sentences, and sequencing events, they amass the skills they need to structure and begin to develop narrative writing. In their EOM original narrative, students apply what they have learned through the sequenced retelling of stories to compose a narrative about how a character's life is changed by books, set in one of the countries from *My Librarian Is a Camel*.

- **Speaking and Listening:** Students begin the year focusing on the give and take of collaborative conversations, learning rules for discussions and how to listen with care and attention. They practice and apply these skills in responding to what others say and listening for pauses through diverse speaking and listening opportunities, including oral retellings of module stories, oral rehearsal for writing, and, more formally, Socratic Seminars.

Standards

FOCUS STANDARDS

Reading Literature	
RL.1.1	Ask and answer questions about key details in a text.
RL.1.2	Retell stories, including key details, and demonstrate understanding of their central message or lesson.
RL.1.3	Describe characters, settings, and major events in a story, using key details.
Reading Informational Text	
RI.1.1	Ask and answer questions about key details in a text.
RI.1.7	Use the illustrations and details in a text to describe its key ideas.
Writing	
W.1.3	Write narratives in which they recount two or more appropriately sequenced events, include some details regarding what happened, use temporal words to signal event order, and provide some sense of closure.
W.1.5	With guidance and support from adults, focus on a topic, respond to questions and suggestions from peers, and add details to strengthen writing as needed.
Speaking and Listening	
SL.1.1.a	Follow agreed-upon rules for discussions (e.g., listening to others with care, speaking one at a time about the topics and texts under discussion).
SL.1.1.b	Build on other's talk in conversations by responding to the comments of others through multiple exchanges.
Language	
L.1.1.b	Use common, proper, and possessive nouns.
L.1.1.f	Use frequently occurring adjectives.
L.1.1.j	Produce and expand complete simple and compound declarative, interrogative, imperative, and exclamatory sentences in response to prompts.
L.1.2.b	Use end punctuation for sentences.

WIT & WISDOM™   G1 > Module 1

CONTINUING STANDARDS

Reading Literature	
RL.1.10	With prompting and support, read prose and poetry of appropriate complexity for Grade 1.
Reading Informational Text	
RI.1.10	With prompting and support, read informational texts with appropriate complexity for Grade 1.
Language	
L.1.6	Use words and phrases acquired through conversations, reading and being read to, and responding to texts, including using frequently occurring conjunctions to signal simple relationships (e.g., *because*).

Major Assessments

Focusing Question Task	Elements that Support Success on EOM Task	Standards
1. Write and draw to retell the story of *Tomás and the Library Lady*, including character, setting, and problem/resolution.	■ Identify character, setting, and problem/ resolution in a narrative. ■ Use Sentence Frames to structure writing.	RL.1.2, RL.1.3, W.1.3, W.1.8, SL.1.1.a
2. Write and draw to retell the story *Waiting for the Biblioburro*, including character, setting, and problem/resolution. Use complete sentences and end punctuation.	■ Use understanding of character, setting, and problem/resolution to retell a story. ■ Apply knowledge of complete sentences with end punctuation to writing.	RL.1.2, RL.1.3, W.1.3, W.1.8, SL.1.1.a, L.1.1.j, L.1.2.b
3. Describe how people get books in your section of *My Librarian Is a Camel* by answering the question: "Using evidence from the photographs, how do people in this country get books?" Be sure to: ■ Include details from the photographs. ■ Write complete sentences. ■ Capitalize proper nouns. ■ Use end punctuation.	■ Include examples about the ways that children around the world borrow books to their original narrative essay. ■ Apply knowledge of complete sentences with end punctuation to writing. ■ Apply knowledge of capitalization of proper nouns to writing.	RI.1.1, RI.1.7, W.1.8, SL.1.1.a, SL.1.2, L.1.1.b, L.1.1.j, L.1.2.b

7

Copyright © 2016 Great Minds®

4. Write and draw to retell the story *That Book Woman*. Be sure to include: - Characters - Setting - Problem - Resolution - Complete sentences. - End punctuation. - A drawing of Cal and one adjective to describe him.	- Use understanding of character, setting, and problem/resolution to retell a story. - Apply knowledge of complete sentences with end punctuation to writing.	RL.1.2, RL.1.3, W.1.3, W.1.8, SL.1.1.a, L.1.1.b, L.1.1.f, L.1.1.j, L.1.2.b
5. Write and draw to retell the story *Green Eggs and Ham*, including characters, setting, and problem/resolution. Also apply the following skills in context: - Use time order words. - Use complete sentences. - Capitalize letters at the beginning of a sentence and proper nouns. - Use end punctuation. - Use an adjective to describe a noun.	- Applying the same craft strategies that they will use in their original narrative gives students an opportunity to practice them and receive feedback. - Writing this task without scaffolds builds students' independence.	RL.1.2, RL.1.3, W.1.3, W.1.8, SL.1.1.a, L.1.1.b, L.1.1.f, L.1.1.j, L.1.2.b

New-Read Assessment	Elements that Support Success on EOM Task	Standards
1. **Text:** *Waiting for the Biblioburro*, Monica Brown Write and draw to formulate a question. After the Read Aloud, write and draw to answer the question.	- Deepens understanding that people in remote areas lack access to books and get books in unconventional ways.	RL.1.1, L.1.1.j, L.1.2.b
2. **Text:** *My Librarian Is a Camel*, Margriet Ruurs Visually explore photographs and illustrations to write and draw to formulate a question.	- Expands and deepens understanding of content directly related to the topic of students' original narrative. - Apply knowledge of complete sentences with end punctuation to writing.	RI.1.1, L.1.1.j, L.1.2.b
3. **Text:** *Green Eggs and Ham*, Dr. Seuss Write and draw to fill in a Story Map after a Read Aloud with support from Story Stones.	- Demonstrates understanding of story elements in a narrative. - Apply knowledge of complete sentences with end punctuation to writing.	RL.1.2, RL.1.7, W.1.8, L.1.1.b, L.1.1.j, L.1.2.b

Socratic Seminars	Elements that Support Success on EOM Task	Standards
1. Respond to what others say in a Socratic Seminar on the Focusing Question: "How does the packhorse librarian change life for Cal?"	<ul><li>Demonstrate an understanding of how books change the lives of characters.</li><li>Recognize the importance of getting books in remote locations.</li></ul>	SL.1.1.a, SL.1.1.b
2. Respond to what others say in a Socratic Seminar on the Focusing Question: "How can books change my life?"	<ul><li>Demonstrate an understanding that books can change their life.</li><li>Recognize that books are read for enjoyment and learning.</li></ul>	SL.1.1.a, SL.1.1.b
3. Respond to what others say in a Socratic Seminar on the Essential Question: "How do books change lives around the world?"	<ul><li>Demonstrate an understanding that books change people's lives around the world.</li><li>Recognize that people value the opportunity to read books.</li></ul>	SL.1.1.a, SL.1.1.b

End-of-Module Task	Criteria for Success	Standards
Write and illustrate a narrative about a character whose life has changed because of books. Be sure to include:<ul><li>Characters.</li><li>Setting from *My Librarian Is a Camel*.</li><li>A problem (the character doesn't have books).</li><li>The resolution to the problem (using the method for getting books from that country).</li></ul>Make sure each page includes:<ul><li>Complete sentences that begin with a capital letter and end with a punctuation mark.</li><li>Capitals at the beginning of proper nouns (names and countries).</li><li>Illustrations to match the words on each page.</li></ul>	<ul><li>Demonstrate an understanding of story elements.</li><li>Use complete sentences.</li><li>Use end punctuation.</li><li>Capitalize the first word in a sentence and proper nouns.</li></ul>	RL.1.2, RL.1.3, W.1.3, W.1.8, SL.1.1.a, L.1.1.b, L.1.1.j, L.1.2.b

G1 > Module 1   WIT & WISDOM™

Module Map

Focusing Question 1: How do library books change life for Tomás?				
Lesson	**Text(s)**	**Content Framing Question**	**Craft Question(s)**	**Learning Goals**
1	*Tomás and the Library Lady*, *Museum ABC*	Wonder What do I notice and wonder about *Tomás and the Library Lady*?		Generate and answer questions about *Tomás and the Library Lady*, using key details from the text. (RL.1.1, RL.1.7) Identify and generate common nouns. (L.1.1.b)
2	*Tomás and the Library Lady*, *Museum ABC*	Organize What's happening in *Tomás and the Library Lady*?	Examine Why is it important to use Sentence Frames in speaking and writing?	Retell *Tomás and the Library Lady*, including key details about characters. (RL.1.2) Ask and answer questions about key vocabulary in *Tomás and the Library Lady*. (L.1.6)
3	*Tomás and the Library Lady*, *Museum ABC*	Organize What's happening in *Tomás and the Library Lady*?	Experiment How does using Sentence Frames in speaking and writing work?	Retell *Tomás and the Library Lady*, including key details about setting. (RL.1.2) Identify and generate common nouns. (L.1.1.b)
4	*Tomás and the Library Lady*, *Museum ABC*	Organize What's happening in *Tomás and the Library Lady*?	Execute How do I use Sentence Frames in speaking and writing?	Retell *Tomás and the Library Lady*, including key details about problem and resolution. (RL.1.2) Write a narrative retelling of *Tomás and the Library Lady* that shows how library books change life for Tomás. (RL.1.2, RL.1.3, W.1.3 W.1.8, L.1.2.b, SL.1.1.a) Identify and generate proper nouns. (L.1.1.b)
5	*Tomás and the Library Lady*	Reveal What does a deeper exploration of the main character reveal in *Tomás and the Library Lady*?	Execute How do I use Sentence Frames in speaking and writing?	Distinguish between what Tomás imagines and what is real in *Tomás and the Library Lady*. (RL.1.3) Compose a narrative retelling using Sentence Frames for structure. (W.1.3) Develop vocabulary knowledge of the word *value*. (L.1.6)

Copyright © 2016 Great Minds®

| 6 | *Tomás and the Library Lady* | Know

How does *Tomás and the Library Lady* build our knowledge of how books change lives? | Excel

How do I improve using Sentence Frames in my writing? | Write and speak about how *Tomás and the Library Lady* adds to knowledge of how books change lives.

Revise a narrative retelling for correct usage of Sentence Frames. (W.1.5)

Develop vocabulary knowledge of the word *value*. (L.1.6) |

Focusing Question 2: How does the Biblioburro change life for Ana?

Lesson	Text(s)	Content Framing Question	Craft Question(s)	Learning Goals
7	*Waiting for the Biblioburro*	Wonder What do I notice and wonder about *Waiting for the Biblioburro*?	Experiment How does reading fluently work?	Generate and answer questions about *Waiting for the Biblioburro*, using key details from the text. (RL.1.1) Identify and generate verbs. (L.1.1.e)
8	*Waiting for the Biblioburro, Museum ABC*	Organize What is happening in *Waiting for the Biblioburro*?		Retell *Waiting for the Biblioburro*, including key details about characters, settings, and major events. (RL.1.3) Ask and answer questions about key vocabulary in *Waiting for the Biblioburro*. (L.1.6)
9	*Waiting for the Biblioburro*	Organize What is happening in *Waiting for the Biblioburro*?	Examine Why is writing complete sentences important?	Retell *Waiting for the Biblioburro*, including key details about characters, settings, and major events. (RL.1.3, RL.1.7) Identify and generate verbs. (L.1.1.e)
10	*Waiting for the Biblioburro*	Reveal What does a deeper exploration of the main character reveal in *Waiting for the Biblioburro*?	Experiment How does writing complete sentences work?	Analyze the main character's dreams using key details in *Waiting for the Biblioburro*. (RL.1.1, RL.1.3) Draft a simple sentence with support. Develop vocabulary knowledge of the word *inspire*. (L.1.6)
11	*Waiting for the Biblioburro*	Know How does *Waiting for the Biblioburro* build my knowledge?	Execute How does writing complete sentences work in writing?	Write a narrative retelling of *Waiting for the Biblioburro* that shows how the Biblioburro changes life for Ana. (RL.1.2, RL.1.3, W.1.3, W.1.8, L.1.1.j, L.1.2.b, SL.1.1.a) Develop vocabulary knowledge of the word *inspire*. (L.1.6)

12	*Waiting for the Biblioburro*	**Know** How does *Waiting for the Biblioburro* build my knowledge?	**Excel** How do I improve my writing by using complete sentences?	Write and speak about how *Waiting for the Biblioburro* adds to knowledge of how books change lives. Edit a narrative retelling paragraph for use of complete sentences. Identify root words and the inflectional ending *-ing*. (L.1.1.e, L.1.4.c)
Focusing Question 3: How do people around the world get books?				
13	*My Librarian Is a Camel, Museum ABC*	**Wonder** What do I notice and wonder about *My Librarian Is a Camel*?		Generate questions about *My Librarian Is a Camel* using key details from the text. (RI.1.1) Create a complete declarative sentence. (L.1.1.j)
14	*My Librarian Is a Camel*	**Organize** What is happening in *My Librarian Is a Camel*?	**Examine** Why are proper nouns important?	Ask and answer questions to help determine or clarify the meaning of words and phrases in *My Librarian Is a Camel*. (RI.1.4) Develop vocabulary knowledge of the word *remote*. (L.1.6)
15	*My Librarian Is a Camel*	**Reveal** What does a deeper exploration of pictures and captions reveal in *My Librarian Is a Camel*?	**Experiment** How do proper nouns work?	Identify how pictures and captions communicate key details in *My Librarian Is a Camel*. (RI.1.7) Develop vocabulary knowledge of the word *mobile*. (L.1.6)
16	*My Librarian Is a Camel*	**Reveal** What does a deeper exploration of quotations reveal in *My Librarian Is a Camel*?	**Execute and Excel** How do I use proper nouns in my writing?	Write, speak, and illustrate how people in different countries borrow books. (RI.1.2, RI.1.7, W.1.2, W.1.8, SL.1.1.a, L.1.1.b, L.1.1.j, L.1.2.b) Demonstrate understanding of grade-level vocabulary. (L.1.6)
Focusing Question 4: How does the packhorse librarian change life for Cal?				
17	*That Book Woman, Museum ABC*	**Wonder** What do I notice and wonder about *That Book Woman*?		Generate and answer questions about *That Book Woman* using key details from the text. (RL.1.1) Generate a variety of adjectives. (L.1.1.f)

18	*That Book Woman*	Organize What is happening in *That Book Woman*?	Examine Why is responding to what others say important?	Retell *That Book Woman*, including key details about characters, settings, and major events. (RL.1.3) Define multiple meanings for words *poke* and *spell*. (L.1.6)
19	*That Book Woman*	Reveal What does a deeper exploration of the main character's feelings reveal in *That Book Woman*?	Experiment How does responding to what others say work?	Analyze the main character's feelings using key details in *That Book Woman*. (RL.1.1, RL.1.7, SL.1.1.f) Develop vocabulary knowledge of the word *scholar*. (L.1.6)
20	*That Book Woman*	Reveal What does a deeper exploration of the main character's feelings reveal in *That Book Woman*?	Examine What is informal language?	Analyze characters using key details in *That Book Woman*. (RL.1.3, RL.1.7) Generate a variety of adjectives. (L.1.1.f)
21	*That Book Woman*	Know How does *That Book Woman* build our knowledge of how books can change lives?	Execute How do I use adjectives in my writing?	Write a narrative retelling of *That Book Woman* that shows how the packhorse librarian changes life for Cal. (RL.1.2, RL.1.3, W.1.3, W.1.8, SL.1.1.a, L.1.1.b, L.1.1.f, L.1.1.j, L.1.2.b) Respond to others and describe the connections among multiple pieces of information about packhorse librarians and cite specific details and key ideas from *That Book Woman* in a Socratic Seminar. (RL.1.3, RI.1.3, SL.1.1.a, SL.1.1.b) Define multiple meanings for words *signs* and *duck*. (L.1.6)
22	*That Book Woman*	Know How does *That Book Woman* build our knowledge of how books can change lives?	Execute How do I improve using adjectives in my writing?	Write and speak about how *That Book Woman* adds to knowledge of how books change lives. Use frequently occurring adjectives to describe visual images. (L.1.1.f)

G1 > Module 1

Focusing Question 5: How can books change my life?				
23	*Green Eggs and Ham, Museum ABC*	<u>Wonder</u> What do I notice and wonder about *Green Eggs and Ham*?		Generate and answer questions about *Green Eggs and Ham* using key details from the text. (RL.1.1) Identify story elements in *Green Eggs and Ham*. (RL.1.2, RL.1.3, RL.1.7, W.1.8, L.1.1.b, L.1.1.f, L.1.1.j, L.2.b)
24	*Green Eggs and Ham, Museum ABC*	<u>Organize</u> What is happening in *Green Eggs and Ham*?	<u>Examine</u> Why is retelling events in sequence important?	Retell *Green Eggs and Ham*, including details about characters, settings, and major events. (RL.1.3) Use sentence-level context as a clue to the meaning of the words *portrait*, *landscape*, and *still life*. (L.1.6)
25	*Green Eggs and Ham, Museum ABC*	<u>Reveal</u> What does a deeper exploration of which character is speaking reveal in *Green Eggs and Ham*?	<u>Experiment</u> How does sequencing events work?	Identify who is telling the story at key points in *Green Eggs and Ham*. (RL.1.3, RL.1.6) Recognize and define imperative sentences. (L.1.1.j)
26	*Green Eggs and Ham*	<u>Distill</u> What is the central message of *Green Eggs and Ham*?	<u>Execute</u> How do I sequence events in writing?	Sequence events in a written narrative summary of *Green Eggs and Ham*. (W.1.3) Determine the central message of *Green Eggs and Ham*. (RL.1.2) Identify temporal words and their use in writing. (L.1.1.i)
27	*Green Eggs and Ham*	<u>Know</u> How can books build my knowledge?	<u>Excel</u> How do I improve sequencing events in my writing?	Respond to what others say in a Socratic Seminar about how books can change your lives. (SL.1.1.a, SL.1.1.b) Identify temporal words in writing, and edit writing for temporal words. (L.1.1.i)

Essential Question: How do books change lives around the world?				
28	*Green Eggs and Ham, Museum ABC*	Distill What is important about *Museum ABC*?	Examine and Experiment Why is using story elements to write a narrative important?	Plan for giving and receiving useful peer feedback on writing. (W.1.5) Demonstrate understanding of grade-level vocabulary. (L.1.6)
29	*Tomás and the Library Lady, Waiting for the Biblioburro, My Librarian Is a Camel, That Book Woman, Green Eggs and Ham, Museum ABC*	Know How does *My Librarian Is a Camel* build my knowledge?	Execute How do I use story elements in a narrative?	Students express understanding of story elements by writing the setting and character for the first sentence in the EOM Task. (RL.1.2, RL.1.3, W.1.3, W.1.8, SL.1.1.a, L.1.1.b, L.1.1.j, L.1.2.b) Make connections between *My Librarian Is a Camel* and other module texts. Edit sentences created in response to a prompt. (L.1.1.b, L.1.1.j, L.1.2.a, L.1.2.b)
30	*Tomás and the Library Lady, Waiting for the Biblioburro, My Librarian Is a Camel, That Book Woman, Green Eggs and Ham, Museum ABC*	Know How do all the Module 1 texts build our knowledge of how books can change lives around the world?	Execute How do I use story elements in a narrative?	Write a sequenced event in a narrative. (W.1.3, W.1.8) Edit and revise sentences created in response to a prompt. (L.1.1.j, W.1.5)
31	*Tomás and the Library Lady, Waiting for the Biblioburro, My Librarian Is a Camel, That Book Woman, Green Eggs and Ham, Museum ABC*	Know How do all the Module 1 texts build our knowledge of how books can change lives around the world?	Execute How do I use story elements in a narrative?	Write the resolution to a narrative. (W.1.3) Edit sentences created in response to a prompt. (L.1.1.j)
32	*Tomás and the Library Lady, Waiting for the Biblioburro, My Librarian Is a Camel, That Book Woman, Green Eggs and Ham, Museum ABC*	Know How do all the Module 1 texts build our knowledge of how books can change lives around the world?	Excel How can I respond to what others are saying in a Socratic Seminar?	Write and speak to show understanding of the module Learning Goals.

WIT & WISDOM™   G1 > M1 > Lesson 1

■ FOCUSING QUESTION: LESSONS 1-6

How do library books change life for Tomás?

| 1 | 2 | 3 | 4 | 5 | 6 | 7 | 8 | 9 | 10 | 11 | 12 | 13 | 14 | 15 | 16 | 17 | 18 | 19 | 20 | 21 | 22 | 23 | 24 | 25 | 26 | 27 | 28 | 29 | 30 | 31 | 32 |

Lesson 1

TEXTS

- *Museum ABC*, The Metropolitan Museum of Art
- *Tomás and the Library Lady*, Pat Mora, Raul Colón

Copyright © 2016 Great Minds®

G1 > M1 > Lesson 1   WIT & WISDOM™

Lesson 1: At a Glance

AGENDA

Welcome (8 min.)

Notice Details in Museum ABC

Launch (5 min.)

Understand the Content Framing
Question

Learn (55 min.)

Define the Listening Goal (5 min.)

Notice Details (25 min.)

Generate and Answer Questions
(25 min.)

Land (5 min.)

Answer the Content Framing
Question

Wrap (2 min.)

**Style and Conventions Deep
Dive: Common Nouns (15 min.)**

STANDARDS ADDRESSED

The full text of ELA Standards can be
found in the Module Overview.

Reading

- RI.1.1, RI.1.7
- RL.1.1, RL.1.7
- RL.1.1

Speaking and Listening

- SL.1.1.a, SL.1.2

Language

- ⬇ L.1.1.b

MATERIALS

- Cut-up pages from Museum ABC
- Speaking and Listening Anchor
  Chart
- Handout 1A: Notice and Wonder
  Prompt Cards
- Wonder Wheel
- Blank Questions and Answers
  Chart
- Sticky notes
- Nouns Chart
- Response Journals
- Volume of Reading Reflection
  Questions

Learning Goals

Generate and answer questions
about *Tomás and the Library Lady*,
using key details from the text.
(RL.1.1, RL.1.7)

✔ Contribute to the Questions
and Answers Chart.

⬇ Identify and generate
common nouns. (L.1.1.b)

✔ Complete Sentence Frames
with common nouns.

✔ Checks for Understanding

Copyright © 2016 Great Minds®

WIT & WISDOM™   G1 > M1 > Lesson 1

Prepare

FOCUSING QUESTION: Lessons 1-6

How do library books change life for Tomás?

CONTENT FRAMING QUESTION: Lesson 1

Wonder: *What do I notice and wonder about* Tomás and the Library Lady?

Students are introduced to how to notice about a text with *Museum* ABC. They begin by gradually exploring select works of art to figure out more about this unique ABC book. Students then learn about whole-body listening, which segues to their first reading of *Tomás and the Library Lady*, where students engage in the core practice of generating and answering questions. The initial exploration of this text elevates the value of authentic questioning while also preparing students to retell and analyze the story in later lessons.

Welcome 8 MIN.

NOTICE DETAILS IN *MUSEUM ABC*

Give each pair one of the illustration pages from *Museum* ABC. Do not show students the words until Lesson 3. Share that these pages all come from the same mystery book, and that students will be exploring different pages each day this week to see what they can figure out about the book.

Explain that when people appreciate a great work of art, they look carefully to see what they notice. Tell students they will learn more about how to do this during the day's lesson, but, first, they will practice with these pages.

Echo Read the question: "What do you notice about your page?"

Students Think-Pair: "What does it mean to notice something?"

- *I notice things when I see them.*
- *Noticing means to pay attention.*

Share that when artists create art, the choices they make guide people to notice special things in the artwork.

Invite students to silently and carefully look at their page for a full minute to see what they notice.

In pairs or small groups, students discuss their page using the Sentence Frames: **I notice _____.**

- *I notice four paintings!*
- *I notice a lot of bare feet on this page.*

19

Copyright © 2016 Great Minds®

G1 > M1 > Lesson 1   WIT & WISDOM™

- *I notice two women with black hair.*
- *I notice that the paint looks cracked.*
- *I notice that their faces look like masks.*
- *I notice lots of colors!*
- *I notice that three of the people are facing sideways.*
- *I notice ladies with crowns.*

Two or three students share their responses with the whole group.

Explain that the things they noticed in the picture are called *details*, and details can help students understand more about the painting. Share that as they find details in more paintings, students will put these clues together to figure out what the mystery book they came from is all about.

Share that details aren't just found in paintings, and that good readers also notice details when they read a book.

Explain that students will use the same process of noticing details as they enjoy the first book of the module, *Tomás and the Library Lady*.

Launch 5 MIN.

UNDERSTAND THE CONTENT FRAMING QUESTION

TEACHER NOTE	The Focusing and Content Framing Questions help students understand their focus for the text and the particular lesson. They will be introduced and displayed in this section of every lesson. Their purpose is to allow for students' productive struggle, scaffolded by repetition, to help students grasp the process of understanding complex texts.

Display the Essential Question. Explain that students will learn more about this question in this module and through many different texts. Students will begin this work by studying a new book, *Tomás and the Library Lady*.

Display the Content Framing Question and Focusing Question. Echo Read the Focusing Question.

Tell students that each time they study the book, they will come closer to answering the Focusing Question, and in each lesson, students will explore a different Content Framing Question to understand more about the book.

Echo Read the Content Framing Question. Remind students that they just practiced noticing using the paintings.

20

Copyright © 2016 Great Minds®

Ask: "What does it mean to wonder?"

Students Think-Pair-Share.

- *I wonder about things I don't know for sure.*
- *When I wonder about something, I have a lot of questions about it.*

Confirm understanding of the words *notice* and *wonder* by sharing a recent reading experience and pointing out what you noticed in the book and something you wondered about in the book. As you share, invite students to put their hands on their head when they hear something you noticed and on their shoulders when they hear something you wondered.

Explain that students will now practice developing their own notices and wonders as they read the first book of this module: *Tomás and the Library Lady*.

DEFINE THE LISTENING GOAL

Whole Group 5 MIN.

Tell students they will have a listening goal to help them listen carefully to *Tomás and the Library Lady*. Display and introduce the Speaking and Listening Anchor Chart.

Students Think-Pair-Share to answer the question: "What does a good listener look like?" Use Equity Sticks to call on two pairs to share their responses.

- *A good listener looks at the person speaking.*
- *A good listener is quiet.*

Explain to students that when you listen with your whole body, you turn your body, look at the speaker, and are quiet. The class will use the information on this chart to become better speakers and listeners. Write *whole body listening* on the Speaking and Listening Anchor Chart.

SPEAKING AND LISTENING ANCHOR CHART

Speaking Goals	Listening Goals
	Whole body listening

Tell students to use their whole bodies to listen to *Tomás and the Library Lady*.

NOTICE DETAILS

Whole Group 25 MIN.

TEACHER NOTE | The pages of *Tomás and the Library Lady* are unnumbered. In this module, pages 1–2 show the illustration of Tomás looking out the window of the car and text that begins, "It was midnight." Write small page numbers in your text for easy reference.

Read the text aloud, including A Note about the Story, without interruptions.

Explain that students will look at the pictures in the story and share what they notice. Remind students how they shared what they noticed in the artwork at the beginning of the lesson, and that they will do the same thing with this book. Model something you notice on the front cover, such as, "I notice a young boy and a woman reading books." Provide an obvious non-example to emphasize this point, such as, "I notice two children playing." Students stand up if your example is a notice and sit down if it is not. Reinforce that what students notice, or their observations, should come from the text; this helps them pay attention and see details as they read.

Distribute cut-up copies of the Notice Prompt Card from Handout 1A: Notice and Wonder Prompt Cards. Explain that the picture of the eye and ear are symbols for noticing. Tell students they will stand up with the prompt card each time they notice something.

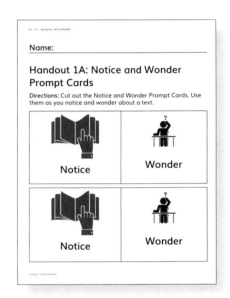

Visually explore the book by slowly, silently flipping through pages. Students stand up with the Notice Prompt Card when they notice details.

Pause every few pages and ask standing students: "What did you notice in the illustrations?" Use Equity Sticks to call on students for their observations.

Alternate Activity

Instead of using a prompt card, create a Nonverbal Signal for *notice*, e.g., pointing to your eyes for notice. Students demonstrate the signal before using it in the lesson.

GENERATE AND ANSWER QUESTIONS

Whole Group 25 MIN.

Students focus on what they wonder by forming questions when they feel curious.

Explain that the class will use a Wonder Wheel to help form and record questions about the text.

Display a blank Wonder Wheel. Read aloud the question words: *who*, *what*, and *where*, and circle or star these words on the chart. Explain that students will focus on these three question words because they will best help students understand the text. However, if questions with other words come to mind, students should feel free to share them.

Students Echo Read the question words they will be focusing on.

TEACHER NOTE

Students might be familiar with the Wonder Wheel from Kindergarten. Using it in this lesson will help access their prior knowledge of question words. In later lessons, students will use a Question Box to help them ask questions.

In this module, the questioning routines will focus on select question words aligned to the particular text. Having groups focus on one question word will ensure a variety of questions are posed.

WONDER WHEEL CHART

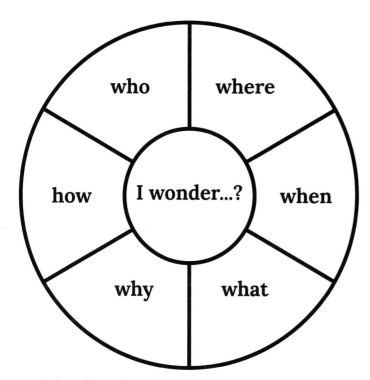

Remind students about the purpose of each question: <u>Who</u> questions ask about people. <u>Where</u> questions ask about places. <u>What</u> questions ask about specific information.

Scaffold

Provide examples of questions about everyday activities using the question words.

G1 > M1 > Lesson 1

Differentiation

Students who think more concretely will be more comfortable forming questions that begin with *who, what, where,* and *when.* Students who are able to think more abstractly will be more comfortable with forming questions beginning with *why* and *how.* Introduce the more abstract question words if students are ready.

Assign pairs one of the three question words.

✔ With copies of the text, pairs generate as many relevant text-based questions as they can using their chosen word. Circulate as pairs discuss, and redirect their questioning as needed to reinforce that their questions should come from the text or illustrations.

Display a blank Questions and Answers Chart to collect student responses. Circulate to find pairs with strong text-based questions. Record their questions on sticky notes and place them on the chart.

Choose a few questions that relate to vocabulary from the text and highlight how asking questions about unknown words is an important reading habit. Briefly define vocabulary words that appear in student-generated questions, modeling how to use context or illustrations to help you.

Read the text aloud again as students listen for answers to their questions.

Students stand up when they hear the answers to the questions. When students stand, flag the page in your copy of the text with a sticky note and record initials of some standing students.

After finishing the story, return to the flagged pages. Call on a student who stood up for that page to respond to a question on the Questions and Answers Chart. As needed, reread that section of the text to confirm and clarify students' thinking. Record the answer on the relevant sticky note. Each time, move sticky notes across the chart to indicate the extent to which each question has been answered. If there are any unanswered questions, explain that students will revisit the chart after they've had more time to explore the text to answer the remaining questions.

TOMÁS AND THE LIBRARY LADY QUESTIONS AND ANSWERS CHART

Questions ?	Answers in progress ⟵⟶	Complete answers ✔
▪ (Q1) Where does Tomás find books? ▪ (Q2) What makes Tomás use his imagination? ▪ (Q3) What does *borrow* mean? ▪ (Q4) Who tells Tomás stories?	▪ (Q2) Tomás uses his imagination when he is reading books (pages 13–14, 17, 21–22, 27–28).	▪ (Q1) Tomás finds books in the library (page 11) and the dump (page 18). ▪ (Q4) Papá Grande tells Tomás stories (pages 7–8).

In future lessons, continue to display the Questions and Answers Chart and allow students to revisit their questions as they work with the text.

WIT & WISDOM™   G1 > M1 > Lesson 1

	As time allows over the course of Lessons 2–5, revisit the Questions and
TEACHER	Answers Chart from Lesson 1 at the close of the Land. Students share the
NOTE	answers they have discovered. For each answer, briefly return to the text to
	reinforce using textual evidence when answering questions.

Land 5 MIN.

ANSWER THE CONTENT FRAMING QUESTION

Wonder: What do I notice and wonder about *Tomás and the Library Lady*?

Invite one student to share something they noticed and another to share something they wondered.

Celebrate the many observations and wonders the students highlighted during the course of the lesson. Remind students that in the lessons to come, they will have many more chances to find answers to the questions they asked as they read the book even more closely.

25

Copyright © 2016 Great Minds®

Wrap 2 MIN.

ASSIGN HOMEWORK

Consult with colleagues to develop a grade-appropriate home-reading routine. Use this time in each lesson to remind students of expectations. Once this routine is in place, distribute and review the Volume of Reading Reflection. Explain that students should consider these questions as they read and explain classroom systems for sharing their responses.

TEACHER NOTE | See the Implementation Guide for a further explanation of Volume of Reading, as well as various ways of using the reflection. Recommended texts for Volume of Reading can be found in Appendix D.

Analyze

Context and Alignment

After generating their own questions, students identify and use text evidence to answer selected student questions (RL.1.1, RL.1.7). Check students' oral responses for the following success criteria:

- Responds to the selected question.
- Uses relevant text evidence from words or pictures.

Next Steps

If students respond with irrelevant evidence, read aloud a small section of text that answers the question. Ask more specific questions that relate to the student-generated one. For example, read the first and fourth sentences on page 18 and ask, "What is Tomás doing? Where is he?"

WIT & WISDOM™   G1 > M1 > Lesson 1

⬇ Lesson 1: Style and Conventions Deep Dive

Finding Common Nouns

- **Time:** 15 min.

- **Text:** *Tomás and the Library Lady*, Pat Mora, Raul Colón

- **Style and Conventions Learning Goal:** Identify and generate common nouns. (L.1.1.b)

- **STYLE AND CONVENTIONS CRAFT QUESTION:** Lesson 1
  Experiment: *What are nouns?*

Launch

Display and read the Craft Question: *What are nouns?*

Students Echo Read the question. Explain that they are going to learn about some creatures they might see in the text. These creatures are different types of words.

Learn

Students Think-Pair-Share about what they know about the word *safari*. Use Equity Sticks to choose two or three volunteers to share their thinking. Help students understand that a safari is a hunt. Explain that their safari or hunt will be through the book *Tomás and the Library Lady* to search for a type of word.

Explain that nouns are words that tell us people, places, things, and objects. These creatures help us to know who the characters are in a book, where the characters are, and the things in the book that they might be using.

Ask students to share what objects, places, and people they see on the pages of *Tomás and the Library Lady*. Explain that this is a lot like the noticing they did earlier this lesson; this time, they are just looking for specific things they notice.

Flip through the text showing students the different pages. Generate a list of words to describe what students see in the images. Record students' responses. To help students put their responses in a complete sentence, use the Sentence Frame: **We see the _____.**

- The car.

- The corn.

- The ball.

- The tree.

- The library.

- The books.

27

Copyright © 2016 Great Minds®

- The grandpa.

Ask students what they notice about the words. Guide students to notice:

- The word *the* in front of each word.
- *Car*, *corn*, *ball*, *tree*, and *books* are things.
- *Library* is a place.
- A *grandpa* is a person.

Explain that these words are called *common nouns*. Common nouns are the words we use for places, things, or ideas. Display the Nouns Chart and have students direct where to write the words on the chart. Save this chart for use later.

Nouns			
Common Nouns ("the _____")			Proper Nouns
People (characters) ▪ Grandpa	Places (setting) ▪ Library	Things ▪ Car ▪ Corn ▪ Ball ▪ Tree ▪ Books	

✔ Send students on a safari, either in pairs or individually, in search of common nouns around the classroom. Have students make a list. Students write answers to complete the Sentence Frame: **We see the _____.** in their Response Journals after they have finished their safari.

Conduct a Whip Around, asking each student to share a sentence they wrote in their Response Journal. Volunteers share nouns to add to the chart.

Land

Instruct students to Think-Pair-Share, and ask: "What are nouns?"

Use Equity Sticks to select two pairs to share their thinking. Use their responses to reinforce that nouns are the words we use for people, places, things, and ideas. Explain that students will learn more about nouns and how they are used in texts.

WIT & WISDOM™   G1 > M1 > Lesson 2

■ FOCUSING QUESTION: LESSONS 1-6

How do library books change life for Tomás?

1 **2** 3 4 5 6 7 8 9 10 11 12 13 14 15 16 17 18 19 20 21 22 23 24 25 26 27 28 29 30 31 32

Lesson 2

TEXTS

- *Museum ABC*, The Metropolitan Museum of Art
- *Tomás and the Library Lady*, Pat Mora, Raul Colón
- "ASL Sign for: yes," *American Sign Language Dictionary*
- "ASL Sign for: no," *American Sign Language Dictionary*

Copyright © 2016 Great Minds®

G1 > M1 > Lesson 2

WIT & WISDOM™

Lesson 2: At a Glance

AGENDA

Welcome (8 min.)

Determine Subject in Museum ABC

Launch (5 min.)

Understand the Content Framing Question

Learn (60 min.)

Identify Characters (25 min.)

Retell the Story (15 min.)

Examine Sentence Frames (15 min.)

Land (5 min.)

Answer the Content Framing Question

Wrap (2 min.)

Vocabulary Deep Dive: Ask and Answer Questions About Vocabulary (15 min.)

STANDARDS ADDRESSED

The full text of ELA Standards can be found in the Module Overview.

Reading

- RI.1.1, RI.1.7

- RL.1.1, RI.1.2, RL.1.3, RL.1.7

Speaking and Listening

- SL.1.1.a, SL.1.2

Language

- ↓ L.1.6

MATERIALS

- One character Story Stone for each pair of students

- Wonder Wheel

- Vocabulary Journal

Learning Goals

Retell *Tomás and the Library Lady*, including key details about characters. (RL.1.2)

✔ Orally retell events of the story through the lens of character.

↓ Ask and answer questions about key vocabulary in *Tomás and the Library Lady*. (L.1.6)

✔ Use new words in sentences to demonstrate understanding.

✔ Checks for Understanding

Copyright © 2016 Great Minds®

WIT & WISDOM™

G1 > M1 > Lesson 2

Prepare

FOCUSING QUESTION: Lessons 1-6

How do library books change life for Tomás?

CONTENT FRAMING QUESTION: Lesson 2

Organize: *What's happening in* Tomás and the Library Lady?

CRAFT QUESTION: Lesson 2

Examine: *Why is it important to use Sentence Frames in speaking and writing?*

Students begin the lesson with *Museum ABC*, determining that a group of paintings are portraits. This connects to their subsequent work with *Tomás and the Library Lady*, where they begin learning about the story element *character*. They identify the characters in the story using Story Stones, a routine they are familiar with from Kindergarten. To further support their understanding, students create Tableaux. Using their whole bodies allows students to experience the text in a meaningful way. Students also discover how Sentence Frames help their speaking and writing as they fill in a Sentence Frame with information about what Tomás did in the story. Providing a model allows students to emulate the features of good writing. It also allows teachers to gradually release responsibility to students as they learn how to write for different purposes.

Welcome 8 MIN.

DETERMINE SUBJECT IN *MUSEUM ABC*

Remind students how they focused on thinking about what they noticed in the artwork. In this lesson they will look carefully at a single painting and try to figure out what is happening in it.

Display the H page of *Museum ABC*.

Echo Read the question: "What's happening in the paintings on this page?"

Highlight that even though this page contains four different paintings, there is one thing that is true for all of the pictures: they are all something that artists call *portraits*.

Ask: "What is the same about all of the paintings on this page?"

- *All of the paintings have faces in them.*
- *The paintings all show one person.*
- *All of the people seem important.*

31

Copyright © 2016 Great Minds®

G1 > M1 > Lesson 2

Focus on the painting *George Washington* from the H page of *Museum ABC*.

Confirm that a portrait is a work of art about a person. Share that artists create portraits to show how that person is important.

Ask: "What details in this painting show how this person is important?"

Students Think-Pair-Share.

- *The man is in the middle of the picture.*
- *The man is wearing fancy clothes.*
- *It looks like the man is looking right at us.*
- *It seems like there is a light shining on him.*
- *I think the man looks like George Washington!*

Choose one or two students to share their responses with the whole group.

Share that details in portraits help you understand how the person is important. Students will try to answer a similar question about *Tomás and the Library Lady*, and finding details will help them understand how the people in the story are important, too.

Launch 5 MIN.

UNDERSTAND THE CONTENT FRAMING QUESTION

Post the Content Framing Question and Focusing Question.

Echo Read the Content Framing Question: "What's happening in *Tomás and the Library Lady*?"

Explain that this question will help students think about the story. In this lesson, they will focus on learning more about the <u>characters</u> in the story.

Ask: "What are characters?"

Volunteers respond.

- *Characters are who the story is about.*

Hold up and Echo Read a card with a simple definition for *character*. Put *character* on the Word Wall as a year-long word. Include the character symbol from the Story Stone as a visual reference.

| TEACHER NOTE | Consider setting aside a dedicated space in the classroom to collect and reference academic vocabulary words for ELA. These words, like *character* in this lesson, are not module-specific and will be useful to reference any time students encounter a literary text. |

Share that the symbol on the card is one they will see often during the lesson as students use Story Stones to retell *Tomás and the Library Lady*.

IDENTIFY CHARACTERS

Whole Group 30 MIN.

Hold up Story Stones as you remind students that they might have used Story Stones in Kindergarten to help retell important parts of a story. Remind them that each Story Stone represents a different element, or important part, of the story. Hold up the character Story Stone and explain that students will focus on character as they determine what is happening in *Tomás and the Library Lady*.

Display a large character Story Stone. Distribute a character Story Stone to each student. As you read the story aloud, pairs will follow along in their copies. Each time the words mention a character, one partner will touch that character in the illustration with the character Story Stone. Partners will take turns, switching each time they turn the page. Model by reading page 2 and touching the picture of Tomás.

Read the story aloud (except the author's note) as students touch pictures of characters with Story Stones.

Display the *Tomás and the Library Lady* Story Map. Students Think-Pair-Share: "Who are the characters in the story?" Use Equity Sticks to call on students. Write and illustrate students' responses on the Story Map.

| TEACHER NOTE | Drawing illustrations or using pictures from the text helps students read the chart. |

G1 > M1 > Lesson 2   WIT & WISDOM™

TOMÁS AND THE LIBRARY LADY STORY MAP

Characters	Setting
▪ Tomás (drawing of Tomás).	
▪ Papá Grande (drawing of Papá Grande).	
▪ Papá (drawing of Papá).	
▪ Mamá (drawing of Mamá).	
▪ Enrique (drawing of Enrique).	
▪ Library lady (drawing of the library lady).	

Problem		Resolution

Guide students to find the main character of the text by asking: "Which character did you see the most?" Students respond chorally. Listen to make sure most students identify Tomás. Explain that Tomás is the main character, or most important character, of the story because he appears most frequently. Place a star next to Tomás on the chart to indicate that he is the main character in the story.

Extension

If you have extra time, small groups of six students can create tableaux to show the characters in the story and indicate in a special way who the main character is.

Students create tableaux using the characters of the story.

- ▪ (Pose as Tomás reading a book.)
- ▪ (Pose as Papá Grande telling a story.)
- ▪ (Pose as the library lady giving away a book.)
- ▪ (Group line up with Tomás in front to demonstrate he is the main character)

As a whole group, ask students: "What did your tableaux show about the story's characters?" Use student responses to reinforce the key idea that Tomás is the main character, or the one who the story is about. Ask: "Who is the main character?" Students chorally respond.

34

Copyright © 2016 Great Minds®

WIT & WISDOM™   G1 > M1 > Lesson 2

RETELL THE STORY

Pairs 15 MIN.

Now that students know who the characters are, pairs will retell the story to each other by telling what happened to Tomás.

Tell students to consider the important things that happened to Tomás when they retell. Ask: "What do you remember from Kindergarten about retelling?" Volunteers respond.

Reinforce that *retelling* means "to name important details from a story in the order they happened."

Think Aloud to model an unimportant detail on pages 1–4, such as Tomás holding on to the car with both hands. Explain that this is not important because the story would still make sense without that detail. Then Think Aloud about an important detail, such as Tomás and his family driving to Iowa.

Invite volunteers to share two to three more important details from the first half of the story. For each detail, ask another student volunteer to retell it.

- *Tomás knew all of Papá Grande's stories.*
- *Tomás went to the library to find more stories.*
- *He met the library lady and read books.*

Invite students to do the same thing in pairs with the second half of the story.

- *He told his family the stories from the books.*
- *Tomás and his family had to go back to Texas.*
- *He said goodbye to the library lady.*
- *Papá Grande said Tomás became the new storyteller.*

✔ Pairs take turns orally retelling the second half of the story through the lens of the main character, Tomás. Students flip through the text for picture support as they retell the story.

Circulate to listen as students orally retell the story to a partner. Highlight a few exemplar answers for the entire class. Explain that the class will continue to work on retelling throughout the year and that one way to get better at retelling is to understand the importance of using complete sentences.

35

Copyright © 2016 Great Minds®

G1 > M1 > Lesson 2   WIT & WISDOM™

EXAMINE SENTENCE FRAMES

Pairs 15 MIN.

Read the Craft Question aloud: "Why is it important to use Sentence Frames in speaking and writing?"

TEACHER NOTE	Using Sentence Frames at the beginning of the year provides a scaffold for beginning writers and speakers including English Language Learners. They allow students to use key vocabulary and content while providing them with a structure beyond what they might be able to produce on their own.

Explain to students that using Sentence Frames will help them learn how to write and speak complete sentences.

Display and Echo Read the Sentence Frame, using a word such as *blank* for the empty line:
Tomás _____.

Explain that blank lines in Sentence Frames tell us that we need to speak or write words on the lines to complete the sentence.

Think Aloud as you model completing the Sentence Frame. Visually explore the text to determine a word or words to complete the Sentence Frame so it tells something that Tomás did.

Ask: "What other words could we use to complete the sentence about what Tomás did in the story?

Pairs visually explore the text to answer the question.

Use Equity Sticks to call on two to three pairs to share their responses.

Write student responses in two to three Sentence Frames. Echo Read the completed frames.

- *Tomás went to the library.*
- *Tomás read books.*
- *Tomás told stories.*

Student Think-Pair-Share: "How do Sentence Frames help me as a speaker and a writer?"

- *Sentence Frames help me write a complete sentence.*
- *Sentence Frames help me say a complete sentence.*

36

Copyright © 2016 Great Minds®

Land 5 MIN.

ANSWER THE CONTENT FRAMING QUESTION

Organize: What is happening in *Tomás and the Library Lady*?

Students Think-Pair-Share: "How did knowing the characters help you retell what happens in the story?"

- I retold the things that happened to the characters to retell the story.
- I told about Tomás because he's the main character. Most things in the story happen to him.

Ask: "Did we answer the Content Framing Question?" Students respond with a Nonverbal Signal, such as ASL signs for *yes* (**http://witeng.link/0400**) and *no* (**http://witeng.link/0401**).

Wrap 2 MIN.

Share that, in the next lesson, students will continue retelling with a new Story Stone.

Analyze

Context and Alignment

Students create tableaux about the characters in the story *Tomás and the Library Lady* in preparation for retelling longer and more detailed scenes later in the module (RL.1.2, RL.1.3).

Check for the following success criterion:

- Accurately represented scene(s) from the text.

Next Steps

Use observational evidence to determine whether students were able to depict the characters they were assigned.

If students experienced difficulty accurately representing the characters in the tableaux:

- Reread the section of text, asking what the character is doing in each scene.
- Form a Fishbowl, allowing students with strong representations to model their assigned character and scene.

G1 > M1 > Lesson 2   WIT & WISDOM™

⤓ Lesson 2 Deep Dive: Vocabulary

Ask and Answer Questions About Key Vocabulary

- **Time:** 15 min.

- **Text:** *Tomás and the Library Lady*, Pat Mora, Raul Colón

- **Vocabulary Learning Goal:** Ask and answer questions about key vocabulary in *Tomás and the Library Lady*. (L.1.6)

Launch

Display the Wonder Wheel. Volunteers respond: "What do we use this for?"

- *We use it to wonder about texts.*

- *We use it to ask questions about texts.*

- *We use it to help us ask questions.*

Remind students of all the wondering they did in the previous lesson. Explain that they can also wonder, or ask questions about, vocabulary and that they are going to practice wondering about vocabulary words in *Tomás and the Library Lady*.

Learn

Display the following words:

- *Storyteller*

- *Borrow*

- *Eager*

Display the following Sentence Frames.

- **What does _____ mean?**

- **How does _____ work?**

- **What is _____?**

Explain that you are going to use one of these Sentence Frames to ask a question about one of the vocabulary words. Point to the word *storyteller*. Model asking a question about the word *storyteller*.

38

Copyright © 2016 Great Minds®

Storyteller. **This is a word I am unsure of. I need to make sure I ask a question about this word. I will choose one of the Sentence Frames to help me ask a question about this word. "How does *storyteller* work?" I don't think that sounds quite right. When I look at the picture of the storyteller, it doesn't look like it really does anything by itself. Maybe another question would sound better. "What does *storyteller* mean?" That sounds like a better question for this word.**

Read the sentences with the word *storyteller* on page 8 of the text. Students Think-Pair-Share about what they think the word means. Use Equity Sticks to choose volunteers to share their thinking.

- *Someone who likes to tell stories.*
- *Someone who is good at telling stories.*

Confirm that the word *storyteller* means "someone who likes and is good at telling stories." Capture the definition next to the word and draw a quick sketch to help students remember what the word means. Students Think-Pair-Share about someone they know who is a storyteller. Model how to use the word in a sentence and have partners practice using the word in a sentence. Volunteers share their responses.

- *My dad is a storyteller because he loves to tell me stories at bedtime.*
- *I am a storyteller because I love to tell stories to my friend.*

In a similar fashion, model how to ask a question about the word *borrow*.

Borrow. **This is a word I am unsure of. I need to make sure I ask a question about this word. The first Sentence Frame we'll try is: "How does *borrow* work?" Does this sound right to you? Stand up if this sounds like the correct question. It doesn't sound right to me either. I will choose a different question. "What is *borrow*?" Does this question sound correct to you? Stand up if you think it is the correct question to use. That doesn't sound quite right to me either. I will choose another question. "What does *borrow* mean?" Stand up if this sounds right to you.**

Read the sentence with the word *borrow* on page 16 of the text. Students Think-Pair-Share what they think the word means. Use Equity Sticks to choose volunteers to share their thinking.

- *Take something.*
- *Check out something.*
- *Check out books.*
- *Bring something back.*

Confirm that the word *borrow* means "to take something with the intention of returning it." Capture the definition next to the word and draw a quick sketch to help students remember what the word means. Student Think-Pair-Share about something they have borrowed before. Model using the word in a sentence and have partners practice using the word in a sentence. Volunteers respond.

- *My sister always borrows my clothes.*
- *I borrow books from the library.*
- *My friend borrows my pencil when she doesn't have one.*

Read the next vocabulary word, *eager*. Students Think-Pair-Share about a question they could ask about the meaning of this word using the Sentence Frame. Use Equity Sticks to choose volunteers to respond.

- *What is eager?*
- *What does eager mean?*

Read the sentence with the word *eager* on page 16 of the text. Students Think-Pair-Share about the answer to their question. Use Equity Sticks to choose volunteers to share their thinking.

- *In a hurry.*
- *Wanting something a lot.*

Confirm that the word *eager* means "excited about something." Capture the definition next to the word and draw a quick sketch to help students remember what the word means.

✔ Partners work together to use their new words in sentences. Circulate to scaffold students as necessary.

Scaffold

Provide the following Sentence Frames only if needed to help students understand how to use their word in a sentence.
- I was eager when _____.
- I am eager to _____.

Land

Use Equity Sticks to choose volunteers to share a sentence their partner told them using the word. Students record their words in their Vocabulary Journals, along with the definition and sketch.

Remind students that they ask questions about words in a text to learn more about them.

WIT & WISDOM™   G1 > M1 > Lesson 3

■ FOCUSING QUESTION: LESSONS 1-6

How do library books change life for Tomás?

1 2 **3** 4 5 6 7 8 9 10 11 12 13 14 15 16 17 18 19 20 21 22 23 24 25 26 27 28 29 30 31 32

Lesson 3

TEXTS

- *Museum ABC*, The Metropolitan Museum of Art
- *Tomás and the Library Lady*, Pat Mora, Raul Colón
- "ASL Sign for: yes," *American Sign Language Dictionary*
- "ASL Sign for: no," *American Sign Language Dictionary*

Copyright © 2016 Great Minds®

G1 > M1 > Lesson 3   WIT & WISDOM™

Lesson 3: At a Glance

AGENDA

Welcome (8 min.)

Determine Subject in Museum ABC

Launch (5 min.)

Understand the Content Framing Question

Learn (55 min.)

Identify Settings (15 min.)

Sequence Settings (15 min.)

Retell the Story (10 min.)

Experiment with Using Sentence Frames (15 min.)

Land (5 min.)

Answer the Content Framing Question

Wrap (2 min.)

Style and Conventions Deep Dive: Finding Common Nouns (15 min.)

STANDARDS ADDRESSED

The full text of ELA Standards can be found in the Module Overview.

Reading

- RI.1.1, RI.1.2, RI.1.7

- RL.1.1, RI.1.2, RL.1.3, RL.1.7

Writing

- W.1.2, W.1.8

Speaking and Listening

- SL.1.1.a, SL.1.2

Language

- ⬇ L.1.1.b

MATERIALS

- One setting Story Stone per pair of students

- *Tomás and the Library Lady* Story Map

- Illustrated signs for settings

- Handout 3A: Tomás Sentence Frame

- Nouns Chart

- Handout 3B: Nouns Chart

- Response Journals

Learning Goals

Retell *Tomás and the Library Lady,* including key details about setting. (RL.1.2)

✔ Orally retell events of the story through the lens of setting.

⬇ Identify and generate common nouns. (L.1.1.b)

✔ Identify common nouns for setting.

✔ Checks for Understanding

Copyright © 2016 Great Minds®

WIT & WISDOM™   G1 > M1 > Lesson 3

| Prepare |

FOCUSING QUESTION: Lessons 1-6

How do library books change life for Tomás?

CONTENT FRAMING QUESTION: Lesson 3

Organize: *What's happening in* Tomás and the Library Lady?

CRAFT QUESTION: Lesson 3

Experiment: *How does using Sentence Frames in speaking and writing work?*

Students resume their study of *Museum ABC* as they figure out that the common subject among key paintings is landscape. This work aligns with their continued learning about story elements as they identify the settings using Story Stones. Students physically sequence the settings to show how they change throughout the story. Then, students orally retell the story through the lens of both setting and character. Students continue to work with Sentence Frames, as they fill in a Sentence Frame with information about places Tomás went in the story.

Welcome 8 MIN.

DETERMINE SUBJECT IN *MUSEUM ABC*

Remind students of how, in the previous lesson, they focused on portraits. Explain that they will look carefully at a single page of paintings about a different subject and try to figure out what is happening in it.

Display the Y page of four paintings from *Museum ABC*. Cover the right half of the page so only the two paintings on the left side are visible.

Ask: "What's happening in these two paintings?"

Highlight that even though this page shows two different paintings, there is one thing that is true for both of the pictures: they are something that artists call *landscapes*.

Ask: "What is the same about both of these paintings?"

- *Both of the paintings have skies.*
- *Both of the paintings are outside.*
- *Both of the paintings have trees.*

Focus on the painting *Autumn River* (bottom left) from the Y page of *Museum ABC*.

43

Copyright © 2016 Great Minds®

Confirm that a *landscape* is "a work of art that shows a natural scene as the artist sees or imagines it." Share that artists sometimes create landscapes to show the beauty of nature.

Ask: "What details in this painting show the beauty of nature?"

Instruct students to Think-Pair-Share.

- *The blue sky shows the beauty of nature.*
- *The ground looks golden with beautiful flowers or grass.*
- *The green and gold trees make it look like fall!*

Choose one or two students to share their responses with the whole group. Highlight that landscapes show a wide view of natural scenery such as mountains, valleys, trees, and rivers.

Share that details in landscapes help you see what the artist saw in nature. Explain that students will try to answer a similar question about *Tomás and the Library Lady* and that finding details will help them understand more about where the story happened.

Launch 5 MIN.

UNDERSTAND THE CONTENT FRAMING QUESTION

Post the Content Framing Question and Focusing Question.

Echo Read the Content Framing Question: *What is happening in* Tomás and the Library Lady?

Explain that this question will help students think about how things are organized. In this lesson, they will focus on learning more about the setting to retell what happens in the story.

Students Think-Pair-Share: "What is a setting?"

- *A setting is a place where the characters do things.*
- *A setting is where and when the story takes place.*

Use Equity Sticks to choose one or two volunteers to share their thinking.

Decide on a simple definition for *setting*. Put *setting* on the Word Wall as a year-long word. Include the setting symbol from the Story Stone as a visual reference.

Learn 55 MIN.

IDENTIFY SETTINGS

Pairs 15 MIN.

Remind students that they used the character Story Stones in the previous lesson, and now they are going to use the setting Story Stone.

Display a large setting Story Stone. Explain that setting is another element in a story. Repeat the definition of *setting*: where and when the story takes place.

Distribute a setting Story Stone to each student. Explain that pairs will look at each illustration in the story, touching a detail about the setting with the Story Stone and stating the setting on that page. Partners will take turns, switching each time they turn the page. Model the task on the first page.

Use Equity Sticks to call on students to share with the group different settings they found in the text.

- Road
- House
- Fields
- Library
- Dump

> *Scaffold*
>
> If students name an imaginary scene as a setting, reread the text where Tomás uses his imagination (e.g., pages 13-14, 21-22, and 27-28). Ask students: "Where is Tomás? Listen to the words for clues. Why does the illustration show a different place?" Follow up by asking: "What clues tell you that Tomás is imagining these settings?"

Write and illustrate students' responses on the class *Tomás and the Library Lady* Story Map.

As each setting is written on the Story Map, ask: "Where is this place located in the world?" Students whisper to respond. Confirm they are all in Iowa, except the car, which takes place between Texas and Iowa. Add this information to the map.

G1 > M1 > Lesson 3   WIT & WISDOM™

TOMÁS AND THE LIBRARY LADY STORY MAP

Characters	Setting
• Tomás (drawing of Tomás) • Papá Grande (drawing of Papá Grande) • Papá (drawing of Papá) • Mamá (drawing of Mamá) • Enrique (drawing of Enrique) • Library lady (drawing of the library lady)	• Car (between Texas and Iowa) (drawing of car) • House (Iowa) (drawing of house) • Fields (Iowa) (drawing of fields) • Library (Iowa) (drawing of library) • Dump (Iowa) (drawing of dump)

Problem		Resolution
	→	

SEQUENCE SETTINGS

Whole Group 15 MIN.

Label different areas of the room with illustrated signs for each setting: road, house, fields, library, dump. Explain that students will move to the designated area of the room to show the order in which the settings change.

Reread sentences aloud that describe a change in setting (pages 3, 4, 5, 9, 11, 16, 17, 18, 19, 25).

After each excerpt, students point to the sign that shows the new setting. If answers differ, ask a student pointing to the correct location: "What details in the text show this setting?" Once they confirm the location, students move to the appropriate sign.

Scaffold

If students struggle with retelling the story, reread the entire text. Repeated readings help students remember details accurately.

As a whole group, ask students: "What did moving between signs show you about the story's setting?"

46

Copyright © 2016 Great Minds®

WIT & WISDOM™   G1 > M1 > Lesson 3

- *There are many settings in the story.*
- *Tomás went to the library a lot.*

Use student responses to reinforce the key ideas that the story's setting changes between different places.

RETELL THE STORY

Pairs 10 MIN.

Now that students understand the settings, pairs will retell the story by telling what happened in the different settings.

Remind students to consider the important things that happened when they retell the story, and reiterate the two-step process they used in the previous lesson: 1) identify a detail, and 2) retell what happened using that detail.

✔ Pairs take turns orally retelling the story. Students flip through the text for picture support as they retell the story.

- *Tomás and his family rode in the car to Iowa. When it was hot in the fields, Papá Grande told stories in the field under a big tree but Tomás knew all the stories. Tomás went to the library and met the library lady. She gave him books to read. He went home and told the stories to his family. When they went to the town dump, Tomás looked for more books. Tomás went to the library to say goodbye to the library lady and she gave him a book. His family drove to Texas. Papá Grande said he was the new storyteller.*

Circulate to listen as students orally retell the story to a partner.

EXPERIMENT WITH USING SENTENCE FRAMES

Individuals 15 MIN.

Share the Craft Question: *How does using Sentence Frames in writing and speaking work?*

Explain to students that the class is going to use a Sentence Frame to create sentences about setting.

Display and read aloud the Sentence Frame:

Tomás went to _____.

Distribute Handout 3A: Tomás Sentence Frame.

> **Handout 3A: Tomás Sentence Frame**
>
> Directions: Write and illustrate to describe one setting in *Tomás and the Library Lady.*
>
> Tomás went to _____
>
> _____

47

Copyright © 2016 Great Minds®

G1 > M1 > Lesson 3   WIT & WISDOM™

Explain to students that they will experiment with writing the words for the settings they found in the story on the blank line of the Sentence Frame.

Students use the Sentence Frame to write and illustrate a complete sentence. If time allows, have students share their sentence with a partner.

Call on one or two volunteers to share their responses using the Sentence Frame by placing their handout on the document projector.

- *Tomás went to Iowa.*
- *Tomás went to the dump.*
- *Tomás went to Texas.*
- *Tomás went to the library.*

Read the sentences aloud.

Differentiation

Students needing additional support may be writing squiggly lines, letter streams, or not writing at all. Scribe, underwrite, or provide students with a Sentence Strip depending on the writing level of each student.

Scribe

Write word-for-word what the student says, spelling out each word as it is written. Students touch and Echo Read each word in the sentence.

Underwriting

Underwriting: Write word-for-word under what the student says their marks mean. Spell out each word as you write it. Students touch and Echo Read each word in the sentence.

Land 5 MIN.

ANSWER THE CONTENT FRAMING QUESTION

Organize: *What is happening in* Tomás and the Library Lady?

Students Think-Pair-Share: "How did knowing the settings help you retell what happens in the story?"

- *I told about different places where things happen.*

Ask: "Did we answer the Content Framing Question?" Students respond with a Nonverbal Signal such as ASL signs for *yes* (**http://witeng.link/0400**) and *no* (**http://witeng.link/0401**).

Wrap 2 MIN.

In the next lesson, students will add two more Story Stones to use in their retelling.

Analyze

Context and Alignment

Pairs orally retell *Tomás and the Library Lady* by telling what happened in the different settings. (RL.1.2, RL.1.3, RL.1.7). Check for the following success criterion:

- Students retell the story in the order the settings occurred, using the text to support them.

Next Steps

If students do not retell the story in sequence using the settings, meet with each student and have them retell as they turn each page. If students miss key events in certain settings, reread the page and ask them, "What happened in this setting?"

G1 > M1 > Lesson 3

⬇ Lesson 3: Style and Conventions Deep Dive

Finding Common Nouns

- **Time:** 15 min.

- **Text:** *Tomás and the Library Lady*, Pat Mora, Raul Colón

- **Style and Conventions Learning Goal:** Identify and generate common nouns. (L.1.1.b)

- **STYLE AND CONVENTIONS CRAFT QUESTION:** Lesson 3
  Experiment: *What do nouns tell us about the setting?*

Launch

Display and read the Craft Question: *What do nouns tell us about the setting?*

Students Echo Read the question. Explain that they will go on a safari through *Tomás and the Library Lady* to find more nouns to add to their chart. The nouns they will look for will be places or the different settings in the book.

Learn

Students Think-Pair-Share to answer the question: "What do you remember about nouns?" Choose two or three students to share their answers.

- They are people.

- They are places.

- They are things.

Students Think-Pair-Share to answer the question: "What is another word for *place* that we learned today?" Volunteers respond.

■ *Setting*

Explain that today they will go on a safari through *Tomás and the Library Lady* to find nouns that are places or the different settings in the book.

Students work in pairs with their pages from the book to hunt for nouns that represent the different settings in the book. Provide each student with Handout 3B: Nouns Chart so they can write or draw their responses.

Handout 3B: Nouns Chart

Directions: Write the nouns from the class Nouns Chart and place in Response Journal.

Nouns			
Common Nouns ("the _____")			Proper Nouns
People (characters)	Places (settings)	Things	

50

Copyright © 2016 Great Minds®

Nouns			
Common Nouns ("the _____")			Proper Nouns
People (characters) ▪ Grandpa	Places (setting) ▪ Library	Things ▪ Car ▪ Corn ▪ Ball ▪ Tree ▪ Books	

✔ Send students on a safari, either in pairs or individually, in search of common nouns that represent different settings, such as the library corner or the gathering place. Students record these on their charts that will be stapled into their Response Journals.

Use Equity Sticks to choose volunteers to share places or settings that can be added to the class chart.

Land

Instruct students to Think-Pair-Share, and ask: "What do nouns tell us about setting?"

Use Equity Sticks to select two pairs to share their thinking. Use their responses to reinforce that nouns are the words we use for places and that places can also be the setting in the stories we read and write. Explain that students will continue to learn about nouns and how to use them in their writing.

FOCUSING QUESTION: LESSONS 1-6

How do library books change life for Tomás?

Lesson 4

TEXTS

- *Museum ABC*, The Metropolitan Museum of Art
- *Tomás and the Library Lady*, Pat Mora, Raul Colón
- "ASL Sign for: yes," *American Sign Language Dictionary*
- "ASL Sign for: no," *American Sign Language Dictionary*

G1 > M1 > Lesson 4   WIT & WISDOM™

Lesson 4: At a Glance

AGENDA

Welcome (10 min.)

Identify Text Structure in Museum ABC

Launch (10 min.)

Understand the Content Framing Question

Learn (50 min.)

Identify the Problem and Resolution (25 min.)

Retell the Story (10 min.)

Execute Using Sentence Frames (15 min.)

Land (3 min.)

Answer the Content Framing Question

Wrap (2 min.)

Style and Conventions Deep Dive: Finding Proper Nouns (15 min.)

STANDARDS ADDRESSED

The full text of ELA Standards can be found in the Module Overview.

Reading

- RI.1.1, RI.1.2, RI.1.7

- RL.1.1, RL.1.2, RL.1.3, RL.1.7

Writing

- W.1.3, W.1.8

Speaking and Listening

- SL.1.1.a, SL.1.2

Language

- ⬇ L.1.1.b

MATERIALS

- Large and medium sticky notes

- One Problem and Resolution Story Stone for each pair of students

- *Tomás and the Library Lady* Story Map

- Handout 4A: Focusing Question 1 Prompt

- Assessment 4: Focusing Question Task 1

- Nouns Chart

- Handout 4B: Noun Cards

- Response Journals

Learning Goals

Retell *Tomás and the Library Lady*, including key details about problem and resolution. (RL.1.2)

✔ Retell events of the story through the lens of problem and resolution.

Write a narrative retelling of *Tomás and the Library Lady* that shows how library books change life for Tomás. (RL.1.2, RL.1.3, W.1.3, W.1.8, L.1.2.b, SL.1.1.a)

✔ Complete the first part of Focusing Question Task 1.

⬇ Identify and generate proper nouns. (L.1.1.b)

✔ Complete Handout 4B to sort common and proper nouns.

Copyright © 2016 Great Minds®

✔ Checks for Understanding

WIT & WISDOM™   G1 > M1 > Lesson 4

Prepare

FOCUSING QUESTION: Lessons 1-6

How do library books change life for Tomás?

CONTENT FRAMING QUESTION: Lesson 4

Organize: *What's happening in* Tomás and the Library Lady?

CRAFT QUESTION: Lesson 4

Execute: *How do I use Sentence Frames in speaking and writing?*

Students review what they've learned about *Museum ABC* as a whole to determine the alphabetic structure of the book. This segues to organizing what is happening with *Tomás and the Library Lady* as students learn about the final story elements—*problem* and *resolution*. They identify these elements using Story Stones. They then Tableaux the problem and resolution and orally retell the story through the lens of problem and resolution. This scaffolded instruction around story elements and retelling further supports students' understanding in these areas. Students apply their knowledge as they begin work on Focusing Question Task 1, using Sentence Frames to orally retell the story.

Welcome 10 MIN.

IDENTIFY TEXT STRUCTURE IN *MUSEUM ABC*

Show the cover and read aloud the title of *Museum ABC*. Share that this is the book that contains all the paintings students have studied in the lessons so far.

Echo Read the question: "What's happening in *Museum ABC*?" Explain that now that students have practice with finding details, students will organize their thinking about the whole text.

Cover the letters A through D with large sticky notes. Display the first page. Ask: "What is the same about all four pictures on this page?" Use student responses to confirm all the pictures show apples. Write *apple* on the sticky note. Repeat the procedure for the B, C, and D pages.

Students Echo Read the words on the sticky notes. Ask: "What do you notice about the order of the words?" If needed, follow up with questions like, "Look at the first letter of each word. What other letters go in that order?"

Use student responses to confirm that the book tells about topics in alphabetical order, as suggested by the title *Museum ABC*. Read aloud the entire book, inviting students to Choral Read as they are able.

55

Copyright © 2016 Great Minds®

G1 > M1 > Lesson 4   WIT & WISDOM™

Explain that it's important to think about what happens in a whole text, not just small parts. Next, students will organize their thinking about what happens throughout the whole story of *Tomás and the Library Lady*.

Launch 10 MIN.

UNDERSTAND THE CONTENT FRAMING QUESTION

Post the Content Framing Question and Focusing Question.

Echo Read the Content Framing Question.

Explain that this question will help students think about how things are organized. In this lesson, they will focus on learning more about the problem and resolution to retell what happens in the story.

Ask: "What does it mean to have a problem?" Volunteers respond.

- *The problem is something that challenges or causes trouble for the character.*
- *It's the challenge for the character.*

Use Equity Sticks to choose one or two volunteers to share their thinking.

Post a simple definition along with the Story Stone symbol for *problem*. Put *problem* on the Word Wall as a year-long word.

Ask: "What is a resolution?" Volunteers respond.

- *The resolution is how the problem is fixed.*
- *It's the end of the problem.*

Use Equity Sticks to choose volunteers to share their thinking.

> **Alternate Activity**
>
> Develop a relatable problem-resolution scenario for students. Introduce the terms as you present the scenario. Then, define the terms and use prompting to support students in generating examples of problems and resolutions.

Post a simple definition along with the Story Stone symbol for *resolution*. Put *resolution* on the Word Wall as a year-long word.

56

Copyright © 2016 Great Minds®

Extension

Ask follow-up questions, such as:
- What's a recent problem you have had?
- How did you solve it?

Explain that stories have a problem and resolution. Problems are things that challenge the main character. Things happen that change that problem. By the end of the story, the problem is solved—which is the resolution.

Remind students that they already know about the main character, so in this lesson they will learn what challenges him, or is the problem, and how that problem ends, or the resolution.

| TEACHER NOTE | Gesture to the posted story elements as you reiterate their meanings. If time allows, develop Nonverbal Signals for each story element and encourage students to use them when they hear a specific story element throughout the lesson. |

Learn 50 MIN.

IDENTIFY THE PROBLEM AND RESOLUTION

Whole Group 25 MIN.

Remind students that they used the character and setting Story Stones in the previous lessons, and now they are going to use the problem and resolution Story Stones. Display the large problem and resolution Story Stones.

Distribute a problem Story Stone to each student. Explain that as the story is read aloud, pairs will follow along in their copies. They will place the appropriate stone on the text when they hear details about the problem or resolution. Both students will shake their problem stones in the air when they notice the problem changing in the story. As needed, model ways to do this in a careful manner.

Read aloud page 8, with students following along with Story Stones.

Instruct students to Think-Pair-Share: "What is the problem, or what challenges Tomás?"

- *The problem is that Tomás knows all of Papá Grande's stories.*

Write and illustrate the problem on the Story Map.

G1 > M1 > Lesson 4   WIT & WISDOM™

Before continuing with the Read Aloud, remind students to listen for when the problem changes and shake their problem Story Stone when they hear details about the problem changing.

Pause on page 14 to Think Aloud to explain a moment that helps change the problem. For example:

Remember the problem is that Tomás knows all of Papá Grande's stories. What happens in the story that helps change Tomás's problem? On page 9, Tomás goes to the library. He meets the library lady and discovers books to read. This helps change the problem of knowing all of Papá Grande's stories because Tomás learns new stories in the library books.

Record details under the arrow column on the Story Map.

TEACHER NOTE	In this module, students do not need to independently identify the event(s) that change the problem. Provide details about the changes so students can focus on the problem and resolution.

Start reading aloud again beginning on page 23, reminding students to use their Story Stones when they hear details about the resolution. Continue reading the remainder of the story (except the author's note). Pause after page 25 for students to Think-Pair-Share: "What is the resolution, or how does the problem end?"

Use Equity Sticks to call on students to share with the group the problem and resolution from the text.

  ▪ *The resolution is that Tomás becomes the family's new storyteller.*

Write and illustrate the resolution on the class *Tomás and the Library Lady* Story Map.

58

Copyright © 2016 Great Minds®

WIT & WISDOM™   G1 > M1 > Lesson 4

TOMÁS AND THE LIBRARY LADY STORY MAP

Characters	Setting
▪ Tomás (drawing of Tomás). ▪ Papá Grande (drawing of Papá Grande). ▪ Papá (drawing of Papá). ▪ Mamá (drawing of Mamá). ▪ Enrique (drawing of Enrique). ▪ Library lady (drawing of the library lady).	▪ Car (between Texas and Iowa) (drawing of car). ▪ House (Iowa) (drawing of house). ▪ Fields (Iowa) (drawing of fields). ▪ Library (Iowa) (drawing of library). ▪ Dump (Iowa) (drawing of dump).

Problem		Resolution
▪ Tomás knows all of Papá Grande's stories. (draw a speech bubble with an X)	▪ Tomás reads books from the library. (draw books)	▪ Tomás becomes the new storyteller of the family. (draw a speech bubble with a book inside)

Extension

Assign small groups either problem or resolution. Groups will make tableaux to show their assigned story element. Review how to make tableaux as needed.

- *(Problem: One student poses as Papá Grande telling a story. Another student poses as Tomás telling the story's ending. Another student holds their arms over the other students to represent the tree.)*

- *(Resolution: One student poses as Tomás reading a book to the rest of the students, who represent his family.)*

Circulate to observe students demonstrating the problem and resolution.

Share details from the tableaux to reinforce the key ideas: Stories have problems, which are things that challenge the main character. A story's resolution is when the problem is solved at the end.

RETELL THE STORY

Pairs 10 MIN.

Now that students understand the problem and resolution, pairs will retell the story to each other by telling what happened with the problem and resolution.

Remind students to consider the important things that happened when they retell the story.

✔ Pairs take turns orally retelling the story, including key details about the problem and resolution. Students flip through the text for picture support as they retell the story.

> *Tomás and his family rode to Iowa. In Iowa, Papá Grande told stories to Tomás and Enrique. The problem was Tomás already knew all of his stories. So Tomás went to the library and met the library lady. She gave him books to read. He went home and told the stories to his family. Tomás went to the library to say goodbye to the library lady and she gave him a book. His family drove to Texas. The resolution was that Tomás became the new storyteller.*

Circulate to listen as students orally retell the story to a partner.

> *Extension*
>
> Ask: "How have the summaries been different for each of the three lessons?"
>
> Instruct students to Think-Pair-Share to reflect on how each summary has changed.

EXECUTE USING SENTENCE FRAMES

Individuals 15 MIN.

Remind students that they have been studying the importance of speaking and writing in complete sentences. In this lesson they will use this important skill in their Focusing Question Task.

Read the Craft Question: "How do I use Sentence Frames in speaking and writing?" Explain to students will use the Sentence Frames to complete Focusing Question Task 1.

Display Handout 4A: Focusing Question 1 Prompt.

Read aloud the Focusing Question: *How do library books change life for Tomás?*

Students Echo Read:

> *Write and draw to retell the story* Tomás and the Library Lady.

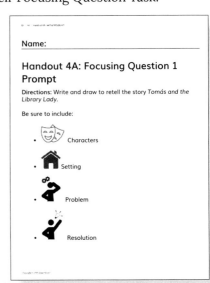

Include key details about:

- *Characters*
- *Setting*
- *Problem*
- *Resolution*

Display and distribute Assessment 4: Focusing Question Task 1. Post the Story Map for *Tomás and the Library Lady*.

Call on students using Equity Sticks.

- *I notice the pictures from the Story Map and Story Stones.*
- *I notice there are three lines in the Sentence Frame.*

Remind students that the story symbols represent the most important parts of a story. They will use the same symbols and Sentence Frames to help retell the story in writing.

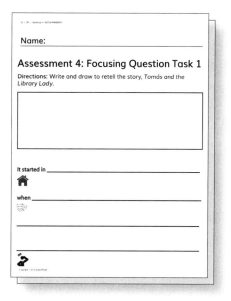

Students point to each word as they Echo Read the Sentence Frame, using a filler word like "blank" or "hmm" for the missing words.

Point to the setting icon in the Sentence Frame. Ask "What does this picture mean on the Story Map?" Silently count to three, allowing students to chorally respond. Point to Settings on the Story Map. Read the information, then remind students where they can find it.

Repeat the process for characters and the problem. Remind students to use the main character and main setting when writing their retelling.

Ask students to point to the illustration box at the top of the page. Tell students to illustrate their sentence after they complete the Sentence Frame.

✔ Pairs use the Sentence Frames to orally rehearse their sentence before independently completing page 1 of Focusing Question Task 1.

Scaffold

- Some students may need additional assistance in the form of underwriting or scribing to complete the Sentence Frame.
- Students Echo Read the sentence as they identify the story symbols.

Gather materials as needed and tell students they will continue this work in the next lesson.

Land 3 MIN.

ANSWER THE CONTENT FRAMING QUESTION

Organize: *What is happening in* Tomás and the Library Lady?

Hold up the problem and resolution Story Stones as you ask: "How did knowing the problem and resolution help you retell what happens in the story?" Use Equity Sticks to choose students to answer and prompting questions to help students build on each other's thinking.

- *The problem and resolution are important parts of the story.*

Ask: "Did we answer the Content Framing Question?" Students respond with a Nonverbal Signal, such as ASL signs for *yes* (**http://witeng.link/0400**) and *no* (**http://witeng.link/0401**).

Wrap 2 MIN.

In the next lesson, students will find out more about the main character, Tomás, by looking at key parts of the book more closely.

Analyze

Context and Alignment

Students write independently as they use information on the Story Map to complete the Sentence Frames in Focusing Question Task 1 in preparation for drafting independent narrative retelling later in the module. (RL.1.2, RL.1.3, W.1.3, SL.1.1.a)

Check for the following success criteria:

- Draws setting and character(s).
- Writes the setting, main character, and the problem.

Next Steps

If students do not illustrate details about the setting and characters, direct them to specific pages in the text to help them add details to one of those categories.

If students struggle to use the Story Map to complete the Sentence Frames, model the process one line at a time using evidence from the Story Map to complete the frame.

G1 > M1 > Lesson 4   WIT & WISDOM™

⬇ Lesson 4: Style and Conventions Deep Dive

Finding Proper Nouns

- **Time:** 15 min.

- **Text:** *Tomás and the Library Lady*, Pat Mora, Raul Colón

- **Style and Conventions Learning Goal:** Identify and generate proper nouns. (L.1.1.b)

- **STYLE AND CONVENTIONS CRAFT QUESTION:** Lesson 4
  Experiment: *What is the difference between a common noun and a proper noun?*

Launch

Display and read the Craft Question: *What is the difference between a common noun and a proper noun?*

Students Echo Read the question. Remind students that they have found common nouns and added them to their chart. Review the chart and explain that they will learn about proper nouns in this lesson and add them to their chart.

Learn

Students Think-Pair-Share to answer the question, "Who are the characters in our book?" Use Equity Sticks to choose volunteers to share their thinking. Capture relevant responses.

- *Tomás*
- *Mamá*
- *Papá*
- *The library lady*
- *Enrique*
- *Papá Grande*

Students Think-Pair-Share to answer the question, "What do you notice that is the same about all these words we listed?" Volunteers respond.

- *They are all names.*
- *They all have a big, or capital, letter.*
- *They are all people.*
- *They are all nouns.*

Affirm correct answers and explain that students are going to learn about a special type of noun called a proper noun.

Explain that proper nouns are names of specific people and places, and one way we can tell they are

64

Copyright © 2016 Great Minds®

proper nouns is that they have a capital letter. Explain that sentences also begin with a capital letter so they should look for words in different parts of the sentence that begin with a capital letter.

Students work in pairs to go on a safari to find proper nouns in the text. As they find proper nouns, they should mark the page with a sticky note. Since students will be limited in the number of proper nouns they will find on the pages, encourage them to add other proper nouns by looking around the classroom or thinking of other examples. Use Equity Sticks to choose volunteers to share the words they located in the text and add them to the chart. Help students read these words as needed.

Nouns			
Common Nouns ("the ")			Proper Nouns
People (characters) - Grandpa	Places (setting) - Library	Things - Car - Corn - Ball - Tree - Books	(characters and setting) - Papá - Mamá - Papá Grande - Tomás - Library lady - Texas - Iowa

Students add the new proper nouns to their charts in their Response Journals.

✓ Distribute word cards from Handout 4B: Noun Cards to pairs, along with the chart. Echo Read the words with the students to ensure they know what each card says. Have the pairs sort the cards into the correct column on the chart.

Land

Instruct students to Think-Pair-Share, and ask: "What is the difference between a common noun and a proper noun?"

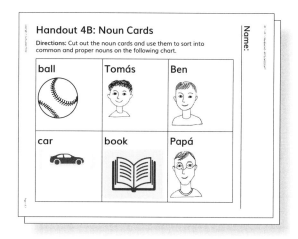

Use Equity Sticks to select two pairs to share their thinking. Use their responses to reinforce that proper nouns name a specific person, place, or thing, and that they are capitalized. Explain that students will continue to use these nouns in their writing and look for them in the texts they are reading.

WIT & WISDOM™   G1 > M1 > Lesson 5

■ FOCUSING QUESTION: LESSONS 1-6

How do library books change life for Tomás?

1 2 3 4 **5** 6 7 8 9 10 11 12 13 14 15 16 17 18 19 20 21 22 23 24 25 26 27 28 29 30 31 32

Lesson 5

TEXT

- *Tomás and the Library Lady*, Pat Mora, Raul Colón

Copyright © 2016 Great Minds®

G1 > M1 > Lesson 5   WIT & WISDOM™

Lesson 5: At a Glance

AGENDA

Welcome (3 min.)

Define Imagination

Launch (5 min.)

Understand the Content Framing Question

Learn (60 min.)

Dramatize the Main Character's Imagination (30 min.)

Execute Using Sentence Frames (30 min.)

Land (5 min.)

Answer the Content Framing Question

Wrap (2 min.)

Vocabulary Deep Dive: Frayer Model for *Value* (15 min.)

STANDARDS ADDRESSED

The full text of ELA Standards can be found in the Module Overview.

Reading

- RL.1.1, RL.1.2, RL.1.3, RL.1.7

Writing

- W.1.3. W.1.8

Speaking and Listening

- SL.1.1.a, SL.2

Language

- ⬇ L.1.6

MATERIALS

- Assessment 4: Focusing Question Task 1
- *Tomás and the Library Lady* Story Map
- Enlarged copy of the Frayer Model
- Handout 5A: Frayer Model
- Vocabulary Journals

Learning Goals

Distinguish between what Tomás imagines and what is real in *Tomás and the Library Lady*. (RL.1.3)

✔ Act out sensory details of Tomás's imagination in small groups.

Write a narrative retelling of *Tomás and the Library Lady* that shows how library books change life for Tomás. (RL.1.2, RL.1.3, W.1.3, W.1.8, L.1.2.b, SL.1.1.a)

✔ Complete the second part of Focusing Question Task 1.

⬇ Develop vocabulary knowledge of the word *value*. (L.1.6)

✔ Complete Sentence Frames in Vocabulary Journal.

Copyright © 2016 Great Minds®

✔ Checks for Understanding

WIT & WISDOM™   G1 > M1 > Lesson 5

Prepare

FOCUSING QUESTION: Lessons 1-6

How do library books change life for Tomás?

CONTENT FRAMING QUESTION: Lesson 5

Reveal: *What does a deeper exploration of the main character reveal in* Tomás and the Library Lady?

CRAFT QUESTION: Lesson 5

Execute: *How do I use Sentence Frames in speaking and writing?*

Students focus on learning more about Tomás. They study key parts of *Tomás and the Library Lady* to differentiate Tomás's imagination from reality and dramatize Tomás's actions. Acting out scenes from the book provides an active and meaningful way to deepen understanding of what is happening in the text. They explore Tomás as a character through his imagination and make connections between the beginning and the end. Students also complete Focusing Question Task 1, using Sentence Frames to finish orally retelling the story.

Welcome 3 MIN.

Ask: "What do you think about when you hear the word *imagination*?"

Instruct students to Think-Pair-Share.

- *I use my imagination when I pretend.*
- *I think about dreaming.*
- *Artists use their imagination when they draw a picture.*

Define *imagination* as "making a picture in your mind of something that you are not experiencing in real life."

Put *imagination* on the Word Wall, along with a simple picture as a visual cue, as a year-long word.

Tell students to listen for the word *imagination* in the day's lesson.

69

Copyright © 2016 Great Minds®

Launch 5 MIN.

UNDERSTAND THE CONTENT FRAMING QUESTION

Post the Content Framing Question and Focusing Question. Echo Read the Content Framing Question.

Ask: "What is an *exploration*?" A volunteer responds.

Reinforce that explorations are adventures and that readers take explorations through text as they closely study the important information. Explain that this allows them to uncover hidden information. A deeper exploration of a text can reveal new information.

Define the word *reveal* as "to show or make known."

Post the word and definition on the Word Wall with a visual such as an image of a magician's hat or a magnifying glass to help students remember the meaning of *reveal*.

Ask students: "According to our Content Framing Question, what are we exploring more deeply in our book today?"

- *We are exploring the main character.*
- *Tomás is the main character. We'll think more about him.*

Learn 60 MIN.

DRAMATIZE THE MAIN CHARACTER'S IMAGINATION

Whole Group 30 MIN.

Explain that students will closely read four parts of the book to learn more about Tomás. Read aloud the second half of page 11, starting with "What would you like to read about?" Read the first sentence of page 13. Ask the following Text-Dependent Question (TDQ).

1 What just changed for Tomás?

- *He starts thinking about dinosaurs.*
- *He imagines he is in the book. On the page before, he was thinking about the library.*

WIT & WISDOM™   G1 > M1 > Lesson 5

Use students' responses to confirm that page 11 describes Tomás's real-life situation, while page 13 describes a situation he imagines.

Share that if students look carefully at what Tomás imagines, it gives them clues about what the main character is thinking and feeling.

Explain that students will keep reading parts of the story. Tell them they will stand up when the text describes Tomás's imagination and sit down when the text describes his real life. Students practice standing up and sitting down as you read a few sentences from pages 11 and 13.

Alternate Activity

Create sets of prompt cards with symbols to represent reality and imagination. Reality could be represented by a globe, and imagination by a thought bubble. Students use the cards to indicate if a detail relates to reality or imagination.

Tell students that to explore Tomás's imagination and reality even more deeply, they will use their bodies to act out Tomás's actions. Model how to act out a couple of sentences on page 11, such as Tomás drinking water and looking at the ceiling.

Reread the last paragraph on page 11, with students acting out Tomás's actions. You might act out the library lady's actions to help students show Tomás's interactions with her.

- *(Students look at the ceiling and wall.)*
- *(Students pick up and open an imaginary book.)*

Continue reading on page 13, making sure students remember to stand up when the text describes an imaginary scene. You might act out the animals' actions to help students show Tomás's reactions to them.

- *(Students bring their hands to their ears to indicate hearing and flap their arms to imitate a snakebird.)*
- *(Students use their hands to hold on to an imaginary dinosaur.)*

Read pages 21 and 25–27 aloud.

✔ As students listen to the pages read aloud, they stand up and sit down when Tomás's attention shifts between reality and imagination, and dramatize Tomás's actions.

Page 21: "He smelled the smoke at an Indian camp. He rode a black horse across a hot, dusty desert."

- *(Students point to their noses to indicate smelling.)*
- *(Students fan themselves with their hands to indicate heat.)*

Page 27: "He saw the dinosaurs drinking cool water long ago. He heard the cry of the wild snakebird. He felt the warm neck of the dinosaur as he held on tight for a bumpy ride."

- *(Students bring their hands to their brow to indicate looking at dinosaurs drinking water.)*
- *(Students bring their hands to their ears to indicate hearing a snakebird.)*
- *(Students bounce up and down to represent riding on a dinosaur.)*

71

Copyright © 2016 Great Minds®

Flip to the beginning of the story to compare it with the end. Read page 3 aloud, starting with "Year after year." Students Think-Pair-Share about the following TDQs.

2 **How is this part of the beginning similar to the end? How is it different?**

- *On both pages, Tomás is riding in the car. In the beginning, he pays attention to real life. In the end, he imagines he's in a book.*
- *He bumps in the beginning and the end. First, the car bumps. At the end, the car bumps again. Tomás pretends it's a dinosaur.*
- *Both times, he thinks about water. In the beginning, he wants a glass of water because it's hot. At the end, he imagines dinosaurs drinking cold water.*

3 **What do you notice about how Tomás uses his imagination?**

- *Tomás imagines that he is inside the books. He is part of the action.*
- *He enjoys the stories and imagines he is there.*
- *He forgets about Iowa and Texas. He imagines being in different places.*

Scaffold

Before students dramatize Tomás's actions, briefly review the five senses for students by asking: "What are the five senses?" Call on student volunteers for responses. Follow up by asking students to point to what they see/touch/taste/smell/feel/hear with.

Encourage students to pay attention to the sensory details of Tomás's imagination before acting them out.

Students individually act out details, focusing on what Tomás experiences with his senses.

Extension

Further explore details about water, a motif used throughout the story.

Read aloud the text, and together annotate for details about water using sticky notes. Discuss the details and their significance.

- *Page 3: Tomás wants cold water to drink and pour on his face when he is hot and tired in the car ride.*
- *Page 5: Tomás and Enrique bring water to Papá and Mamá in the fields.*
- *Page 11: The library lady offers Tomás cold water to drink before he reads books.*
- *Page 19: Tomás has to drink water before reading new books.*
- *Page 23: Tomás will miss the cool water in the library.*
- *Page 27: In his imagination, Tomás sees the dinosaurs drinking cool water.*
- *Water is in many places in the story.*
- *Water appears in real life and in Tomás's imagination.*

WIT & WISDOM™   G1 > M1 > Lesson 5

EXECUTE USING SENTENCE FRAMES

Pairs 30 MIN.

Display the prompt for Focusing Question Task 1, and the *Tomás and the Library Lady* Story Map. Ask: "What did we do for our Focusing Question Task in the previous lesson?" Call on a volunteer to respond.

Display and distribute Assessment 4: Focusing Question Task 1, pages 2–3.

Students Echo Read page 2 as they touch each word. This page tells when the problem started changing in the story. Remind students that their job on this page is to illustrate what the words say.

Students turn to page 3. Ask: "Which story element icon do you see on this page?" Count to three and ask students to loud-whisper the answer. Ask students to point to where they can find the information to complete the Sentence Frame. Read the information on the Story Map. Remind students to illustrate the resolution.

✔ Pairs use the Sentence Frames to orally rehearse their sentence before independently completing pages 2–3 of Focusing Question Task 1.

> *Scaffold*
>
> Some students may need additional assistance in the form of underwriting or scribing to complete the Sentence Frame.

Land 5 MIN.

ANSWER THE CONTENT FRAMING QUESTION

Reveal: *What does a deeper exploration of the main character reveal in* Tomás and the Library Lady?

Ask: "What did we learn about Tomás today?" Volunteers respond.

Instruct students to Think-Pair-Share, and read the Content Framing Question.

- *Things happen to Tomás in real life and Tomás also imagines things from books.*
- *Tomás has a big imagination.*
- *Tomás imagines with all his senses.*

Wrap 2 MIN.

In the next lesson, students will find connections between the author's note and the story in *Tomás and the Library Lady*.

Analyze

Context and Alignment

Students write independently as they use information on the Story Map to complete the Sentence Frames in Focusing Question Task 1 in preparation for drafting independent narrative retellings later in the module (RL.1.2, RL.1.3, W.1.3, W.1.8, SL.1.1.a).

Check for the following success criteria:

- Illustrates when the problem changes and the resolution.
- Writes the resolution to the problem.

Next Steps

If students do not illustrate details about the problem change and the resolution, direct them to specific pages in the text to help them add details to one of those categories.

If students struggle to use the Story Map to complete the Sentence Frame for the resolution, model the process using evidence on the Story Map to complete the frame.

WIT & WISDOM™   G1 > M1 > Lesson 5

⬇ Lesson 5: Vocabulary Deep Dive

Vocabulary Strategies: Frayer Model for *Imagination*

- **Time:** 15 min.

- **Text:** *Tomás and the Library Lady*, Pat Mora, Raul Colón

- **Vocabulary Learning Goal:** Develop vocabulary knowledge of the word *imagination*. (L.1.6)

Launch

Remind students of how they listened for *reality* and *imagination* in their lesson and explain that now they will learn more about the word *imagination*.

Ask students to close their eyes and think of a place they would like to visit. Students Think-Pair-Share and discuss the place they saw in their minds.

Ask students to close their eyes and think of a character in their favorite story. Students draw the character they saw in their minds.

Students Think-Pair-Share about what they used to help them think of the places they wanted to visit and their favorite characters. Use Equity Sticks to choose volunteers to share their thinking.

- *Our minds.*
- *Our imaginations.*

Learn

Post a large copy of the Frayer Model for students to see. Write the word *imagination* in the center circle. Read the word for the students and have them repeat it several times.

Begin to complete the chart by writing a definition in the first quadrant. Tell students that *imagination* is thinking about something that is pretend or not real. Ensure that students understand this definition before writing it on the class chart.

As a class, generate a list of facts and characteristics for *imagination*. Remind students how Tomás uses his imagination in the story. Use pages from the text to help students begin to generate their list. Possible responses may include:

- *Characters you see in your mind from a story.*
- *A place you see in your mind that you have never been to.*
- *A place you made up that you want to make someday.*

75

Copyright © 2016 Great Minds®

After generating the list of characteristics, work with the class to generate examples that fit the characteristics. Encourage students to think of things they have seen in their imaginations while reading books or listening to stories. In a similar fashion, generate a list of non-examples.

✔ Partners look through their books and find evidence of when Tomás used his imagination while reading books. Students mark their pages with sticky notes.

Land

Use Equity Sticks to choose volunteers to share their evidence from the book. Encourage them to use complete sentences when sharing.

Students add the word *imagination* to Handout 5A: Frayer Model from the Student Edition, and place this in their Vocabulary Journals.

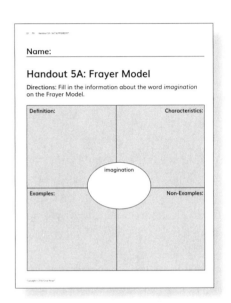

WIT & WISDOM™   G1 › M1 › Lesson 6

■ FOCUSING QUESTION: LESSONS 1–6

How do library books change
life for Tomás?

| 1 | 2 | 3 | 4 | 5 | 6 | 7 | 8 | 9 | 10 | 11 | 12 | 13 | 14 | 15 | 16 | 17 | 18 | 19 | 20 | 21 | 22 | 23 | 24 | 25 | 26 | 27 | 28 | 29 | 30 | 31 | 32 |

Lesson 6

TEXT

- *Tomás and the Library Lady*, Pat Mora, Raul Colón

- "ASL Sign for: same," *American Sign Language Dictionary*

Copyright © 2016 Great Minds®

G1 > M1 > Lesson 6

WIT & WISDOM™

Lesson 6: At a Glance

AGENDA

Welcome (5 min.)

Draft Portrait

Launch (5 min.)

Understand the Content Framing Question

Learn (60 min.)

Relate the Author's Note to the Story (20 min.)

Excel Using Sentence Frames (10 min.)

Record Knowledge (20 min.)

Reflect on the Essential Question (10 min.)

Land (3 min.)

Answer the Content Framing Question

Wrap (2 min.)

Vocabulary Deep Dive: Frayer Model for *Value* (15 min.)

STANDARDS ADDRESSED

The full text of ELA Standards can be found in the Module Overview.

Reading

- RL.1.1, RL.1.3

- RI.1.1, RI.1.3

Speaking and Listening

- SL.1.1.a, SL.1.6

Language

- ⬇ L.1.6

MATERIALS

- Speaking and Listening Anchor Chart

- Essential Questions Chart

- Handout 6A: Essential Questions Chart

- Blank word cards

- *Tomás and the Library Lady* Story Map

- Knowledge Journal

- Sticky flags

- World Map

- Enlarged copy of the Frayer Model

- Handout 6B: Frayer Model

- Vocabulary Journals

Learning Goals

Write and speak about how *Tomás and the Library Lady* adds to knowledge of how books change lives.

✔ Contribute to the Knowledge Journal.

Revise a narrative retelling for correct usage of Sentence Frames.

✔ Revise Focusing Question Task 1.

⬇ Develop vocabulary knowledge of the word *value*. (L.1.6)

✔ Use Sentence Frames to demonstrate map understanding of the word *value*.

✔ Checks for Understanding

Copyright © 2016 Great Minds®

WIT & WISDOM™   G1 > M1 > Lesson 6

Prepare

FOCUSING QUESTION: Lessons 1-6

How do library books change life for Tomás?

CONTENT FRAMING QUESTION: Lesson 6

Know: *How does* Tomás and the Library Lady *build our knowledge of how books change lives?*

CRAFT QUESTION: Lesson 6

Excel: *How do I improve using Sentence Frames in my writing?*

Students wrap up work with Tomás by drawing his portrait. Students then relate two key pieces of information in the author's note to the story *Tomás and the Library Lady*. This provides them with background about Tomás Rivera and the powerful understanding that the story they read is based on a true story. Students also begin to fill in the Essential Questions Chart, which holds key information about how books change lives for many of the texts in the module. Students learn to revise their writing by improving their sentences in Focusing Question Task 1. Finally, they are introduced to the Knowledge Journal, where they include important knowledge gained throughout their work with this text.

Welcome 5 MIN.

DRAFT A PORTRAIT

Now that students know both what a portrait is and lots of details about the main character Tomás, they will put this knowledge to use by drawing a portrait of Tomás reading a book.

Distribute a blank drawing frame to each student. Students use what they know about Tomás from the text to draft a portrait of Tomás reading a book. Remind students to refer to the text for ideas, and point out the definition of *portrait* on the Word Wall for reference.

Explain that this portrait will be the first of four illustrations they create to include on the cover page for their EOM project.

79

Copyright © 2016 Great Minds®

Launch 5 MIN.

UNDERSTAND THE CONTENT FRAMING QUESTION

TEACHER NOTE | Typically, students will work through all five Content Stages, focusing on Distill before proceeding to Know. However, you will note that the first few Focusing Question arcs of this module skip the Distill stage. This intentional delay allows students to build confidence in retelling complex stories. They will apply this skill later in the module to a more independently accessible text, *Green Eggs and Ham*, when they learn about central message.

Post the Content Framing Question and Focusing Question.

Echo Read the Content Framing Question.

Students Think-Pair-Share: "What does *knowledge* mean?"

- *Information we learn.*
- *We know things are true.*

In this lesson students explore everything they have learned from reading *Tomás and the Library Lady* in order to understand how books change lives.

Learn 60 MIN.

RELATE THE AUTHOR'S NOTE TO THE STORY

Whole Group 20 MIN.

Explain that students will read a new part of the book to build their knowledge. Remind students that during a Read Aloud they should practice their best listening.

* Display the Speaking and Listening Anchor Chart.

---

* *This icon indicates an opportunity to practice Speaking and Listening skills.*

WIT & WISDOM™   G1 > M1 > Lesson 6

TEACHER NOTE	Tomás Rivera, the real person who inspired Pat Mora to write *Tomás and the Library Lady*, was an amazing author and educator who wrote great works of fiction and poetry and became the chancellor of the University of California, Riverside. He grew up in poverty and experienced discrimination as a Mexican-American educator and writer. Learn about Rivera for yourself to deepen your student's appreciation of his inspiring life.

Read aloud "A Note about the Story" on page 24.

Tell student's that this information is known as an author's note. Ask, "What does this author's note explain?"

Explain that an author's note is informational text. This note provides information about Tomás Rivera, the main character of the story. In real life, Tomás Rivera was "a migrant worker who valued education" and became a successful author and education leader.

Tell students you will read the note again as they listen for information that connects to, or is the same as, the story. Students indicate what is the same by using a Nonverbal Signal, such as the ASL sign for *same* (**http://witeng.link/0272**).

Use student responses to highlight important connections. Illustrate two important connections on word cards:

- A migrant worker (drawing of a migrant worker).
- Encouraged to read by a librarian in Iowa (drawing of a boy reading next to a librarian).

Define the words *encourage* and *migrant*. Tell students that a *migrant worker* is "a person who moves to different places looking for work," and *encourage* means "to cheer someone on."

Post cards with the word, definition, and illustration for the words *migrant* and *encouraged* on opposite sides of the room.

TEACHER NOTE	Students will reference these cards in the next part of the activity. At the end of the lesson, put the words on the Word Wall as module words.

Scaffold

Show photographs or a brief video about migrant workers.

Now that students know the words, as you reread the story aloud, students listen for connections between the story and the author's note. When students notice a connected detail in the story, they will signal the appropriate card on the Word Wall.

81

Copyright © 2016 Great Minds®

Read key parts of the story aloud, such as pages 2, 3–4, 5, 11, 13, 16, 19, 23. After each excerpt, students signal toward the card that shows the connection. If answers differ, ask a student signaling to the correct location, "What details in the text show this connection?"

Connections to "migrant worker":

- *Pages 1–2: The illustration shows Tomás in a car at night with his family, traveling from one state to another for work.*

- *Page 3: The text says, "They pick fruit and vegetables for Texas farmers in the winter and for Iowa farmers in the summer." The family has to move every summer.*

- *Page 3: They travel "year after year" for work.*

- *Page 4: This page shows an illustration of Tomás sleeping on a small cot and the text explains that the workers share a small house with other workers. They move into a temporary house.*

Connections to "encouraged to read by a librarian in Iowa":

- *Page 11: Tomás is encouraged to read by the library lady in Iowa just like Tomás Rivera was encouraged by a librarian.*

- *Page 12: The library lady helps Tomás get books from the library, just like a librarian inspired Tomás Rivera.*

- *Page 19: Tomás spends time reading with the library lady, just like Tomás Rivera was encouraged to read by a librarian.*

WIT & WISDOM™   G1 > M1 > Lesson 6

Extension

Extension: Before the Read Aloud, write and illustrate a third important detail from the author's note on a card:
- Valued education (drawing of books inside a heart).

During the Read Aloud, students identify and discuss connections to all three details.

Connections to "valued education":

- *Page 8: Papá Grande tells Tomás stories. The family values stories and shares them.*

- *Page 8: Papá Grande suggests that Tomás go to the library to find new stories. He encourages Tomás to spend time there to learn.*

- *Page 11: The librarian gives Tomás books for him to read and learn from.*

- *Page 16: The librarian encourages Tomás to take books home to read to his family and learn.*

- *Page 17: Tomás's family wants him to share everything that he reads. The family gathers around to listen and shows how deeply they care about Tomás's interest in reading. The family spends time reading and learning from one another.*

- *Page 18: Tomás looks for books at the town dump. This shows how much he values reading and learning.*

- *Pages: 13–14, 21–22, and 27–28: Tomás gets so interested in the stories and he imagines all the details.*

- *Page 23: Papá Grande comes to the library to thank the librarian for sharing books and reading with Tomás. He is grateful to the librarian for inspiring Tomás.*

- *Page 26: As they leave Iowa, the illustration shows Papá Grande and Tomás reading in the back of the car.*

EXCEL USING SENTENCE FRAMES

Pairs 10 MIN.

Share the Craft Question for the lesson: "How do I improve using Sentence Frames in my writing?"

In this lesson students revise the first sentence of Focusing Question Task 1 to make sure they used the Sentence Frames well to retell *Tomás and the Library Lady*.

Define the word *revise* for students. *Revise* means "to do over." Write the word and definition on a word card, and place it on the interactive Word Wall.

Tell students the first step in revising is to reread your writing to see if it makes sense. The second step is to correct the mistakes on your draft.

Display the Story Map and page 1 of the Focusing Question Task. Echo Read the sentence on page 1. Ask: "What word did you write to tell about the setting?" Students share their writing with a partner.

Select two students to share their responses and tell where they found the information.

83

Copyright © 2016 Great Minds®

G1 › M1 › Lesson 6   WIT & WISDOM™

✔ Students stand and air-write any new words, then correct their draft. Students may also revise or add to their illustration. Students repeat this process in pairs for character and problem.

| TEACHER NOTE | The amount of revising done by students early in the school year will vary. Revise according to the developmental level of your students. |

Revisit the Craft Question. Students Think-Pair-Share: "How do I improve using Sentence Frames in my writing?"

- *First, reread your writing to see if it makes sense with the frame.*
- *Fix the mistakes.*

RECORD KNOWLEDGE

Whole Group   20 MIN.

Explain that learners keep track of what they have learned. Remind students of how much they have already learned, including information and skills, or how to do things.

Display a blank Knowledge Journal.

| TEACHER NOTE | To set up the Knowledge Journal, display two pieces of chart paper side-by-side to create the image of an open journal. When scribing information, include images to maximize accessibility and encourage independence. If possible, use different colors for each lesson in which students create Knowledge Journal entries. This will highlight the progression of knowledge and skills over the course of the module. |

Ask: "What is a journal? Why do people keep them?" Volunteers respond.

Reinforce that journals are places where people write important things they want to remember, including what they have learned.

Explain that the Knowledge Journal is a good place to record what they have learned.

Label the left-hand side of the Knowledge Journal "What I know" and include a picture to cue students.

Explain to students that this part of the Knowledge Journal is for the new information they have learned in these lessons.

Instruct students to Think-Pair-Share, and ask: "What did you learn about books from reading *Tomás and the Library Lady*? Explain your answers with details from the text."

84

Copyright © 2016 Great Minds®

WIT & WISDOM™   G1 > M1 > Lesson 6

■ *You can get books from a library. Tomás borrowed books from the library lady.*

■ *Books tell about different things. Tomás read about dinosaurs, tigers, and cowboys.*

■ *You can imagine things in books, like Tomás did when he read books at the library.*

■ *You can tell other people stories from books. Tomás told his family the stories he read in books.*

Scaffold

Ask more concrete questions to prompt students and encourage application of key vocabulary:
- What did you learn about Tomás?
- What did you learn about stories?
- Why are our books important?

Explain that, while all students' thoughts and contributions are valuable, the Knowledge Journal is where students record learning they most need to remember. Use Equity Sticks to call on pairs to share responses. After each response, students stand up if they predict they will need to remember the information, and remain seated if they disagree or are unsure.

Use votes to choose three to four refined responses to record in the Knowledge Journal.

TEACHER NOTE	Students will gradually take more ownership over which information goes into the Knowledge Journal. To support this process, briefly explain the rationale behind the responses you chose.

Label the right-hand side of the Knowledge Journal "What I can do" and include a picture to cue students.

Explain that this column is for things they can now <u>do</u>—in their heads, out loud, or on paper. Reread the "What I can do" side of the Knowledge Journal and encourage students to think about <u>how</u> they learned these things. Revisit artifacts from previous lessons, including Anchor Charts, Response Journal entries, and Focusing Question Task 1.

✔ Instruct students to Think-Pair-Share, and ask: "What did you learn to do as a writer? What did you learn to do as a reader?"

Scaffold

Ask more concrete questions to prompt students and encourage application of key vocabulary:
- What did you do the first time you read *Tomás and the Library Lady*?
- What do we do when we are listening?
- What did you use to write a complete sentence?

Repeat the process detailed above to engage students in a class vote and record refined responses.

85

Copyright © 2016 Great Minds®

What I know	What I can do
▪ I learned books can help you imagine things. ▪ Books can tell you new stories. ▪ I learned you can get books at a library. ▪ I learned librarians can help you find books. ▪ I learned migrant workers move year to year for work.	▪ I know that there is a main character in a story. ▪ I learned that the settings in a story can change. ▪ I can talk about the characters, setting, problem, and resolution when I retell a story. ▪ I know that a problem is the challenge the main character faces, and the resolution is the end of the problem.

Explain to students that they will continue to add to this chart throughout this module so they can track everything they have learned and are now able to do.

REFLECT ON THE ESSENTIAL QUESTION

Whole Group 10 MIN.

Now that they have recorded knowledge about Tomás Rivera, students will build knowledge about the module topic. Display and Echo Read the Essential Question. Explain to students that they will create a chart and continue adding to it throughout the module to track their knowledge about the Essential Question.

Display the Essential Questions Chart and distribute Handout 6A: Essential Questions Chart. Explain that you will be asking students questions to help them complete this chart. Ask: "What are some examples of question words?" Volunteers respond. Tell students to listen carefully to the question words included in each question so that they can understand what the question is asking them.

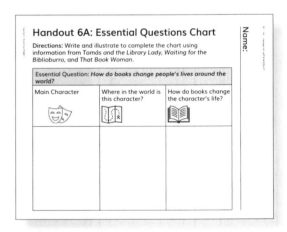

Ask: "Who is the main character of the story?"

Volunteers respond. Write *Tomás* in the Main Character column.

Explain that the middle column is for the place in the world where the story happens. Ask: "Where are most of the settings in the book located?" If students struggle to name states, show page 1 and point out that Tomás's family was driving from Texas to Iowa on the first page. Write *Texas and Iowa* on the chart.

Share that Texas and Iowa are two different states in the United States of America. Add a sticky flag with the name of the location written on it to the class world map. Explain that the class will continue to mark locations on the world map throughout the module as they read new texts and explore different places.

WIT & WISDOM™   G1 > M1 > Lesson 6

Students Think-Pair-Share: "The Essential Question of the module is 'How do books change people's lives around the world?' How do books change Tomás's life in the story?"

- *Tomás can share new stories with his family.*
- *The books help Tomás use his big imagination.*

Ask students to share two to three refined responses. Record sentences and illustrations on the class chart.

ESSENTIAL QUESTIONS CHART

Essential Question: *How do books change people's lives around the world?*		
Main Character	**Where in the world is the character?**	**How do books change the character's life?**
▪ *Tomás*	▪ *Iowa and Texas.*	▪ *Books give Tomás new stories to tell his family. (drawing of book inside speech bubble).* ▪ *Books open Tomás's imagination. (drawing of thought bubble).*

TEACHER NOTE

Students will distill the essential meaning of texts more explicitly when they study *Green Eggs and Ham* later in the module. Recording these big ideas on the Essential Questions Chart is a scaffolded first step to inform their later work with central message. They will revisit this Essential Questions Chart near the end of the module to consider central message for the other texts once they have the context.

Explain to students that they will revisit this chart throughout the module.

87

Copyright © 2016 Great Minds®

 3 MIN.

ANSWER THE CONTENT FRAMING QUESTION

Knowledge: *How does* Tomás and the Library Lady *build our knowledge of how books change lives?*

Students Mix and Mingle: "What did we learn about how books change lives from reading *Tomás and the Library Lady*?" Remind students to consider: "What part of the text helped you learn that?"

Use Equity Sticks to call on two students to share.

- *I learned that you can find more stories in books. Tomás found more stories to tell his family.*
- *Books can help you learn and open your imagination, like when Tomás imagined what he was reading about.*

 2 MIN.

In the next lesson, students start reading a new text, *Waiting for the Biblioburro*.

Analyze

Context and Alignment

Students demonstrate understanding of how the text *Tomás and the Library Lady* adds to their knowledge of how books change lives by discussing and by participating in a shared writing experience (RL.1.1, RL.1.3, RL.1.7, SL.1.1.a, SL.1.2). Check for the following success criterion:

- Actively participates in the discussion.

Next Steps

If students do not actively participate in the discussion, analyze if it is a knowledge or language problem. If it is a language problem, provide students with Sentence Frames to begin their sentences and pair them with a fluent partner. If students experience difficulty making connections to how the text added to their knowledge about books changing lives, review pages 13–14, 17, 21, and 25. After reading each page, ask students, "How are books changing Tomás's life on this page?"

WIT & WISDOM™   G1 › M1 › Lesson 6

⬇ Lesson 6: Vocabulary Deep Dive

Vocabulary Strategies: Frayer Model for *Value*

- **Time:** 15 min.

- **Text:** *Tomás and the Library Lady*, Pat Mora, Raul Colón

- **Vocabulary Learning Goal:** Develop vocabulary knowledge of the word *value*. (L.1.6)

Launch

Remind students of how they explored a new section of the text—the "Note About the Story" in the back of the text. Reread the text and write the word *valued* in a visible place. Have students Think-Pair-Share what they think *valued* means as it is used in the note.

Use Equity Sticks to choose two volunteers to discuss their thinking. Ensure they understand that *valued* here means "how important something is."

Read the "Note About the Story" a second time and help students locate evidence that Tomás Rivera valued education. Remind them that since he valued education, he felt it was very important. Students Think-Pair-Share about how the jobs Rivera held show that he valued education. Use Equity Sticks to choose two or three volunteers to discuss their thinking.

Learn

Post a large copy of the Frayer Model for students to see. Write the word *value* in the center circle. Read the word for the students and have them repeat it several times.

Begin to complete the chart by writing a definition in the first quadrant. Tell students that when you value something, you think it is very important. Ensure that students understand this definition before writing it on the class chart.

As a class, generate a list of facts and characteristics for things that they value. Use pages from the text to help students begin to generate their list. Possible responses may include:

- *Something important that you do.*
- *Something important that you have.*
- *Someone important that you know and love.*

After generating the list of characteristics, work with the class to generate examples that fit the characteristics. Encourage students to think of things they value or that Tomás valued in the text. Remind them that something doesn't need to be expensive to be valued. In a similar fashion, generate a list of non-examples, such as garbage, or when students are mean to one another.

89

Copyright © 2016 Great Minds®

G1 > M1 > Lesson 6

✓ Students fill in the following Sentence Frames in their Vocabulary Journals.

- I value _____ because _____.
- I do not value _____ because _____.

Land

Students Mix and Mingle to share their answers to the Sentence Frames.

Students add the word to Handout 6B: Frayer Model and place this in their Vocabulary Journals.

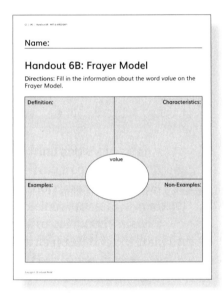

WIT & WISDOM™   G1 > M1 > Lesson 7

■ FOCUSING QUESTION: LESSONS 7-12

How does the Biblioburro change life for Ana?

1 2 3 4 5 6 **7** 8 9 10 11 12 13 14 15 16 17 18 19 20 21 22 23 24 25 26 27 28 29 30 31 32

Lesson 7

TEXT

- *Waiting for the Biblioburro*, Monica Brown, John Parra

Copyright © 2016 Great Minds®

G1 > M1 > Lesson 7

WIT & WISDOM™

Lesson 7: At a Glance

AGENDA

Welcome (10 min.)

Experiment with Fluency

Launch (5 min.)

Understand the Content Framing Question

Learn (55 min.)

Complete a New-Read Assessment (35 min.)

Notice Details and Answer Questions (20 min.)

Land (3 min.)

Answer the Content Framing Question

Wrap (2 min.)

Assign Fluency Homework

Style and Conventions Deep Dive: Finding Verbs (15 min.)

STANDARDS ADDRESSED

The full text of ELA Standards can be found in the Module Overview.

Reading

- RL.1.1, RL.1.2, RL.1.3
- RI.1.1, RI.1.7

Speaking and Listening

- SL.1.1.a, SL.1.2

Language

- L.1.1.j, L.1.2.b
- ⬇ L.1.1.e

MATERIALS

- Fluent Readers Chart
- Handout 7A: Fluency Homework
- Assessment 7: New-Read Assessment 1
- Handout 1A: Notice and Wonder Cards
- Blank Questions and Answers Chart
- Verbs Chart
- Response Journals

Learning Goals

Generate and answer questions about *Waiting for the Biblioburro*, using key details from the text. (RL.1.1)

✔ Complete a New-Read Assessment.

⬇ Identify and generate verbs. (L.1.1.e)

✔ Hunt for verbs and complete a Sentence Frame.

✔ Checks for Understanding

Copyright © 2016 Great Minds®

WIT & WISDOM™   G1 > M1 > Lesson 7

Prepare

FOCUSING QUESTION: Lessons 7–12

How does the Biblioburro change life for Ana?

CONTENT FRAMING QUESTION: Lesson 7

Wonder: *What do I notice and wonder about* Waiting for the Biblioburro?

CRAFT QUESTION: Lesson 7

Experiment: *How does reading fluently work?*

Students are introduced to the components of fluent reading and begin practicing reading with fluency. This leads to students' first encounter with the text *Waiting for the Biblioburro* as they form questions about the book independently through a New-Read Assessment using Sentence Frames. They then continue with the questioning routine, finding answers to the questions they formed in the assessment. These activities help students further develop this independence of monitoring their reading by becoming aware of their notices and wonders.

Welcome 10 MIN.

EXPERIMENT WITH FLUENCY

Display the Fluent Readers Chart. Explain to students that this chart is also on their fluency homework and will remind them how to read fluently. Explain that *fluent* means "being able to read or speak easily or naturally." Students Echo Read the chart. Briefly explain that we will add a new component each day, but for this lesson the focus is on reading without stumbling.

FLUENT READERS CHART

Fluent readers read:
▪ Without stumbling.

Display and read page 17 in *Waiting for the Biblioburro*, beginning with, "Someone should write a story about your burros." Read fluently, emphasizing reading without stumbling. Track the print to model.

Students use Nonverbal Signals to respond to the following question: "Did I read without stumbling?"

93

Copyright © 2016 Great Minds®

G1 > M1 > Lesson 7   WIT & WISDOM™

Distribute Handout 7A: Fluency Homework. Remind students to share the passage with their family. The passage is from the text *Waiting for the Biblioburro*.

Explain that for this lesson's fluency homework, students will practice reading without stumbling. Ask: "What does it mean to read without stumbling?" Volunteers respond.

Reinforce that reading without stumbling means to read smoothly without mistakes. Students point to and underline "read without stumbling" on their homework sheet.

Read the homework passage aloud while students follow along with their fingers. Chorally read the passage. Pairs may stand elbow to elbow while doing the fluency practice.

Name:

Handout 7A: Fluency Homework

Directions: Have an adult initial each day that you read the passage three to five times. Optional: Have a peer sign on the second row of boxes, checking your progress below.

"Someone should write a story about your burros," Ana tells the librarian, rubbing Alfa's nose and feeding more grass to Beto.

"Why don't you?" he asks. Then he packs up the books and is off.

"Enjoy!" he calls to the children. "I will be back."

45 words

Brown, Monica. *Waiting for the Biblioburro*. New York: Random House, 2011. 19. Print.

Day 1	Day 2	Day 3	Day 4	Day 5	Day 6

Launch 5 MIN.

UNDERSTAND THE CONTENT FRAMING QUESTION

Post the Content Framing Question and Focusing Question. Echo Read the Focusing Question.

Ask students: "What is different about this Focusing Question compared to our last Focusing Question?" Repeat the previous Focusing Question if necessary.

Call on one or two volunteers to respond. Confirm that instead of "librarian" and "Tomás," the current Focusing Question says "Biblioburro" and "Ana."

Explain that students will explore a new book, *Waiting for the Biblioburro*, for the next five lessons. And just like with the last text, students will use the Content Framing Questions to help them understand the story and get closer to answering the Focusing Question.

Echo Read the Content Framing Question. Ask a student to remind the class what it means to notice. Ask another student to remind the class what it means to wonder.

Ask: "According to our Content Framing Question, what are we noticing and wondering about?"

Student Echo Read the title of the text as you hold it up.

- *We are noticing and wondering about our new book,* Waiting for the Biblioburro.

94

Copyright © 2016 Great Minds®

G1 > M1 > Lesson 7

Learn 55 MIN.

COMPLETE A NEW-READ ASSESSMENT

Pairs 35 MIN.

This New-Read Assessment assesses whether students can ask and answer questions about a new text, *Waiting for the Biblioburro*.

Explain that the first thing students will do with *Waiting for the Biblioburro* will be to ask questions in order to show everything they have learned about asking and answering questions.

Display and distribute Assessment 7: New-Read Assessment 1 and the text *Waiting for the Biblioburro*.

Explain that students will explore the text *Waiting for the Biblioburro* visually with a partner. Then, they will use one Sentence Frame to create a question they have about the text. After listening to the story, they will answer their question.

Ask: "What are we doing first?" A volunteer responds.

Reinforce that first students will visually explore the text with a partner and then use Sentence Frames to ask questions.

Display and Echo Read the Sentence Frames. Remind students that they have used the words to ask questions about *Tomás and the Library Lady*.

Who _____?

Where _____?

When _____?

Remind students:

- <u>Who</u> questions tell you about people.
- <u>Where</u> questions tell you about places or locations.
- <u>When</u> questions tell you about a time.

✔ Students choose one Sentence Frame and orally rehearse their question with a partner. Individually, students write and draw to formulate a question.

95

Copyright © 2016 Great Minds®

TEACHER NOTE   As students ask questions during the New-Read Assessment, choose four to six student-generated questions to record on sticky notes labeled with students' initials. Create the Wonder Chart, adhere the notes, and share student questions as time is available.

Tell students that you will reread the text aloud to help them answer their question. Remind students to listen carefully for the answer to their question as the story is read aloud.

Read the text aloud, including the author's note, without interruptions.

Students write and draw to answer their question.

> *Differentiation*
>
> Underwriting or scribing may be necessary for some students. Encourage students to use phonetic spelling as they write to ask and answer their questions.

NOTICE DETAILS AND ANSWER QUESTIONS

Whole Group 20 MIN.

TEACHER NOTE   The pages of *Waiting for the Biblioburro* are unnumbered. In this module, pages 1–2 have text that begins "On a hill behind a tree" and show the illustration of a house on a hill. Write small page numbers in your text for easy reference.

Explain that students will look at the pictures in the story and share what they notice, just as they did with *Tomás and the Library Lady*. Remind students that good readers notice as they read a text because it helps them pay attention and see details.

Students retrieve their Notice Prompt Card from Handout 1A: Notice and Wonder Prompt Cards. Tell students they will stand up with the prompt card each time they notice something.

Visually explore the book by slowly, silently flipping through pages. Students stand up with the Notice Prompt Card when they notice details.

Students Think-Pair-Share: "What do you notice in the illustrations?" Use Equity Sticks to call on students for their observations. Use the text to clarify any responses to model appropriate notices.

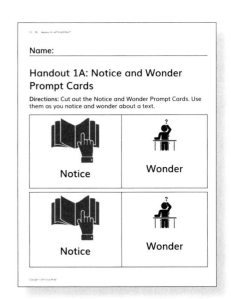

Display the Questions and Answers Chart with the questions you captured from the New-Read Assessment.

Students Echo Read the questions you added to the chart.

Read the text aloud again as students listen for answers to their questions.

Students stand up when they hear the answers to their questions. When they stand, flag the page in your copy of the text with a sticky note and record initials of some standing students.

After finishing the story, return to the flagged pages. Call on a student who stood up for that page to respond to a question on the Questions and Answers Chart. As needed, reread that section of the text to confirm and clarify students' thinking. Record the answer on the relevant sticky note. Each time, move sticky notes across the chart to indicate the extent to which each question has been answered. If there are any unanswered questions, explain that students will revisit the chart after they've had more time to explore the text to answer the remaining questions.

WAITING FOR THE BIBLIOBURRO QUESTIONS AND ANSWERS CHART

Questions ?	Answers in progress ⟷	Complete answers ✓
▪ (Q1) Where does Ana live? ▪ (Q2) Who brings the books to Ana's village? ▪ (Q3) When is Ana using her imagination?	▪ (Q3) On pages 15–16 Ana is imagining she is part of the stories she is telling.	▪ (Q1) Ana lives on a farm in a village in the hills (pages 1–4). ▪ (Q2) The librarian and his two donkeys, Alfa and Beto (pages 11–12).

In future lessons, continue to display the Questions and Answers Chart and allow students to revisit their questions as they work with the text.

Extension

Students label one page in their Response Journals with an "N" for things they notice, and another page with a "W" for things they wonder. Students draw and write sentences about what they notice and wondered about Ana on the pages. Students Think-Pair-Share their entries.

Land 3 MIN.

ANSWER THE CONTENT FRAMING QUESTION

Wonder: *What do you wonder and notice about* Waiting for the Biblioburro?

Invite a volunteer to share one notice they heard from a classmate. Invite a second volunteer to share one wonder they heard from a classmate in the day's lesson.

- *I notice Ana has a lot to do in the morning before breakfast, like bathe her brother, feed, goats, and collect eggs to sell.*
- *I wonder who will read Ana's book next.*

Celebrate the great notices and wonders the students shared. Remind students that in the lessons to come, they will have many more chances to find answers to the wonderful questions they asked as they read the book even more closely.

Wrap  2 MIN.

ASSIGN FLUENCY HOMEWORK

Remind students to share the homework passage from *Waiting for the Biblioburro* with their family, and to practice reading without stumbling.

> ### Analyze
>
> **Context and Alignment**
>
> Students work independently to complete a New-Read Assessment (RL.1.1, L.1.1.j, L.1.2.b). Each student:
>
> - Visually explores *Waiting for the Biblioburro*.
> - Constructs a question using a Sentence Frame.
> - Listens to the story read aloud to answer their question.
>
> **Next Steps**
>
> If students are unable to complete the assessment, consider the following errors: Is the student unable to construct a question? Can they answer the question by drawing and writing? In small groups, provide students additional support by modeling how to ask a question using only one of the Sentence Frames, or construct Sentence Frames using additional words to support students.
>
> Some students may be able to ask and answer questions orally, but not in writing. Model using phonetic spelling and words in the room as you underwrite or scribe.

WIT & WISDOM™   G1 > M1 > Lesson 7

⤓ Lesson 7: Style and Conventions Deep Dive

Finding Verbs

- **Time:** 15 min.

- **Text:** *Waiting for the Biblioburro*, Monica Brown, John Parra

- **Style and Conventions Learning Goal:** Identify and generate verbs. (L.1.1.e)

- **STYLE AND CONVENTIONS CRAFT QUESTION:** Lesson 7
  Experiment: *What is a verb?*

Launch

Display and read the Craft Question: *What is a verb?*

Students Echo Read the question. Explain that in this lesson they will learn about a new type of creature they will see in the text. This creature is different than the last creature they found on their safari, and has a very different function in the text.

Learn

Remind students of how they looked at words that ended in *–ed*. Ask: "What kind of words were those? What did the *–ed* mean?" Volunteers respond. Explain that in this lesson they will look more carefully at verbs. Display the following words on the board:

- Dream

- Wait

- Walk

- Work

- Read

- Write

Echo Read the words with the students. Students Think-Pair-Share about what they notice about all these words. Use Equity Sticks to choose volunteers to share their thinking.

- *They are all things I can do.*
- *They are all things Ana does in the book.*
- *They are all things Tomás does in his book.*
- *They are things my mom does.*

Ensure students understand that all these words are actions or things that can be done. Explain that today they are going to go on a Grammar Safari to find these creatures called *verbs*.

Ask students to share what things they see Ana doing on the pages of *Waiting for the Biblioburro*.

99

Copyright © 2016 Great Minds®

G1 > M1 > Lesson 7

WIT & WISDOM™

Flip through the text showing students the different pages. Generate a list of words to describe what students see in the images. Record students' responses. Use the sentence frame to help them put their responses in complete sentences: **We see Ana** _____. Responses could include the following.

- Read
- Write
- Sit
- Work
- Walk
- Wish
- Imagine

Ask students what they notice about all these words. Guide students to notice that these words are actions or things they can do. Explain that action words are called *verbs*. Verbs are the words we use to tell what we are doing, and when we are doing it. Capture their responses on a Verbs Chart similar to the one below. Save this chart to use in later lessons.

Verbs	
Verbs tell us what we are doing and when we are doing it.	
Present (right now) • Read • Write • Sit • Work • Walk • Wish • Imagine	Past (we already did something)

Explain that these verbs tell what Ana would be doing right now or in the present.

✔ Send students on a safari, either in pairs or individually, in search of verbs around the classroom. During this safari they are looking at their classmates and anything else that does things, like a class pet, to write down their actions. Students write answers to complete the Sentence Frame **We see (Classmate)** _____. in their Response Journals after they have finished their safari.

Conduct a Whip-Around, asking each student to share a sentence they wrote in their Response Journal. Volunteers share verbs to add to the chart.

100

Copyright © 2016 Great Minds®

Land

Instruct students to Think-Pair-Share, and ask: "What is a verb?"

Use Equity Sticks to select two pairs to share their thinking. Use their responses to reinforce that verbs are the words we use to tell what we are doing and when we are doing it. Explain that students will continue to learn about verbs and how to use them in their writing and look for them in the texts they are reading.

Copyright © 2016 Great Minds®

WIT & WISDOM™   G1 > M1 > Lesson 8

■ FOCUSING QUESTION: LESSONS 7-12

How does the Biblioburro change life for Ana?

1 2 3 4 5 6 **7 8 9 10 11 12** 13 14 15 16 17 18 19 20 21 22 23 24 25 26 27 28 29 30 31 32

Lesson 8

TEXTS

- *Museum ABC*, The Metropolitan Museum of Art
- *Waiting for the Biblioburro*, Monica Brown, John Parra

Copyright © 2016 Great Minds®

G1 > M1 > Lesson 8

Lesson 8: At a Glance

AGENDA

Welcome (10 min.)

Determine Subject in Museum ABC

Launch (5 min.)

Understand the Content Framing Question

Learn (55 min.)

Identify the Characters and Settings (25 min.)

Dramatize the Characters and Settings (15 min.)

Retell the Story (15 min.)

Land (2 min.)

Answer the Content Framing Question

Wrap (3 min.)

Homework Check-in

Vocabulary Deep Dive: Ask and Answer Questions about Vocabulary (15 min.)

STANDARDS ADDRESSED

The full text of ELA Standards can be found in the Module Overview.

Reading

- RL.1.1, RL.1.2, RL.1.3, RL.1.7

- RI.1.1, RI.1.7

Speaking and Listening

- SL.1.a, SL.1.2

Language

- ⬇ L.1.6

MATERIALS

- One character and setting Story Stone for each pair of students

- Blank *Waiting for the Biblioburro* Story Map

- Wonder Wheel

Learning Goals

Retell *Waiting for the Biblioburro*, including key details about characters, settings, and major events. (RL.1.3)

✔ Retell events of the story through the lens of character and setting.

⬇ Vocabulary Learning Goal: Ask and answer questions about key vocabulary in *Waiting for the Biblioburro*. (L.1.6)

✔ Use key vocabulary in sentences to demonstrate understanding.

✔ Checks for Understanding

Copyright © 2016 Great Minds®

WIT & WISDOM™   G1 > M1 > Lesson 8

Prepare

FOCUSING QUESTION: Lessons 7-12

How does the Biblioburro change life for Ana?

CONTENT FRAMING QUESTION: Lesson 8

Organize: *What is happening in* Waiting for the Biblioburro?

Students continue to figure out what is happening in groups of paintings in *Museum ABC*, this time learning about still lifes. They transition to understanding what is happening in *Waiting for the Biblioburro*, identifying the characters and settings using Story Stones, with more independence. After they dramatize the characters and settings, they orally retell the story, highlighting those elements.

Welcome 10 MIN.

Remind students of how, in previous lessons about *Museum ABC*, they learned about portraits and landscapes and that both of those words describe types of subjects, or what the painting is about. In this lesson they will look carefully at a single page of paintings about a different subject and try to figure out what is happening.

Display the V page of four paintings from *Museum ABC*. Cover the right half of the page so only the two paintings on the left side are visible.

Ask: "What's happening in these two paintings?"

Highlight that even though this page shows two different paintings, there is one thing that is true for both of the pictures: they are something that artists call *still lifes*.

Ask: "What is the same about both of these paintings?"

- *Both of the paintings have vegetables.*
- *Both of the paintings show things that are placed on a table.*

Focus in on the painting *Still Life: Balsam Apple and Vegetables* (bottom left) from the V page of *Museum ABC*.

Confirm that a still life is a work of art about a group of everyday objects on display. Instead of painting people or places, artists who create still life paintings paint things.

Put the word, definition, and an illustration of objects on a table for the phrase *still life* on the Word Wall as a module term.

105

Copyright © 2016 Great Minds®

G1 > M1 > Lesson 8   WIT & WISDOM™

Ask: "What details in this painting show everyday objects arranged in a still life?"

Instruct students to Think-Pair-Share.

- *I see a big, leafy cabbage in the middle.*
- *I see green pod vegetables in the corner at the bottom.*
- *I see small, round, red things in the other bottom corner.*

Choose one or two students to share their responses with the whole group.

Share that details in still lifes help you see things arranged just as the artist saw them.

Explain that, students will try to answer a similar question about *Waiting for the Biblioburro* and that noticing details in the story will help them understand it better.

Launch 5 MIN.

UNDERSTAND THE CONTENT FRAMING QUESTION

Post the Content Framing Question and Focusing Question.

Remind students that this question will help them think about how things are organized in the story. In this lesson, they will focus on learning more about the characters and setting to retell the story.

Ask: "What did we learn about characters and setting when we read *Tomás and the Library Lady*?" Volunteers respond.

Reinforce that they have learned that characters are who the story is about and that a setting is where and when the story takes place.

Hold up the character and setting Story Stones as you ask: "According to our Content Framing Question, what are we going to tell about in the story?" Students name the Story Stones and then volunteers share additional insights.

- *We are telling about the characters and settings in* Waiting for the Biblioburro.
- *We are retelling what happened in the book.*

106

Copyright © 2016 Great Minds®

Learn 55 MIN.

IDENTIFY THE CHARACTERS AND SETTINGS

Whole Group 25 MIN.

Display a blank *Waiting for the Biblioburro* Story Map.

Distribute a character Story Stone to each student. Explain that as the story is read aloud, pairs will follow along in their copies. Each time the words mention a <u>new</u> character, one partner will touch that character in the illustration with the Story Stone. Partners will take turns, switching each time they find a new character.

Read the story aloud (except the author's note) as students touch pictures of characters with Story Stones.

Students Think-Pair-Share: "Who are the characters in the story?"

Use Equity Sticks to call on students to share the characters in the text. Write and illustrate students' responses on the class *Waiting for the Biblioburro* Story Map.

Ask: "How do we know if a character is a main character?" Volunteers respond.

Reinforce that the main character of a text shows up most frequently. Listen to make sure students identify Ana. Draw a star next to Ana's name on the Story Map.

Distribute a setting Story Stone to each student. As the story is read aloud, pairs follow along in their copies. Each time the words mention a <u>new</u> setting, one partner will touch that setting in the illustration with their Story Stone. Partners will take turns, switching each time they find a new setting.

Reread the story aloud as students touch pictures of settings with Story Stones.

Students Think-Pair-Share: "What are the settings in the story?" Use Equity Sticks to call on students to share with the group different settings they found in the text. Write and illustrate students' responses on the class *Waiting for the Biblioburro* Story Map.

Differentiation

If students name an imaginary or dream scene as a setting, reread the text where Ana uses her imagination or dreams to clarify their thinking. For example, pages 7–8, pages 15–16, and pages 21–22. Ask students, "Where is Ana? Listen to the words for clues. Why does the illustration show a different place?" Follow up by asking: "What clues tell you that Ana is (imagining or dreaming) these settings?"

G1 > M1 > Lesson 8   WIT & WISDOM™

WAITING FOR THE BIBLIOBURRO STORY MAP

Characters	Setting
• Ana (drawing of Ana).	• House
• Mami (drawing of mother).	• Farm
• Papi (drawing of father).	• Bedroom
• Little brother (drawing of little brother).	• Village
• Teacher (drawing of teacher).	
• Bibliotecario (librarian).	
• Alfa (drawing of donkey).	
• Beto (drawing of donkey).	
• Children in the village (drawing of children).	

Problem		Resolution
	⟶	

DRAMATIZE THE CHARACTERS AND SETTINGS

Small Groups 15 MIN.

Remind students that acting a text out can often help them. Explain that small groups will create tableaux for either the characters or settings in the story. Assign small groups either characters or settings using the Story Stone images.

The character-assigned groups choose a few of the characters to represent, including the main character, and indicate in a special way who the main character is. The setting-assigned groups represent all the settings.

Small groups of students create tableaux of either the characters or settings of the story.

Characters:
- *(Pose as Ana writing a book.)*
- *(Pose as the bibliotecario riding or walking a donkey.)*
- *(Pose as Alfa and/or Beto carrying books on their backs.)*
- *(Group gathers together in a circle and points to Ana in the middle to indicate she is the main character.)*

108

Copyright © 2016 Great Minds®

WIT & WISDOM™   G1 > M1 > Lesson 8

Settings:

- *(Pose as a house using arms as a triangular roof.)*
- *(Create a farm scene by posing as plants sprouting from the ground.)*
- *(Create a bedroom by lying flat to pose as a bed.)*
- *(Pose as hills in the village by bending over in a row.)*

Circulate as small groups work together asking scaffolding questions as needed.

As a whole group, ask students assigned to character: "What did your tableaux show about the story's characters?"

- *Ana is the main character.*
- *There are other characters in the story, too.*

As a whole group, ask students assigned to setting: "What did your tableaux show about the story's settings?"

- *There are many settings in the story.*
- *The settings changed.*

Use student responses to reinforce the key ideas that Ana, just like Tomás, is the main character and that there are also other characters in the story. Also, just like *Tomás and the Library Lady*, there is more than one setting in the story and the settings changed.

RETELL THE STORY

Pairs 15 MIN.

Now that students understand the characters and settings, pairs will retell the story to each other by telling about what happened to Ana in the different settings.

Remind students to consider the important things that happened to Ana when they retell. Ask students: "What is one important detail of the story to include in a retelling?" Call on volunteers to respond.

- *An important detail is when the biblioburro comes to Ana's village with books.*
- *Another important detail is when Ana writes a book.*

Highlight a response that models an important detail, such as when the biblioburro came to Ana's village. Explain that this detail is important to the story because the story would not make sense without it.

✔ Pairs take turns orally retelling the story through the lenses of the character and the different settings. Students flip through the text for picture support as they retell the story.

109

Copyright © 2016 Great Minds®

G1 > M1 > Lesson 8

Scaffold

Prepare images representing the different settings in the text, and provide these pictures to support struggling students as a visual reminder of their choices.

- *Ana lives with her family in a village. Ana loves books but only has one book that was given to her by her teacher who moved away. There are no other books in her village, but then the Biblioburro comes to the village. The librarian reads to the children and Ana gets new books to read. She waits a long time for him to come back and decides to write a book about the Biblioburro. She shares the book with the librarian and he shares it with other children.*

Circulate to listen as students orally retell the story to a partner.

Land

ANSWER THE CONTENT FRAMING QUESTION

Organize: *What is happening in* Waiting for the Biblioburro?

Ask: "What did you learn about characters in this text? About setting?" Volunteers respond.

Remind students that knowing the characters and settings helps you retell the story.

Wrap — 3 MIN.

Share that in the next lesson, students will determine the problem and resolution of the story.

HOMEWORK CHECK-IN

Continue home reading routine. Check Fluency Homework from the previous lesson, and remind students to continue to practice reading without stumbling.

Analyze

Context and Alignment

Students create tableaux for sections of text relating to character and setting (RL.1.3, RL.1.7).

Check for the following success criteria for each student:

- Uses illustrations to determine poses.
- Uses text evidence to identify characters and their actions, or settings in the story.

Next Steps

If students struggle with identifying key details in sections of the text, support them by rereading corresponding sections of the text one page at a time. Use the words and the illustrations to identify what is happening on each page. During the Tableaux, review what each character is doing or which setting is being portrayed.

G1 > M1 > Lesson 8   WIT & WISDOM™

⬇ Lesson 8: Vocabulary Deep Dive

Ask and Answer Questions About Key Vocabulary

- **Time:** 15 min.

- **Text:** *Waiting for the Biblioburro*, Monica Brown, John Parra

- **Vocabulary Learning Goal:** Ask and answer questions about key vocabulary in *Waiting for the Biblioburro*. (L.1.6)

Launch

Display the Wonder Wheel. Volunteers respond: "What do we use this for?"

- *We use it to wonder about texts.*

- *We use it to ask questions about texts.*

- *We use it to help us ask questions.*

- *We use it to ask questions about words we aren't sure of.*

Students Mix and Mingle as you call out a word on the Wonder Wheel. Students partner up when a word is called out and ask their partner a question about a word they know. Their partner either answers the question or asks for the answer to the question, then they switch.

Explain that students will use the Wonder Wheel to ask questions about four new words from the *Waiting for the Biblioburro*, using the texts and pictures on the page to help them figure out what the words mean.

Learn

Display the following words:

- Village

- Burros

- Market

- Collect

WIT & WISDOM™   G1 › M1 › Lesson 8

Echo Read the words three times to be sure students can read them. Remind students about the following Sentence Frames. Display the frames only if needed to scaffold the discussion.

- **What does _____ mean?**

- **How does _____ work?**

- **What is _____?**

Explain that you are going to use one of these Sentence Frames to ask a question about one of the vocabulary words. Point to the word *village*. Students Think-Pair-Share about a question they could ask about the word *village*. Model asking a question about the word *village* if necessary to scaffold. Use Equity Sticks to choose volunteers to share their thinking.

- *What is a village?*

- *Where is a village?*

- *What does* village *mean?*

Capture relevant responses. Read the sentence with the word *village* on page 6 of the text. Model how to use the words in the sentence and the pictures on the page to determine the meaning of the word *village*.

I notice that the sentence with the word *village* talks about her teacher moving far away, and that there are children in her village. I also see in the pictures on the page that the teacher is in a place with buildings, and Ana is on the ground by a tree. I know buildings are in very large cities, and places with lots of trees and grass are out in the country. So if the teacher is far away and Ana is in her village, I think that a *village* is a place where people live that is small. I am going to confirm my answer by looking through the rest of the books at the pictures where Ana lives.

Students look through the book and identify evidence for the meaning of the word *village*. Write the definition next to the word and draw a quick sketch to help students remember the definition.

Read the word *burros*. Explain that this word is a Spanish word and that students might not know what this word means. Students Think-Pair-Share about a question to ask about this word. Volunteers respond. Capture relevant responses.

- What are *burros*?

- What is a *burro*?

- What does *burro* mean?

Read the text on pages 10 and 11 about the *burros*. Students Think-Pair-Share about what they think the word means and what they see on the pages that help them understand the meaning of the word. Use Equity Sticks to choose volunteers to share their thinking.

- *Donkeys*

- *The animals carrying the books.*

Confirm that the word *burro* does mean "donkey." Capture the definition next to the word and draw a quick sketch to help students remember what the word means. Student Think-Pair-Share about

113

Copyright © 2016 Great Minds®

G1 > M1 > Lesson 8

WIT & WISDOM™

what they know about donkeys and if the text tells them anything new. Use Equity Sticks to choose volunteers to respond.

In a similar fashion go through the words *market* and *collect*. Explain that a *market* is "a location where things are bought and sold," and that *collect* means "to bring things together." Demonstrate what this looks like if necessary.

✔ Partners work together to use their new words in sentences. Circulate to scaffold students as necessary.

Land

Use Equity Sticks to choose volunteers to share a sentence their partner told them using the word. Students record their words in their Vocabulary Journals, along with the definition and sketch.

Remind students that they ask questions about words in a text to learn more about them.

WIT & WISDOM™

G1 > M1 > Lesson 9

■ FOCUSING QUESTION: LESSONS 7-12

How does the Biblioburro change life for Ana?

| 1 | 2 | 3 | 4 | 5 | 6 | 7 | 8 | 9 | 10 | 11 | 12 | 13 | 14 | 15 | 16 | 17 | 18 | 19 | 20 | 21 | 22 | 23 | 24 | 25 | 26 | 27 | 28 | 29 | 30 | 31 | 32 |

Lesson 9

TEXT

- *Waiting for the Biblioburro*, Monica Brown, John Parra

G1 > M1 > Lesson 9

WIT & WISDOM™

Lesson 9: At a Glance

AGENDA

Welcome (10 min.)

Fluency Check-in

Launch (5 min.)

Understand the Content Framing Question

Learn (55 min.)

Identify the Problem and Resolution (20 min.)

Dramatize the Problem and Resolution (15 min.)

Retell the Story (10 min.)

Examine Complete Sentences (10 min.)

Land (3 min.)

Answer the Content Framing Question

Wrap (2 min.)

Style and Conventions Deep Dive: Verbs in the Past (15 min.)

STANDARDS ADDRESSED

The full text of ELA Standards can be found in the Module Overview.

Reading

- RL.1.1, RL.1.3, RL.1.7

Speaking and Listening

- SL.1.1.a, SL.1.2, SL.1.6

Language

- ⬇ L.1.1.e

MATERIALS

- Fluent Readers Chart
- One problem and resolution Story Stone for each pair of students
- *Waiting for the Biblioburro* Story Map
- Complete Sentences Anchor Chart
- Verbs Chart
- Sticky flags
- Handout 9A: Past Tense

Learning Goals

Retell *Waiting for the Biblioburro*, including key details about characters, settings, and major events. (RL.1.3., RL.1.7)

✔ Create tableaux for the problem and resolution of the story.

⬇ Identify and generate verbs. (L.1.1.e)

✔ Add *-ed* to verbs to make them past tense.

✔ Checks for Understanding

Copyright © 2016 Great Minds®

WIT & WISDOM™   G1 > M1 > Lesson 9

Prepare

FOCUSING QUESTION: Lessons 7-12

How does the Biblioburro change life for Ana?

CONTENT FRAMING QUESTION: Lesson 9

Organize: *What is happening in* Waiting for the Biblioburro?

CRAFT QUESTION: Lesson 9

Examine: *Why is writing complete sentences important?*

Students continue reading with fluency, focusing on their phrasing and pausing when reading excerpts of *Waiting for the Biblioburro*. They identify the problem and resolution using Story Stones and create tableaux for these elements. Finally, students orally retell the story, focusing on the problem and resolution. Students continue to gain confidence in their ability to retell, honing in on the important information in the text. Finally, students examine complete sentences, specifically looking at the important role of subjects and verbs.

Welcome 10 MIN.

FLUENCY CHECK-IN

Students Think-Pair-Share to discuss the question: "Did you read without stumbling on your homework? If you did stumble, what did you do?"

Ask a few students to share their responses. Chorally read the passage, reading without stumbling.

Display the Fluent Readers Chart. Explain to students that their homework assignment will concentrate on another component of the chart—reading with appropriate phrasing and pausing. Students Echo Read the first and second criteria.

Point to the second criterion as you display and read page 5 from the text, beginning with, "Ana has read her book." Demonstrate appropriate phrasing and pausing.

Students use Nonverbal Signals to respond to the following question: "Did I read the words and phrases smoothly, pausing where I noticed punctuation?"

Students underline the new component on their homework sheet. Students chorally read and partner read the homework passage, concentrating on reading with appropriate phrasing and pausing. Remind students to pay attention to their phrasing and pausing when completing their fluency homework.

117

Copyright © 2016 Great Minds®

G1 > M1 > Lesson 9   WIT & WISDOM™

Share that reading a passage fluently helps students understand the text better, and it will help them figure out what is happening in this story.

Launch 5 MIN.

UNDERSTAND THE CONTENT FRAMING QUESTION

Post the Content Framing Question and Focusing Question.

Remind students that this question will help them think about how things are organized in the story. In this lesson, they will focus on learning more about the problem and resolution to retell the story.

Ask: "What did we learn about problem and resolution when we read *Tomás and the Library Lady*?" Volunteers respond.

Reinforce that the problem is the main character's challenge and a resolution is the end of the problem.

Hold up the problem and resolution Story Stones as you ask: "According to our Content Framing Question, what are we going to tell about in the story?" Students name the Story Stones, and then volunteers share additional insights.

- *We are telling about the problem and resolution in* Waiting for the Biblioburro.
- *We are retelling what happened in the book.*

Learn 55 MIN.

IDENTIFY THE PROBLEM AND RESOLUTION

Whole Group 20 MIN.

Display the *Waiting for the Biblioburro* Story Map.

Distribute a problem and resolution Story Stone to each student. As you read the story aloud, pairs will follow along in their copies. When students hear the problem, they hold their problem stones in the air. When they notice the problem changing, they shake their problem stones in the air, and when they hear the resolution, they hold their resolution stones in the air. Call out each response as students practice.

118

Copyright © 2016 Great Minds®

Read the story aloud, pausing after page 5 for students to Think-Pair-Share: "What is the problem, or what challenges Ana?" Students discuss the problem and place the stone.

Use Equity Sticks to call on students to share with the group the problem they found from the text.

   ▪ *The problem is that Ana has only one book and there is no one to teach her.*
   ▪ *Ana wants more books to read but her village doesn't have any books and her teacher is gone.*

Write and illustrate the problem on the class *Waiting for the Biblioburro* Story Map.

Before continuing with the Read Aloud, remind students to listen for when the problem changes and to shake their problem Story Stone when they hear details about the problem changing. Pause after reading page 13 to Think Aloud to explain the moment that helps change the problem. For example:

Remember the problem is that Ana wants more books to read. What happens in the story that helps change her problem? On page 9, I see that the Biblioburro has arrived with books. On page 11, the librarian is reading to Ana and the other children in the village. On page 13, the librarian says Ana can pick out some books. These things help change the problem because Ana gets to read new books.

Record details under the arrow column between the problem and resolution on the Story Map.

Continue reading the story. If students hold up the resolution Story Stone too early, continue reading and explain that the class will look to see if there is anything else that might change the problem.

On page 20, pause briefly to explain that the problem changed again. After getting books from the Biblioburro, Ana is eager to get more books and has to wait. Tell students the problem can change throughout the story. At first, the problem was just that Ana didn't have books, but the problem changed when she has to wait for more books.

Alternate Activity

Use prompting questions to support students in arriving at the above conclusions. Return to the text to reinforce the observation.

Remind students to use their Story Stones when they hear details about the resolution. Continue reading aloud the remainder of the story (except the author's note). Pause on page 28 for students to Think-Pair-Share: "What is the resolution, or how the problem is fixed?" Remind students that the problem is not just that Ana wants new books to read but also that other children have to wait for books, too. Students discuss the resolution and place the stone.

Use Equity Sticks to call on students to share with the group the problem and resolution from the text.

   ▪ *Ana writes a book to give to the Biblioburro.*
   ▪ *The resolution is that Ana writes a book and gives it to the librarian to share with other children so they have books to read, too.*

Write and illustrate the resolution on the class *Waiting for the Biblioburro* Story Map.

G1 > M1 > Lesson 9   WIT & WISDOM™

WAITING FOR THE BIBLIOBURRO STORY MAP

Characters	Setting
- Ana *(drawing of Ana).* - Mami *(drawing of mother).* - Papi *(drawing of father).* - Little brother *(drawing of little brother).* - Teacher *(drawing of teacher).* - Bibliotecario *(librarian).* - Alfa *(drawing of donkey).* - Beto *(drawing of donkey).* - Children in the village *(drawing of children).*	- House - Farm - Bedroom - Village

Problem		Resolution
- Ana has only one book and there are no other books in the village. - Ana's teacher moved away and there is no one to teach her or the other children. - Ana wants new books to read. (draw a book with a strike through it to represent no books)	**The Biblioburro comes to the village to share books with the children. Ana reads new books.** **Ana and other children have to wait a long time for books to come.** (draw the Biblioburro coming to the village and a clock to represent waiting)	- Ana writes her own book to give to the Biblioburro to share with other children. (draw a book and small figures for children)

DRAMATIZE THE PROBLEM AND RESOLUTION

Small Groups   15 MIN.

Ask: "After we add to the Story Map, how else do we talk about what's happening?" Volunteers respond.

Reinforce that acting a text out is a great way to identify the problem and resolution. Assign small groups either problem or resolution. Explain that groups will create tableaux to show their assigned event.

120

Copyright © 2016 Great Minds®

WIT & WISDOM™   G1 > M1 > Lesson 9

Review the problem and resolution recorded on the Story Map.

✔ Small groups create tableaux for the problem or resolution.

  ▪ *Problem: One student poses as Ana, and the other students pose as the children in the village, with their shoulders shrugged and hands up to represent that they don't have books.*

  ▪ *Resolution: One student poses as Ana writing a book. Another student poses as the librarian receiving Ana's book. Other students pose as the children asleep in their beds waiting for Ana's book.*

Circulate to check for understanding of the task.

As a whole group, ask students: "What did you notice about the problem and resolution by doing the activity?"

  ▪ *The problem happened to the main character, Ana.*

  ▪ *The resolution came at the end and solved the problem.*

Use student responses to reinforce the key ideas that stories have problems, which are things that challenge the main character. The resolution is when the problem is solved at the end. Reference the story elements posted in the room as you recap students' learning.

RETELL THE STORY

Pairs 10 MIN.

Now that students understand the problem and resolution, pairs will retell the story to each other by telling what happened in the problem and resolution and when they occurred in the story.

Remind students to consider the important things that happened when they retell the story.

Pairs take turns orally retelling the story through the lens of the problem and resolution. Students reference the Story Map for support as they retell the story.

  ▪ *Ana lives with her family in a village. The problem is that Ana loves books but only has one book that her teacher gave her. Her teacher moved away and there is no one to teach Ana or the other children, and there are no books in the village. Then, the Biblioburro comes to the village. The librarian reads to the children and Ana gets new books to read. But then Ana has to wait a long time for the Biblioburro to come back. She dreams about sharing stories with other children. The resolution is when Ana decides to write a book about the Biblioburro and she gives the book to the librarian who shares it with other children.*

Circulate to listen as students orally retell the story to a partner.

121

Copyright © 2016 Great Minds®

G1 > M1 > Lesson 9 WIT & WISDOM™

EXAMINE COMPLETE SENTENCES

Whole Group 10 MIN.

Share the Craft Question: "Why is writing complete sentences important?"

Remind students that they have looked at both nouns and verbs in the Deep Dives so far and that this, in addition to their Sentence Frame work, has prepared them well for writing in complete sentences.

Display and Echo Read the Complete Sentences Anchor Chart.

COMPLETE SENTENCES ANCHOR CHART

Complete Sentences:
- Tell a complete thought.
- Begin with a capital letter.
- End with a punctuation mark.
- Have a subject and a verb.

Explain that there are two parts to a complete sentence. There is the subject, which tells who or what the sentence is about, and there is a verb. The subject is a noun.

As needed, post some examples of verbs from the Deep Dives and ask: "What is a verb?" Volunteers respond.

Post and read the sentence: "Ana feeds goats."

Think Aloud as you model checking the sentence against the criteria: "The sentence is a thought, begins with a capital letter, and has a period at the end. The sentence is about Ana. Ana is the subject of the sentence. *Feeds* is the action word. *Feeds* is the verb."

Display and Echo Read the following sentences:

1. Ana reads books.

2. The librarian reads.

3. Alfa and Beto walk.

Collectively check the sentences against the criteria for complete sentences. For each sentence, ask: "How would the meaning of this sentence be different if I only had the subject or the verb?" Use Equity Sticks to choose volunteers to respond. Reinforce that subjects and verbs work together to provide important information to readers.

Students Think-Pair-Share to determine the subject and verb in each sentence. Use Equity Sticks to call on students. Use Nonverbal Signals to agree or disagree with student responses. Underline the subject and circle the verb. Students stand and air-write a large check, indicating the sentence meets the criteria.

122

Copyright © 2016 Great Minds®

WIT & WISDOM™   G1 > M1 > Lesson 9

Students Think-Pair-Share the Craft Question: "Why is it important to write a complete sentence?" Choose two pairs to share their thinking.

Land 3 MIN.

ANSWER THE CONTENT FRAMING QUESTION

Organize: *What is happening in* Waiting for the Biblioburro?

Ask: "What story elements did we focus on today?" Volunteers respond.

Students Pair-Share: "How did knowing the problem and resolution help you retell what happens in the story?

▪ *I told about the problem and resolution to retell the important parts of the story.*

Circulate and choose two pairs to share their thinking.

Wrap 2 MIN.

In the next lesson, students explore sections of the text to discover the meaning behind the dreams in *Waiting for the Biblioburro.*

Analyze

Context and Alignment

Students create tableaux for sections of text relating to problem and resolution (RL.1.3, RL.1.7).

Check for the following success criteria for each student:

- Uses illustrations to determine poses.
- Uses text evidence to identify the problem and the resolution.

Next Steps

If students struggle with identifying key details in sections of the text, support them by rereading corresponding sections of the text one page at a time. Use the words and the illustrations to identify what is happening on each page. During the Tableaux review what is happening in the scene.

123

Copyright © 2016 Great Minds®

G1 > M1 > Lesson 9

WIT & WISDOM™

⬇ Lesson 9: Style and Conventions Deep Dive

Verbs in the Past

- **Time:** 15 min.

- **Text:** *Waiting for the Biblioburro*, Monica Brown, John Parra

- **Style and Conventions Learning Goal:** Identify and generate verbs. (L.1.1.e)

- **STYLE AND CONVENTIONS CRAFT QUESTION:** Lesson 9
  Experiment: *How do verbs tell us when we are doing something?*

Launch

Display and read the Craft Question: *How do verbs tell us when we are doing something?*

Students Echo Read the question. Explain that students will learn more about verbs and how they function in the texts they are reading and writing.

Learn

Display the chart titled "Verbs." Ask: "What information do verbs give?" Volunteers respond. Reinforce that verbs are words that tell us what we are doing and when we are doing it.

Students Mix and Mingle as you call out the verbs from the chart. When you call out a verb, have the students find a partner and act out the word.

Students Think-Pair-Share about what all these verbs have in common. Volunteers respond to share their thinking. Guide students in understanding that these verbs are happening right now, in the present.

Explain that students will learn about verbs that show when we have already done something in the past.

Verbs	
Verbs tell us what we are doing and when we are doing it.	
Present (right now) - Read - Write - Sit - Work - Walk - Wish - Imagine	Past (we already did something)

124

Copyright © 2016 Great Minds®

WIT & WISDOM™   G1 > M1 > Lesson 9

Read the chart aloud. Explain that since verbs tell us what we are doing and when we are doing it, we have to have a way of showing that the action already happened, or it is in the past. For most verbs we do the same thing to show this: we add an –ed to the end of the word. Some verbs don't follow the rules so we have to do something different for those, and we will talk about those as we find them in our hunt for verbs that show the past.

Display the following sentences:

- I work yesterday.

- We walk to school this morning.

- My sister wish for a toy last week.

Read the first sentence to the students. Students Think-Pair-Share about the sentence. Does it make sense to them? Volunteers respond. Guide them to notice that the action "*work*" happened yesterday, which is in the past. *Work* tells us that we are doing it right now, so we need to fix it.

Model adding the –ed to *work* in the sentence and then read the sentence again.

- I worked yesterday.

Echo Read the second sentence with the students. Students Think-Pair-Share about the sentence. Does it make sense to them? Students indicate with a Nonverbal Signal whether they think it makes sense or not. Students Think-Pair-Share about what they think needs to be done to show that the action *walk* happened in the past. Volunteers respond.

Model adding the –ed to *walk* in the sentence and then read the sentence again.

- We walked to school this morning.

In a similar fashion change the third sentence to make the verb past tense. Add all three words to the Verbs Chart on the past tense side.

Verbs	
Verbs tell us what we are doing and when we are doing it.	
Present (right now) ▪ Read ▪ Write ▪ Sit ▪ Work ▪ Walk ▪ Wish ▪ Imagine	Past (we already did something) ▪ Worked ▪ Walked ▪ Wished

125

Copyright © 2016 Great Minds®

Distribute the word cards from Handout 9A: Past Tense. Echo Read the words with the students two or three times to ensure they can read them.

✔ Students work with partners to add the *-ed* ending to their word cards. Partners take turns reading the words in the past tense to each other.

Use Equity Sticks to choose students to read a verb and then read it in the past tense. Add the past tense words to the chart.

Land

Instruct students to Think-Pair-Share, and ask: "How do verbs tell us when we are doing something?"

Use Equity Sticks to select two pairs to share their thinking. Use their responses to reinforce that adding the ending of *-ed* to verbs shows that something has happened in the past. Explain that students will continue to learn about how verbs tell us when something is happening (or has happened) and how to use them in their writing and look for them in the texts they are reading.

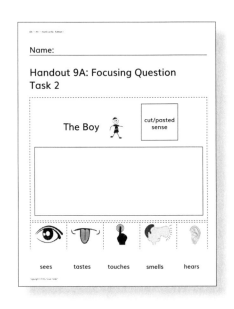

WIT & WISDOM™   G1 > M1 > Lesson 10

■ FOCUSING QUESTION: LESSONS 7-12

How does the Biblioburro change life for Ana?

| 1 | 2 | 3 | 4 | 5 | 6 | 7 | 8 | 9 | 10 | 11 | 12 | 13 | 14 | 15 | 16 | 17 | 18 | 19 | 20 | 21 | 22 | 23 | 24 | 25 | 26 | 27 | 28 | 29 | 30 | 31 | 32 |

Lesson 10

TEXT

- *Waiting for the Biblioburro*, Monica Brown, John Parra

Copyright © 2016 Great Minds®

G1 > M1 > Lesson 10   WIT & WISDOM™

Lesson 10: At a Glance

AGENDA

Welcome (10 min.)

Fluency Check-in

Launch (5 min.)

Understand the Content Framing Question

Learn (50 min.)

Dramatize the Main Character's Dreams (25 min.)

Experiment with Sentences (25 min.)

Land (8 min.)

Answer the Content Framing Question

Wrap (2 min.)

Vocabulary Deep Dive: Adding the Inflectional Ending *-ing* to Root Words (15 min.)

STANDARDS ADDRESSED

The full text of ELA Standards can be found in the Module Overview.

Reading

- RL.1.1, RL.1.2, RL.1.3, RL.1.7

Writing

- W.1.8

Speaking and Listening

- SL.1.1.a, SL.1.2

Language

- L.1.1.j, L.1.2.b
- ⬇ L.1.4, L.1.6

MATERIALS

- Fluent Readers Chart
- Illustrated signs for the words *reality* and *imagination*
- Response Journals

Learning Goals

Analyze the main character's dreams using key details in *Waiting for the Biblioburro*. (RL.1.1, RL.1.3)

✔ Act out key details of dreams in small groups.

Draft a simple sentence with support.

✔ Compose a sentence in their Response Journals.

⬇ Vocabulary Learning Goal: Identify root words and the inflectional ending *-ing*. (L.1.4.c)

✔ Identify the word with an *-ing* ending with a partner and write and illustrate the meaning in Vocabulary Journals.

✔ Checks for Understanding

Copyright © 2016 Great Minds®

WIT & WISDOM™   G1 > M1 > Lesson 10

Prepare

FOCUSING QUESTION: Lessons 7-12

How does the Biblioburro change life for Ana?

CONTENT FRAMING QUESTION: Lesson 10

Reveal: *What does a deeper exploration of the main character reveal in* Waiting for the Biblioburro?

CRAFT QUESTION: Lesson 10

Experiment: *How does writing complete sentences work?*

Continuing instruction about reading with fluency, the lesson begins with learning about reading with expression. Students focus on learning more about the main character by studying Ana's dreams and reality, and using their bodies to act out Ana's actions in each. They compare Ana's dream at the beginning of the book with the dream at the end of the book to uncover deeper meaning in the text. They also practice writing complete sentences, looking at capitalization, punctuation, and the inclusion of a subject and verb.

Welcome 10 MIN.

FLUENCY CHECK-IN

Choral Read the homework passage with appropriate phrasing and pausing. Students check in with Nonverbal Signals indicating how they felt they did on the homework.

Display the Fluent Readers Chart. Students Echo Read the first three criteria.

Point to the third criterion as you explain that students will concentrate on reading with appropriate expression. Share that reading with expression means reading with feeling. Display and read pages 9–10, from the text beginning with, "One morning, Ana wakes up." Begin the demonstration by reading without expression. Stop after a few sentences and ask, "Did I read with appropriate expression?" Students Think-Pair-Share to respond to the question.

Read the rest of the page with expression.

Students underline the new component on their homework sheet. Choral read and partner read the homework passage, concentrating on reading with expression. Remind students to pay attention to their expression when completing this lesson's fluency homework.

129

Copyright © 2016 Great Minds®

G1 > M1 > Lesson 10   WIT & WISDOM™

Launch 5 MIN.

UNDERSTAND THE CONTENT FRAMING QUESTION

Post the Content Framing Question and Focusing Question. Echo Read the Content Framing Question.

Ask: "What does *reveal* mean?"

Call on volunteers to respond.

- *Reveal means "to find the information that is hidden."*

Remind students of the meaning of *reveal* with a visual such as an image of a magician's hat or opening a closed fist.

Ask: "According to our Content Framing Question, what are we exploring more deeply in our book today?" Volunteers respond.

- *We are exploring the main character to find out more information.*
- *Ana is the main character. We'll think more about her.*

Learn 50 MIN.

DRAMATIZE THE MAIN CHARACTER'S DREAMS

Whole Group 25 MIN.

Explain that students will closely read three parts of the book to learn more about Ana. Read pages 1 and 3 aloud, starting with "In the house, there is a bed." Ask the following TDQ:

1 **What just changed for Ana?**

- *Ana is dreaming and then she wakes up and does work on her family's farm.*
- *Ana is sleeping and dreaming about the world outside of her village in the beginning before waking up to help her family on the farm.*

2 **What does Ana's dream tell us about what she might want?**

- *Ana's dream tells us she wonders about the places outside her village.*

130

Copyright © 2016 Great Minds®

WIT & WISDOM™   G1 › M1 › Lesson 10

  ▪ *She is curious about the world.*

  ▪ *She might want to know more about what is happening outside her village.*

Use students' responses to confirm that page 1 describes Ana dreaming about the outside world, while on page 3 she is awake and helping out on the farm. Near students' eye level, post an illustrated sign for *dreams*. Near ground level, post an illustrated sign for *reality*.

Alternate Activity

Create sets of prompt cards with symbols to represent reality and dreams. Dreams could be represented by a thought bubble and reality by a globe. Students use the cards to indicate if a detail relates to dreams or reality.

Tell students that to explore Ana's dreams and reality even more deeply, they will use their bodies to act out Ana's actions. Model how to act out a couple of sentences on page 1, such as Ana's head down and eyes closed.

Reread page 3, with students acting out Ana's actions.

  ▪ *(Students pick up an imaginary basket and pretend to collect eggs.)*

  ▪ *(Students pretend to scatter food for the goats.)*

  ▪ *(Students pretend to pick up and wash a baby.)*

Read aloud pages 22 and 23.

✔️ Students stand up and sit down when Ana's actions shift between dreams and reality, and dramatize Ana's actions to express important evidence from the text.

As you read aloud the first paragraph on page 22, make sure students remember to stand up when the text describes a dream scene.

  ▪ *(Students stretch their arms out pretending to fly.)*

  ▪ *(Students bring their fingers from their mouths to the floor to indicate stories flying out to children below.)*

As you read aloud the second paragraph on page 22 and the text on page 23, students stand up when the text describes reality.

  ▪ *(Students pick up an imaginary pencil and paper and pretend to write a book.)*

  ▪ *(Students hold an imaginary book and pretend to present it to the librarian.)*

Before reading the third part of the book, students Think-Pair-Share about the following TDQ. Use Equity Sticks to call on two to three students to share with the group.

---

3 **What do you notice about Ana's dreams? (If needed, follow up with: "What does Ana dream about?")**

  ▪ *Ana dreams about the outside world.*

  ▪ *Ana dreams about telling stories to the children waiting all around the country.*

131

Copyright © 2016 Great Minds®

G1 > M1 > Lesson 10   WIT & WISDOM™

Explain that students will read one final portion of the book to find out how another dream connects to Ana. Read pages 26 and 28 aloud.

Flip to the beginning of the story to compare it with the end. Reread aloud page 1 before students Think-Pair-Share about the following TDQ.

4 How are the beginning dreams similar to the dreams at the end? How are they different?

- *In the beginning, Ana is dreaming about people and places outside her village.*
- *Ana wants to be connected to the outside world.*
- *In the end, the boy is dreaming about the Biblioburro and all the stories he will bring, including Ana's story.*
- *It begins with Ana's dreams and ends with where her book is traveling.*
- *Ana dreams about the world and her book helps connect her to the rest of the world.*

Use student responses to summarize how the beginning and ending dream scenes fit together. In the beginning, Ana dreams about the world. Then, she dreams about telling stories to other kids. At the end, a boy is dreaming about the story that she wrote. Her book helps connect Ana to the rest of the world.

TEACHER NOTE	The goal here is to have as much of the analysis and connections come from what the students generated while promoting a clear understanding and accurate interpretation. If students provide responses that are accurate and well-conceived, consider having them synthesize and reiterate the learning. If the responses are not accurately rooted in the text, use this time to model your thinking to help students internalize this deep analysis work.

EXPERIMENT USING COMPLETE SENTENCES

Whole Group 25 MIN.

Share the Craft Question: *How does writing complete sentences work?*

Activate student memories by displaying the Complete Sentences Anchor Chart introduced in lesson 9. Students Think-Pair-Share to answer the question: "What does a complete sentence need?" Use Equity Sticks to call on two pairs to share their responses.

- *Sentences start with a capital letter.*
- *Sentences end with a punctuation mark.*
- *Complete sentences need a subject and a verb.*

132

Copyright © 2016 Great Minds®

WIT & WISDOM™   G1 > M1 > Lesson 10

Post the following:

- ana ran to the village

Think Aloud and model checking the sentence against the criteria and inviting volunteers to share their observations.

Explain to students that in this lesson they will practice writing complete sentences in their Response Journals.

Write *Ana* on chart paper. Ask: "Which part of a complete sentence is this?" A volunteer responds.

Reinforce that students have named the subject of the sentence and that now they must add a verb. Students Think-Pair-Share to identify something Ana did in the story, or a verb. Record student responses. Highlight the verbs, reminding students that their sentence needs a subject (Ana) and a verb.

Write: Ana slept in bed. Think Aloud as you check your sentence against the criteria on the chart.

Collaboratively, write a second sentence. Check the sentence against the criteria.

✔ Individuals write a sentence in their Response Journals about Ana using student-generated words on the chart.

Display the Sentence Frame:

- **Ana _____.**

Remind students to use the Complete Sentence Chart to check their sentence.

Students stand in concentric circles to pair read their sentences. The circles turn in opposite ways, providing students with another partner.

Differentiation

Encourage advanced students to write more than one sentence. Students experiencing difficulty may need scribing, underwriting, or Sentence Frames.

If students are experiencing difficulty writing words phonetically, assist them in segmenting the sounds in the word. Write lines for each sound heard when segmenting. For example: Ana wrote a story. The word *wrote* may be written phonetically, r-o-t.

Explain that students are now ready to apply their understanding of complete sentences to their Focusing Question Task in the next lesson.

133

Copyright © 2016 Great Minds®

G1 > M1 > Lesson 10   WIT & WISDOM™

Land   8 MIN.

ANSWER THE CONTENT FRAMING QUESTION

Reveal: *What does a deeper exploration of the main character reveal in* Waiting for the Biblioburro?

Students Think-Pair-Share: "What did you notice about the dream scenes in the book? What did you learn about Ana?"

- *The first two dreams were Ana's dreams, and the last dream was a different boy's dream.*
- *I noticed two of them were about stories and books, when Ana dreams about telling stories to other kids and when the boy dreams about her book.*
- *At first, Ana dreams about the world outside her village. Then at the end, the boy is dreaming about her book.*
- *She dreams about telling stories to other kids and writes her own story about waiting for books.*
- *Ana wants other children to be able to get stories.*
- *Ana wants to be connected to the outside world.*
- *Writing her book connected Ana to the world and shared her story.*

Wrap   2 MIN.

In the next lesson, students have the opportunity to demonstrate what they've learned about story elements when they complete Focusing Question Task 2.

Analyze

Context and Alignment

Students use key details from the text to draft a simple sentence about Ana using a Sentence Frame for guidance (RL.1.3, RL.1.7, L.1.1.j, L.1.2.b). Check for the following success criteria:

- Writes a complete sentence using a Sentence Frame.
- Uses text evidence to inform writing.

Next Steps

If students do not draw details about the main character Ana, visually explore each page asking questions such as, "What is Ana doing on this page?" Write down student responses that include verbs. Students use a group-generated word to complete their Sentence Frame.

134

Copyright © 2016 Great Minds®

WIT & WISDOM™   G1 > M1 > Lesson 10

↓ Lesson 10: Vocabulary Deep Dive

Adding the Inflectional Ending
-ing to Root Words

- **Time:** 15 min.

- **Text:** *Waiting for the Biblioburro*, Monica Brown, John Parra

- **Vocabulary Learning Goal:** Identify root words and the inflectional ending *–ing*. (L.1.4.c)

Launch

Display the following words:

- Reading

- Writing

- Skipping

- Hugging

- Flying

- Moving

- Rubbing

- Feeding

Echo Read the words with students to ensure they know each word. Students Think-Pair-Share about what these words have in common with one another.

Use Equity Sticks to choose two to three students to share their thinking. Students should notice these words all have the ending *–ing*. Remind students that they have already learned about how the ending *–ed* changes words, and explain that now they will learn how adding another ending to a root word changes when that word is happening.

Learn

Make word cards for the following pairs of words:

- Reading, read

- Writing, write

- Skipping, skip

- Hugging, hug

- Flying, fly

135

Copyright © 2016 Great Minds®

G1 > M1 > Lesson 10   WIT & WISDOM™

- Moving, move

- Rubbing, rub

- Feeding, feed

Students Think-Pair-Share about how to sort these words into categories. Remind them that when we sort things into categories we look at what words have in common and place them in groups based on what they have in common.

Tell students they can have only two categories for their words. Students work in pairs to sort their words into two categories. Use Equity Sticks to choose groups to explain their sorting.

Explain to students that –ing is an ending or chunk that is sometimes added to the end of words. When a verb, or action word, has the –ing added to the end, we know that the action is happening right now. Remind them that the word that connects to the ending is called the root word.

Students Think-Pair-Share about what their categories should be labeled. Reinforce that one group are words with the –ing ending that are happening right now, and the other group are the root words the chunk is added to.

Show the following sentences from the text.

- There is a little girl named Ana, fast asleep, dreaming about the world outside and beyond the hill.

- Ana picks up book after book and finds pink dolphins and blue butterflies, castles and fairies, talking lions and magic carpets.

- Stories fly from her mouth and fingers like magic, falling into the hands of the children waiting below.

✔ Students work with partners to identify the word in the sentence that has an –ing ending. They write the word in their Vocabulary Journal. After finding the word, they take away the ending and write the root word next to the word in their Vocabulary Journal. Next to the two words, the students will draw a picture to illustrate the meaning of the word with the inflectional ending.

Land

Students do a quick Gallery Walk to share the illustrations in their Vocabulary Journals. Use Equity Sticks to choose two or three students to share the illustrations they really liked as they did the Gallery Walk. Remind students that when they add –ing to the end of root words, it changes when something is happening to right now.

136

Copyright © 2016 Great Minds®

FOCUSING QUESTION: LESSONS 7-12

How does the Biblioburro
change life for Ana?

1 2 3 4 5 6 7 8 9 10 11 12 13 14 15 16 17 18 19 20 21 22 23 24 25 26 27 28 29 30 31 32

Lesson 11

TEXT

- *Waiting for the Biblioburro*, Monica Brown, John Parra

G1 > M1 > Lesson 11   WIT & WISDOM™

Lesson 11: At a Glance

AGENDA

Welcome (10 min.)

Fluency Check-in

Launch (5 min.)

Understand the Content Framing Question

Learn (55 min.)

Reflect on the Essential Question (10 min.)

Compare and Contrast Characters (20 min.)

Execute Complete Sentences (25 min.)

Land (3 min.)

Answer the Content Framing Question

Wrap (2 min.)

Vocabulary Deep Dive: Frayer Model for *Inspire* (15 min.)

STANDARDS ADDRESSED

The full text of ELA Standards can be found in the Module Overview.

Reading

- RL.1.1, RL.1.2, RI.1.3

Writing

- W.1.3, W.1.8

Speaking and Listening

- SL.1.1.a, SL.1.2

Language

- L.1.1.j, L.1.2.b
- ⬇ L.1.4, L.1.6

MATERIALS

- Fluent Readers Chart
- Essential Questions Chart
- Handout 6A: Essential Questions Chart
- World map
- Sticky flags
- Sentence Strips
- Red sticky notes, four per pair of students
- *Waiting for the Biblioburro* Story Map
- Handout 11A: Focusing Question 2 Prompt
- Assessment 11: Focusing Question Task 2
- Enlarged copy of the Frayer Model
- Handout 11B: Frayer Model
- Vocabulary Journal

Learning Goals

Write a narrative retelling of *Waiting for the Biblioburro* that shows how the Biblioburro changes life for Ana. (RL.1.2, RL.1.3, W.1.3, W.1.8, L.1.1.j, L.1.2.b, SL.1.1.a)

✔ Complete Focusing Question Task 2.

⬇ Develop vocabulary knowledge of the word *inspire*. (L.1.6)

✔ Verbalize definition, examples, and non-examples to partners.

Copyright © 2016 Great Minds®

✔ Checks for Understanding

WIT & WISDOM™

G1 > M1 > Lesson 11

Prepare

FOCUSING QUESTION: Lessons 7-12

How does the Biblioburro change life for Ana?

CONTENT FRAMING QUESTION: Lesson 11

Know: *How does* Waiting for the Biblioburro *build my knowledge?*

CRAFT QUESTION: Lesson 11

Execute: *How does writing complete sentences work in writing?*

Students continue reading with fluency, focusing on reading at a good rate. They fill out the Essential Questions Chart with information from *Waiting for the Biblioburro*, which segues to comparing main characters Tomás and Ana. Students annotate the texts for two different, scaffolded questions: how each character gets books and how books change their lives. Applying what they've learned about the story elements and retelling, students complete Focusing Question Task 2 using Sentence Frames to retell the story *Waiting for the Biblioburro*.

Welcome 10 MIN.

FLUENCY HOMEWORK CHECK-IN

Small groups read the homework passage with expression. Check in with each group to determine how they are doing with the fluency homework.

Display the Fluent Readers Chart. Students Echo Read the first four criteria.

Point to the fourth criterion as you explain that students will concentrate on reading at a good rate. Reading at a good rate means not reading too fast or too slow, but just right. Display and read the pages 26–28 from the text beginning with, "When it's time to go." Begin the demonstration by reading too fast. Stop after a few sentences and ask, "Am I reading too slow, too fast, or just right?" Students provide a choral response. Read a few more sentences slowly and ask the same question. Read with appropriate pace and ask the question again. Students Think-Pair-Share to answer the question: "Why is it important to read at just the right pace?" Listen in and ask two or three students to respond.

Students underline the new component on their homework sheet. Choral read and partner read the homework passage, concentrating on reading at an appropriate pace. Remind students to pay attention to their reading rate while completing this lesson's fluency homework.

139

Copyright © 2016 Great Minds®

Launch 5 MIN.

UNDERSTAND THE CONTENT FRAMING QUESTION

Post the Content Framing Question and Focusing Question. Echo Read the Content Framing Question.

Ask students: "What did you learn about books from reading *Waiting for the Biblioburro*?" Call on volunteers for responses.

- *Libraries can move around from place to place. The Biblioburro traveled around the country.*
- *You can imagine things in books, like Ana (and Tomás) did when she read books at the library.*
- *You can write your own book, just like Ana did.*

As students respond, follow up by asking: "What part of the text helped you learn that?"

Explain that, with this Content Framing Question, students will look at how books change lives using information they've learned from *Waiting for the Biblioburro*.

Learn 55 MIN.

Reflect on the Essential Question Whole Group 10 MIN.

💬 Display and reference the Speaking and Listening Anchor Chart.

Explain that now that students have built knowledge about *Waiting for the Biblioburro*, they will build knowledge about the module topic. Display the Essential Questions Chart.

Point to the Character column, and ask: "What information goes here?" Invite a volunteer to respond.

Ask: "Who is the main character of the story?" Count to three and ask the class to answer in a loud whisper. Fill in *Ana* in the Main Character column.

Explain that the middle column is for the place in the world where the story takes place.

Explain that while we know the story takes place in and around Ana's house and village, all of those settings are in a place called Colombia. Show page 29 and point to the name of the country in the author's note.

Write *Colombia*, modeling and noting the use of the capital C to indicate that a country is a proper noun. Students Echo Read the word.

WIT & WISDOM™   G1 > M1 > Lesson 11

Share that Colombia is a country in South America. Add a small sticky flag with the name of the location written on it to the class world map.

Students Think-Pair-Share: "The Essential Question of the module is 'How do books change people's lives around the world?' How do books change Ana's life in the story?"

- *The books the Biblioburro brings change Ana's life because they open up her imagination.*
- *The books inspire Ana to write her own book to share with other children.*
- *Ana's book helps connect her to the rest of the world.*

Ask students to share two to three refined responses. Record sentences and illustrations on the chart.

ESSENTIAL QUESTIONS CHART

Essential Question: How do books change people's lives around the world?		
Main Character	**Where in the world is the character?**	**How do books change the character's life?**
▪ *Ana*	▪ *Colombia*	Books help connect Ana to the world, open her imagination, and inspire her to write her own book to travel with the Biblioburro for other children to read. (drawing of a globe above *world*, thought bubble above *imagination*, book above *book*, donkey above *Biblioburro*, and children above *children*)

COMPARE AND CONTRAST CHARACTERS

Pairs 20 MIN.

Point to the previous entry in the Essential Questions Chart and remind students that Tomás and Ana have some experiences in common. Show the cover of *Tomás and the Library Lady* and *Waiting for the Biblioburro*. Explain that pairs will look for evidence to compare Tomás and Ana's experiences with books.

Tell students that when they compare things, it means to look at those things closely and see what is the same and what is different about them.

Introduce the first set of questions:

Display the first question on a Sentence Strip written in blue: "How does Tomás get books?" Echo Read the question.

Distribute two blue sticky notes to each pair. Explain that pairs will use these sticky notes to annotate, or mark, important information in the text. Pairs work together in their copies of *Tomás and the Library Lady*, using the illustrations as support. Each member of the pair flags one piece of

141

Copyright © 2016 Great Minds®

G1 > M1 > Lesson 11   WIT & WISDOM™

evidence using one blue sticky note and explains their reasoning to their partner. Pairs share their findings with another pair to discover new evidence. Circulate to listen to pairs share.

- *Page 11 shows that Tomás gets books from a library.*
- *On page 18, Tomás finds books at the dump.*

Display the second question on a Sentence Strip written in blue: "How does Ana get books?" Echo Read the question.

Distribute two blue sticky notes to each pair. Pairs repeat the above procedure with their copies of *Waiting for the Biblioburro.*

- *On page 6, Ana gets one book as a gift from her teacher who moved away.*
- *Ana holding new books from the Biblioburro on page 18.*
- *On page 24, Ana writes her own book.*

Display the third question on a Sentence Strip written in blue: "How is the way Tomás and Ana get books the same and different?" Echo Read the question.

Pairs pair up to form a small group to discuss the answer, comparing both sets of evidence they gathered from their texts. Circulate to listen to students' discussions. Use Equity Sticks to call on groups to offer a comparison.

- *Both Tomás and Ana get books from a library. Tomás gets books from a library that stays in the same place. Ana gets books from the Biblioburro, a library that moves around.*
- *Tomás can find books in the town dump, but there are no books in Ana's village.*
- *Tomás could get new books whenever he wanted. Ana had to wait a long time to get new books.*

Introduce the second set of questions:

Display the fourth question on a Sentence Strip written in red: "How do books change Tomás's life?" Echo Read the question.

Distribute two red sticky notes to each pair. Pairs work together to annotate their copies of *Tomás and the Library Lady*, using the illustrations as support. Pairs then share their findings with another pair to discover new evidence. Circulate to listen to pairs share.

- *Pages 13–14, pages 21–22, and pages 27–28 show that books help Tomás use all his senses to imagine what's happening in the books.*
- *Books give Tomás new stories to tell to his family. Page 17 shows him telling stories to them.*
- *On page 26, books help Tomás become the new storyteller in his family.*

Display the fifth question on a Sentence Strip written in red: "How do books change Ana's life?" Echo Read the question.

Distribute two red sticky notes to each pair. Pairs repeat the above procedure with their copies of *Waiting for the Biblioburro.*

- *Page 9: Books help Ana use her imagination.*

142

Copyright © 2016 Great Minds®

- *Page 9: Books give Ana new stories to tell to her family.*
- *Page 9: Books make Ana want to write her own book to share with other children.*

Display the sixth question on a Sentence Strip written in red: "How is the way books change Tomás and Ana's lives the same and different?" Echo Read the question.

Pairs join together with another pair to form a small group to discuss the answer, comparing both sets of evidence they gathered from their texts. Circulate to listen to students' discussions. Use Equity Sticks to call on groups to offer a comparison.

- *Both Tomás and Ana use their imaginations when reading books.*
- *Books give both Tomás and Ana stories to tell to their families.*
- *Books inspire Ana to write her own book. Tomás doesn't write his own book.*

Differentiation

Introducing one question at a time will help scaffold students' evidence collection. If you feel students can handle two questions, introduce questions one and two at the same time and four and five at the same time.

Congratulate students on their ability to compare and contrast Ana and Tomás using annotation.

EXECUTE USING COMPLETE SENTENCES

Individuals 25 MIN.

Remind students of how they have been learning about story elements and writing in complete sentences. In Focusing Question Task 2, they will demonstrate what they have learned by writing a retelling of the story *Waiting for the Biblioburro*.

Display Handout 11A: Focusing Question 2 Prompt.

Display and Echo Read the Focusing Question: *How does the Biblioburro change Ana's life?*

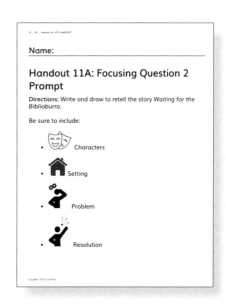

Write and draw to retell the story Waiting for the Biblioburro.

Be sure to include:

- *Characters*
- *Setting*
- *Problem*
- *Resolution*
- *Complete sentences.*
- *End punctuation.*

Distribute Assessment 11: Focusing Question Task 2. Remind students that they used the Sentence Frames for Focusing Question Task 1. Display and tell students to use the Story Map and the Complete Sentences Chart to help them with the task.

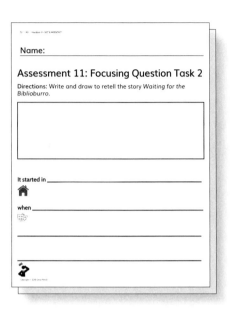

Instruct students to place their hand on the first page of the booklet. Think-Pair-Share: "Which story elements are you going to write and draw about on page 1?" Use Equity Sticks to call on three students to share their responses. Point to the Story Map and refer to the components as students tell about the first page.

- *We are going to write about the setting.*
- *We are going to write about the character.*
- *We are going to write about the problem.*

Remind students to use the main character in their writing.

Echo Read the Sentence Frame as students follow along with their finger. Ask students to point to the illustration box.

Students place their hand on page 2. Echo Read the sentence as students follow along with their finger. Explain that they do not have to complete the Sentence Frames on this page, but they have to illustrate what the sentence says. Students point to the illustration box.

Repeat the procedure with page 3.

Pairs orally process the prompt by retelling the story using the Sentence Frames to guide them.

Students independently complete the prompt.

WIT & WISDOM™   G1 > M1 > Lesson 11

Land 3 MIN.

ANSWER THE CONTENT FRAMING QUESTION

Know: *How does* Waiting for the Biblioburro *build my knowledge?*

Ask: "How did reading this text help you learn more about how books change lives? What did you learn about how books change other people's lives around the world?"

Students draw a response in their Response Journals.

- *(Drawing of a person imagining while reading a book.)*
- *(Drawing of a person writing a book.)*
- *(Drawing of a person getting books at a library.)*

Wrap 2 MIN.

In the next lesson, students meet Luis Soriano Bohórquez, the inspiration for the story *Waiting for the Biblioburro.*

Analyze

Context and Alignment

Students write independently as they use information on the Story Map to complete the Sentence Frames in Focusing Question Task 2 in preparation for drafting independent narrative retellings later in the module (RL.1.2, RL.1.3, W.1.3, W.1.8, SL.1.1.a, L.1.1.j, L.1.2.b).

Check for the following success criterion:

- Draws and writes to complete the Sentence Frames.

Next Steps

If students struggle to retell the story using the Sentence Frames, meet with individuals to hear an oral retelling using Story Stones. Provide support in writing by meeting in a small group to complete the Sentence Frames, referencing the Story Map for each story element page by page.

If students do not draw details about the story elements, direct them to specific pages in the text to help them add details to one of those categories.

145

Copyright © 2016 Great Minds®

⬇ Lesson 11: Vocabulary Deep Dive

Vocabulary Strategies: Frayer Model for *Inspire*

- **Time:** 15 min.

- **Text:** *Waiting for the Biblioburro*, Monica Brown, John Parra

- **Vocabulary Learning Goal:** Develop vocabulary knowledge of the word *inspire*. (L.1.6)

Launch

Explain that students will look closely at a verb that is important to understanding how librarians and the books they provide change lives: *inspire*.

Display a copy of the Frayer Model for students to see. Students Think-Pair-Share about what they remember about this graphic. Ask: "How was this used before?"

Circulate as students discuss and reinforce their responses when bringing the class together. Remind them that the Frayer Model is used to help them deepen their knowledge of a word and that in this lesson they will focus on the word *inspire*.

Learn

Write the word *inspire* in the center circle. Read the word for the students and have them repeat it several times. Students Think-Pair-Share about whether they have heard this word and what it might mean. Remind students that in the author's note, they learned that this book "was inspired by a particular librarian" the author knew.

Begin to complete the chart by writing a definition in the first quadrant. Tell students that to *inspire* means "to encourage to do something." As a class, use this definition to come up with a friendly definition students understand. If necessary, guide students to understand that to *inspire* means "to encourage to do something." Ensure that students understand this definition before writing it in the box on the chart. Offer students examples of someone who inspires you and explain how that person inspires you.

As a class, generate a list of facts and characteristics for ways to inspire someone or what might inspire them. Possible responses may include getting a prize or trophy, making someone happy, etc.

After generating a list of characteristics, work with the class to generate examples that fit the characteristics. In a similar fashion, generate a list of non-examples.

✓ Students verbalize the definition, facts, and examples for the word *inspire* with a partner. Scaffold student discussion by offering the following topics to discuss the following questions:

- In *Waiting for the Biblioburro*, what inspired Ana to write her own book?
- In *Tomás and the Library Lady*, what inspired Tomás to go into the library? What inspired the librarian to help Tomás?
- Think about the art in *Museum ABC*. What do you think inspired the artists to create the art?

Land

Use Equity Sticks to choose two or three pairs to share the definition, facts, and examples for the word *inspire*.

Students add the word to Handout 11B: Frayer Model and fill in the information from the class chart. Students place this in their Vocabulary Journals.

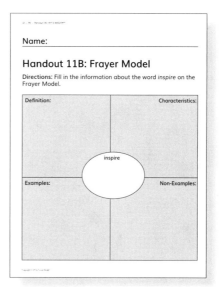

WIT & WISDOM™   G1 > M1 > Lesson 12

■ FOCUSING QUESTION: LESSONS 7-12

How does the Biblioburro change life for Ana?

1 2 3 4 5 6 **7 8 9 10 11 12** 13 14 15 16 17 18 19 20 21 22 23 24 25 26 27 28 29 30 31 32

Lesson 12

TEXTS

- *Waiting for the Biblioburro*, Monica Brown, John Parra
- "CNN Heroes: Luis Soriano" (**http://witeng.link/0627**)
- "ASL Sign for: same," *American Sign Language Dictionary*

Copyright © 2016 Great Minds®

G1 > M1 > Lesson 12

WIT & WISDOM™

Lesson 12: At a Glance

AGENDA

Welcome (10 min.)

Fluency Check-in

Launch (3 min.)

Understand the Content Framing Question

Learn (55 min.)

Relate the Author's Note to the Story (20 min.)

Connect Stories to Real Life (10 min.)

Excel in Writing Complete Sentences (10 min.)

Record Knowledge (15 min.)

Land (5 min.)

Answer the Content Framing Question

Wrap (2 min.)

Vocabulary Deep Dive: Adding the Inflectional Ending *-ing* to Root Words (15 min.)

STANDARDS ADDRESSED

The full text of ELA Standards can be found in the Module Overview.

Reading

- RL.1.1, RL.1.3, RL.1.7

- RI.1.1, RI.1.7

Writing

- W.1.3

Speaking and Listening

- SL.1.1.a, SL.1.2

Language

- ⬇ L.1.4.c

MATERIALS

- Fluent Readers Chart

- Sentence Strips

- Complete Sentences Anchor Chart

- Assessment 11: Focusing Question Task 2

- Knowledge Journal

- Vocabulary Journal

Learning Goals

Write and speak about how *Waiting for the Biblioburro* adds to knowledge of how books change lives.

✔ Contribute to the Knowledge Journal.

Edit a narrative retelling paragraph for use of complete sentences.

✔ Edit Focusing Question Task 2.

⬇ Identify root words and the inflectional ending *-ing*. (L.1.1.e, L.1.4.c)

✔ Work with a partner to identify the correct word to fill in Sentence Frames.

Copyright © 2016 Great Minds®

✔ Checks for Understanding

WIT & WISDOM™   G1 > M1 > Lesson 12

Prepare

FOCUSING QUESTION: Lessons 7-12

How does the Biblioburro change life for Ana?

CONTENT FRAMING QUESTION: Lesson 12

Know: *How does* Waiting for the Biblioburro *build our knowledge of how books change lives?*

CRAFT QUESTION: Lesson 12

Excel: *How do I improve my writing by using complete sentences?*

Students find connections between two key pieces of information in the author's note and the story in *Waiting for the Biblioburro*. Students then compare the information from the author's note to a short video about Luis Soriano Bohórquez, providing more information about the man who inspired this story. Exploring the author's note and video provides students with additional background and the knowledge that the book is based on a real biblioburro. Students also revise their writing from Focusing Question Task 2, focusing on editing for punctuation. Finally, they record knowledge and learning in the Knowledge Journal.

Welcome 10 MIN.

FLUENCY CHECK-IN

Chorally read the homework passage, reading at a good pace. Students check in with Nonverbal Signals, indicating how they felt they did on the homework. Explain to students that if they learn to read fluently, they will be heard and understood, which is the last point on the Fluent Readers Chart.

Students demonstrate all elements of fluency as they perform the homework passage in small groups.

Display the Fluent Readers Chart for students to refer to. Small groups practice the passage before each student has the opportunity to read the passage individually. Circulate to listen to students read, noting students' level of performance.

Small groups determine the actors and readers.

Display page 17 in the text, beginning with: "Someone should write a story." The actors use the illustration to set up the scene.

Four students become silent actors, as the others read the passage. Small groups perform for the rest of the class.

Remind students that this lesson's homework is the final fluency work with *Waiting for the Biblioburro*.

151

Copyright © 2016 Great Minds®

G1 > M1 > Lesson 12   WIT & WISDOM™

Launch 3 MIN.

UNDERSTAND THE CONTENT FRAMING QUESTION

Post the Content Framing Question and Focusing Question.

Echo Read the Content Framing Question.

Explain that students are using the same Content Framing Question to take a closer look at how books change lives using information they've learned from *Waiting for the Biblioburro*.

Ask students: "What did we learn in our last lesson about *Waiting for the Biblioburro* and how it connects to how books change lives?" Call on volunteers for responses.

- *Some people can't get books whenever they want. They have to wait for a library to come to them, like Ana had to wait.*
- *Books are very important to many people, like Ana.*
- *We learned that libraries can move around.*

As students respond, follow up by asking: "What part of the text helped you learn that?"

Learn 55 MIN.

RELATE THE AUTHOR'S NOTE TO THE STORY

Whole Group 20 MIN.

Display and reference the Speaking and Listening Anchor Chart.

💬 Explain that students will read a new part of the book to build their knowledge. Read aloud the author's note on page 29.

Ask: "We know the characters in this book live in a remote village. Where do you think remote places are?" Call on volunteers for responses.

- *I think remote means "far away." Ana's village is far away from other towns.*
- *I think remote means "not close by to other towns." It takes a long time for the Biblioburro to come back to Ana's village.*

Explain that *remote* can describe people or places that are far away.

TEACHER NOTE	Students will do more in-depth work with the word *remote* when they read the text *My Librarian Is a Camel*. For this lesson, briefly define the word.

Remind students of how they read the author's note when reading *Tomás and the Library Lady*. Ask: "What does an author's note explain?" Call on one or two volunteers for their response.

- *An author's note provides facts about the book.*

Reread the author's note as students listen for information that connects to, or is the same as, the story. Students indicate what is the same by gesturing using a Nonverbal Signal, such as the ASL sign for *same* (**http://witeng.link/0272**).

Use student responses to highlight important connections between the text and the author's note. Write and illustrate two important connections on Sentence Strips:

- Libraries that travel (drawing of books moving, such as with "feet" on them).
- Librarian who delivers books to children (drawing of the Biblioburro).

Display the Sentence Strips in two separate areas in the room.

As you reread the story aloud, students will listen for more connections between the story and the author's note. When they notice a connection, they will gesture to the appropriate posted detail written on the Sentence Strip.

Read relevant sections of the story aloud: pages 9–10, 11, 13, 17, 23, 26.

After each excerpt, students gesture to the sign that shows the connection. If answers differ, ask a student pointing to the correct location, "What details in the text show this connection?"

When many students are gesturing, pause to have students Think-Pair-Share: "What connections do you hear in the story?" Call on two to three volunteers to share their thinking.

Connections to "libraries that travel":

- *Page 9: This page shows the Biblioburro arriving at Ana's village.*
- *Page 10: The text says, "This is a moving library."*
- *Page 17: The text says, "Then he packs up the books and is off."*
- *Page 18: The illustration shows the Biblioburro waving to the children in Ana's village as he leaves to go somewhere else.*
- *Page 25: The Biblioburro is traveling again to another village.*

Connections to "librarian who delivers books to children":

- *Page 11: The librarian and Alfa and Beto read to the children.*
- *Page 14: The librarian reads to the children.*

G1 > M1 > Lesson 12

- Page 13: The text says, "Pick out books and in a few weeks I will be back to collect them and bring you new ones." The librarian is giving books to the children.
- Page 24: The illustration shows the librarian came back to give the kids more books.
- Page 28: It says "all the new stories the Biblioburro will bring."

CONNECT STORIES TO REAL LIFE

Whole Group 10 MIN.

TEACHER NOTE	Whenever possible, it's important for students to learn more about the real people and events that inspire a piece of literature. Watching informational videos such as this one can bring diverse perspectives and new appreciation for the story.

Watch the short video about Luis Soriano Bohórquez (**http://witeng.link/0627**).

When students see a connection to the story, they make a Nonverbal Signal for *same*, such as the ASL sign for *same* (**http://witeng.link/0272**).

Explain to students that they should signal briefly when they notice a similarity but then return their attention the video. Students practice signaling.

Students may signal during these moments in the video:

- "In the village, life goes on in a stationary way. There is no change."
- "Reading has made me laugh and dream."
- "Alfa, Beto, and I" (Luis riding on Alfa or Beto and holding the Biblioburro sign).
- "My classroom is not traditional."
- "My Biblioburro consists of books placed in saddles on top of my donkeys."
- "We go to places that are not on the map. Where a child has to walk or ride a donkey for up to forty minutes to reach the closest school."
- "When they learn how to read, the child discovers a new world."
- "[Luis Soriano] has educated a lot of people, [he] has ridden the donkey like no one has."
- "These children need it. Of course they want to learn."

Consider watching the video twice so students are able to find more similarities or affirm the similarities they heard, if time allows.

After the video, students Mix and Mingle: "What was the same in the video and in the story, and what was different?"

WIT & WISDOM™   G1 > M1 > Lesson 12

Use Equity Sticks to call on students.

- *In the video, not much is changing in the villages. That was the same as the story, where not many new things happened in Ana's village.*

- *Reading makes Luis dream in the video. Reading also makes Ana dream in the story.*

- *In the video, Luis has donkeys named Alfa and Beto and carries a Biblioburro sign, just like in the story!*

- *The Biblioburro in the video carries books by putting them in saddles on top of donkeys. That's the same way the books are carried in the story.*

- *Luis in the video said he goes to places that are not on the map, where children live far away from schools. Those places sound similar to Ana's village, which is far away from other places.*

- *The children in the video need the books, they want to learn. That's just like Ana and the children in the village. They love books and are happy when the books come.*

Extension

Students draw one connection between the text and the video in their Response Journals.

EXCEL IN WRITING COMPLETE SENTENCES

Whole Group   10 MIN.

Share the Craft Question with students: "How do I improve my writing by using complete sentences?"

Display the Complete Sentences Anchor Chart and ask: "What are the parts of a complete sentence?" Volunteers respond and then students Echo Read the chart.

Explain that they will edit Focusing Question Task 2 to make sure they included punctuation at the end of sentences. Tell students that edit means to "fix mistakes."

Remind students that when they revised in Lesson 6, they followed two steps. In this lesson they will follow three steps to edit their writing:

- Read the sentence.

- Check for punctuation.

- Correct the error.

Students Echo Read as they follow along with their finger on page 1 of Focusing Question Task 2. Stop at the end of the sentence. Ask: "Does your sentence have a period?" Students stand and Sky Write a period and write a period at the end of their sentence if necessary. Repeat for page 3.

155

Copyright © 2016 Great Minds®

G1 > M1 > Lesson 12   WIT & WISDOM™

Instruct students to Think-Pair-Share, and ask: "How can we edit for end punctuation?"

- *Read the sentence.*
- *Check for punctuation.*
- *Correct the error.*

RECORD KNOWLEDGE

Whole Group   15 MIN.

Congratulate students on how much they have already learned and know how to do and explain that they are now ready to add to the Knowledge Journal.

Display the Knowledge Journal. Point to the left-hand side of the Knowledge Journal, labeled "What I know."

Remind students that this part of the Knowledge Journal is all about the new information they learned in these lessons.

Instruct students to Think-Pair-Share and ask: "What did you learn from our lessons on *Waiting for the Biblioburro*? What did you learn about our Essential Question?"

> #### Scaffold
>
> Ask more concrete questions to prompt students and encourage application of key vocabulary:
> - What did we learn about mobile libraries?
> - What did we learn about how books change lives?

Use Equity Sticks to call on pairs to share responses. After each response, students reach for the sky if they believe the response is important learning and touch their toes if they disagree or are unsure.

Use votes to choose one to three refined responses to record on the Knowledge Journal. Read each response aloud. Point to the right-hand side of the Knowledge Journal, labeled "What I can do."

Remind students that this column is for things we can now do, whether in our heads, out loud, or on paper. Revisit artifacts from previous lessons, including anchor charts, Response Journal entries, and the Focusing Question Task.

✔ Instruct students to Think-Pair-Share, and ask: "What did you learn to do as a writer? What did you learn to do as a reader?"

> #### Scaffold
>
> Ask more concrete questions to prompt students and encourage application of key vocabulary:
> - What did we learn about writing complete sentences?
> - What did we learn about the words *inspire, market, burros,* and *collect*?

156

Copyright © 2016 Great Minds®

Repeat the process detailed above to engage students in a class vote and record refined responses.

What I know	What I can do
[INSERT IMPORTANT KNOWLEDGE] - Books open your imagination. - Books can connect you to the world. - You can write your own book. - I learned some people can't get books whenever they want them. - I learned libraries can travel around the country.	[INSERT IMPORTANT LEARNING– speaking/listening, craft, retelling] - I can compare two characters in two different books. - I can talk about the characters, setting, problem and resolution when I retell a story. - I know that a problem can change more than one time in a story.

Explain to students that they will continue to add to this chart throughout this module so they can track everything they have learned and are now able to do.

ANSWER THE CONTENT FRAMING QUESTION

Knowledge: How does *Waiting for the Biblioburro* build our knowledge of how books change lives?

Choral Read the Content Framing Question.

Students Mix and Mingle: "What did we learn about how books change lives from reading *Waiting for the Biblioburro*?" Remind students to consider the question: "What part of the text helped you learn that?"

Use Equity Sticks to call on students.

- *I learned that you can write your own book and share it with others. Ana did this at the end of the story and gave her book to the Biblioburro to share with other kids.*
- *Books can connect you to the rest of the world. In the text, Ana dreams of the outside world. Then at the end, she writes her book and another kid in a different place in the world gets to read it.*

Wrap

Share that in the next lesson, students read a new informational text, *My Librarian Is a Camel*.

Analyze

Context and Alignment

Students contribute to the Knowledge Journal by discussing how *Waiting for the Biblioburro* adds to their knowledge of how books change lives. Check students' oral responses for the following success criteria:

- Responds accurately to selected questions.
- Uses relevant text evidence in their responses.

Next Steps

If students had difficulty making connections between the text and how books change peoples' lives, consider working with small groups and asking specific questions related to the Content Framing Question. For example, read pages 5 and 9–11. Stop at the end of each page and ask: "What is happening now?" Make connections between why Ana doesn't have books, how she gets them, and what happens as a result.

WIT & WISDOM™   G1 > M1 > Lesson 12

⬇ Lesson 12: Vocabulary Deep Dive

Adding Inflectional Ending *–ing* to Root Words

- **Time:** 15 min.

- **Text:** *Waiting for the Biblioburro*, Monica Brown, John Parra

- **Vocabulary Learning Goal:** Identify root words and the inflectional ending *–ing*. (L.1.1.e, L.1.4.c)

Launch

Remind students that they have learned to pay attention to the ending of verbs.

Display and read the following sentences/phrases from *Waiting for the Biblioburro*:

- Ana, fast asleep, <u>dreaming</u> about the world outside and beyond the hill.

- The book was a gift from her teacher for <u>working</u> so hard.

- What are they <u>carrying</u>?

Students Think-Pair-Share about what they noticed about the underlined words. Students should notice that all of the underlined words have *–ing* at the end.

Students Think-Pair-Share about what they remember about words with *–ing* at the end. Use Equity Sticks to choose two or three volunteers to share what they remember.

   ▪ *The ending means something happening right now.*

   ▪ *The ending is added to a root word.*

   ▪ *The root word is an action word or a verb.*

Affirm correct answers and reinforce that the *–ing* ending is added to the end of a verb to show that the action is happening right now. Explain that they will practice with more words that have this ending.

Learn

Read the word *dreaming* with students. Teach students how to separate the word into syllables. Help them identify the two parts in the word. Have students identify the part of the word that is left when the *–ing* is removed. Write the word *dream* on the board for students to see. Remind students that this is the root word. Repeat the process for *working* and *carrying*.

Show the following Sentence Frames:

159

Copyright © 2016 Great Minds®

G1 > M1 > Lesson 12   WIT & WISDOM™

- I can _____.

- I am _____.

Discuss the difference between *can* and *am* with students. *Can* means "able to do" something, for example, "I can wear tennis shoes." The word *am* means that the action is happening right now, for example, "I am wearing my tennis shoes." Experiment with placing the words from the sentences with and without the ending in the blanks. Guide students to recognizing that adding the *–ing* chunk means the action is happening right now.

✔ Students work with a partner to fill in the following Sentence Frames in their Vocabulary Journal by either using the root word or by adding *–ing* to the end of the word.

- **I am _____ out the window.** (look)

- **I can _____ out the window.** (look)

- **I can _____ dinner with my mom.** (cook)

- **My mom is _____ dinner.** (cook)

- **The boy can _____ my dog.** (walk)

- **The boy is _____ his dog.** (walk)

Land

Use Equity Sticks to choose two or three students to share what they noticed when they added the inflectional ending to the word. Challenge students to make up their own sentence and share it with their partner.

WIT & WISDOM™   G1 > M1 > Lesson 13

■ FOCUSING QUESTION: LESSONS 13-16

How do people around the world get books?

1 2 3 4 5 6 7 8 9 10 11 12 **13 14 15 16** 17 18 19 20 21 22 23 24 25 26 27 28 29 30 31 32

Lesson 13

TEXTS

- *My Librarian Is a Camel*, Margriet Ruurs
- *Museum ABC*, The Metropolitan Museum of Art

Copyright © 2016 Great Minds®

G1 > M1 > Lesson 13   WIT & WISDOM™

Lesson 13: At a Glance

AGENDA

Welcome (10 min.)

Notice and Wonder about Museum ABC

Launch (3 min.)

Understand the Content Framing Question

Learn (55 min.)

Complete a New-Read Assessment (15 min.)

Notice Details (10 min.)

Generate and Answer Questions (15 min.)

Locate Countries (15 min.)

Land (5 min.)

Answer the Content Framing Question

Wrap (2 min.)

Assign Fluency Homework

Style and Conventions Deep Dive: Declarative Sentences (15 min.)

STANDARDS ADDRESSED

The full text of ELA Standards can be found in the Module Overview.

Reading

- RI.1.1

Speaking and Listening

- SL.1.a

Language

- L.1.1.j, L.1.2.b
- ⬇ L.1.1.j

MATERIALS

- Assessment 13: New-Read Assessment 2
- Handout 1A: Notice and Wonder Prompt Cards
- Wonder Wheel
- Blank Questions and Answers Chart
- Sticky notes
- World map
- Sticky flags
- Handout 13A: Fluency Homework
- Noun Chart
- Verb Chart

Learning Goals

Generate questions about *My Librarian Is a Camel* using key details from the text. (RI.1.1)

✔ Complete a New-Read Assessment.

⬇ Create a complete declarative sentence. (L.1.1.j)

✔ Create complete sentences orally.

Copyright © 2016 Great Minds®

✔ Checks for Understanding

WIT & WISDOM™   G1 > M1 > Lesson 13

Prepare

FOCUSING QUESTION: Lessons 13-16

How do people around the world get books?

CONTENT FRAMING QUESTION: Lesson 13

Wonder: *What do I notice and wonder about* My Librarian is a Camel?

Students notice and wonder about *Museum ABC* before seguing into a New-Read Assessment where they look at photos in *My Librarian Is a Camel* to generate questions. Continuing with a gradual release of independence with questioning, students notice and wonder about the pictures of specific countries in the informational text in small groups. They then organize the countries to reveal the alphabetical order and locate them on a map.

Welcome 10 MIN.

NOTICE AND WONDER ABOUT *MUSEUM ABC*

Provide each pair with a new spread of the pages in *Museum ABC*.

TEACHER NOTE	With each new opportunity to notice and wonder with *Museum ABC* spreads, be sure you give each pair a new page. By rotating pages, it keeps the content fresh, and as students get more confident with finding details in the artwork, their notices and wonders will become more nuanced and detailed. This confidence with noticing and wondering without the need to decode words keeps students rooted in the text and builds their capacity to ask and answer questions. In this lesson, they will immediately apply this practice to the New-Read Assessment on their new informational text.

Display the Content Framing Question.

Echo Read the Content Framing Question for *Museum ABC*: *What do you notice and wonder about your page of* Museum ABC?

In pairs, students share the details they notice by putting different artworks on the page into the Sentence Frame: **I notice _____.**

▪ *I see a black and white cat with yellow eyes looking at me.*

163

Copyright © 2016 Great Minds®

G1 > M1 > Lesson 13　　　　　　　　　　　　　　　　　　　　WIT & WISDOM™

- I see three bugs near pink flowers.
- I see a cow with wings and one horn.
- I see a bird with a long tail on a branch.

Two or three students share their responses with the whole group.

Explain that the things the students said they saw in the picture are called *details*, and details can help us understand more about the painting.

Ask: "When you think about the details you found, what do you wonder about the painting on your page?"

If needed, provide a short definition of the word *wonder* or model one or two different examples. Remind students that wonders should come in the form of a question and that they can use their question words from the Wonder Wheel to help them.

Students respond to the different artworks on the page using the Sentence Frame: **I wonder: _____?**

- I wonder: Why is the fluffy cat looking up?
- I wonder: Does the butterfly feel as fuzzy as it looks?
- I wonder: Did the cow just wake up from a nap?
- I wonder: Why does the bird's tail look like it has eyes on it?

Two or three students share their responses with the whole group.

Explain that students will use the same process of noticing and wondering as they enjoy a new book.

Launch 3 MIN.

UNDERSTAND THE CONTENT FRAMING QUESTION

Post the Content Framing Question and Focusing Question.

Read aloud the Focusing Question. Remind students that this is the question they will focus on for the next four lessons to eventually answer the Essential Question of the module.

Ask students: "How does this Focusing Question compare to our other Focusing Questions?"

- This question asks about a lot of people.
- This question is about how people get books.

Reinforce that the other Focusing Questions were about how a particular character's life changed, while this question is about a lot of people and how they get books.

164

Copyright © 2016 Great Minds®

WIT & WISDOM™   G1 > M1 > Lesson 13

Read aloud the Content Framing Question.

Ask: "What do we do the first time we read a book?" Volunteers respond.

- *We notice things in a book.*
- *We wonder about a book and ask questions, just like we did with the paintings.*

Learn 55 MIN.

COMPLETE A NEW-READ ASSESSMENT 15 MIN.

This New-Read Assessment assesses students on whether they can ask and answer questions about a new informational text, *My Librarian is a Camel.*

Explain that the first thing students will do with *My Librarian Is a Camel* is ask questions in order to show everything they have learned about asking and answering questions.

Display and distribute Assessment 13: New-Read Assessment 2 and a two-page spread from *My Librarian is a Camel.*

Explain that students will explore the text *My Librarian Is a Camel* visually with a partner. Then, they will use one Sentence Frame to create a question they have about the text. After listening to the story, they will answer their question.

Ask: "What are we doing first?" A volunteer responds.

Reinforce that first students will visually explore the text with a partner and then use Sentence Frames to ask questions.

Display and Echo Read the Sentence Frames:

Who _____?

Where _____?

Why _____?

Who questions tell you about people.

Where questions tell you about places or locations.

Why questions tell about a reason or cause.

Name: _____

Assessment 13: New-Read Assessment 2

Directions: Write a question you have about a section from the text *My Librarian is a Camel.* Use who, where, or why to begin the question.

Who	Where	Why

Question:

_____
_____
_____
_____
_____
_____

165

Copyright © 2016 Great Minds®

G1 > M1 > Lesson 13

✔ Individually, students write and draw to formulate the question.

| TEACHER NOTE | As students ask questions during the New-Read Assessment, choose four to six student-generated questions to record on sticky notes labeled with students' initials. Create the Wonder Chart, adhere the notes, and share student questions as time is available. |

NOTICE DETAILS

Whole Group 10 MIN.

| TEACHER NOTE | Because of the amount of information in this text, the first read focuses only on exploring sections of the book visually. In subsequent lessons, students will conduct a close read of the introduction and dig deeper into the details of the captions and quotes. This initial viewing serves to engage students, give them a chance to notice the text structure, and provide a sense of the ways children access books in different locations around the world. |

Show students the cover and title of *My Librarian Is a Camel*. Explain that for the first reading of this book, they will notice and wonder about a few of the pages in small groups.

Distribute two to three country page spreads to small groups. Students visually explore the pages, showing the Notice Prompt Card when they notice details. Remind students that when they are noticing, they are paying attention to the text.

| TEACHER NOTE | Cut up the text pages of two books so there is one two-page copy of each country. |

Small groups discuss what they noticed on the pages. Circulate to listen to groups.

- *I see kids reaching for books (pages 8–9).*
- *I notice a woman reading a book to a donkey! (pages 12–13)*
- *There are kids waiting in line to get on a bus with books inside (pages 22–23).*
- *A boy is riding an elephant (page 28).*

Ask: "What clues tell us what type of book this is?" Use Equity Sticks to call on students to share what they noticed.

- There are real photos of people in this book.
- There is a picture of a little map and flag on a lot of the pages.
- Every other page has a big, bold word at the top.

If needed, follow up by asking, "What is different between this book and the others we've read?" Hold up copies of *Tomás and the Library Lady* and *Waiting for the Biblioburro*. Use responses to explain that they are noticing some of the features of an informational text. This type of text has true facts about a specific topic.

GENERATE AND ANSWER QUESTIONS

Small Groups 15 MIN.

Display the Questions and Answers Chart with the questions you captured from the New-Read Assessment.

Students Echo Read the questions you added to the chart.

Students review the pages slowly and look for answers to their questions.

Students stand up when they see the answers to the questions. When students stand, flag the page in your copy of the text with a sticky note and record initials of some standing students.

After finishing the text, return to the flagged pages. Call on a student who stood up for that page to respond to a question on the Questions and Answers Chart. As needed, reread that section of the text to confirm and clarify students' thinking. Record the answer on the relevant sticky note. Each time, move sticky notes across the chart to indicate the extent to which each question has been answered. If there are any unanswered questions, explain that students will revisit the chart after they've had more time to explore the text to answer the remaining questions.

Share that some of the answers might be hidden in the words in the text instead of the pictures, and while we aren't reading all of the pages in this lesson, the more we work with the text, the more we might find out.

G1 > M1 > Lesson 13

WIT & WISDOM™

MY LIBRARIAN IS A CAMEL QUESTIONS AND ANSWERS CHART

Questions ?	Answers in progress ⟵⟶	Complete answers ✓
▪ (Q1) *What are the children holding?* ▪ (Q2) *Where are the children?* ▪ (Q3) *How are the children getting books?*	▪ (Q1) *It looks like the children are holding books on pages 7–9.* ▪ (Q2) *The pictures on different pages look like they were taken in different places. On pages 9–10 the place looks really cold, but on pages 24–25 it looks really warm.* ▪ (Q2) *There are also different little maps on different pages.* ▪ (Q3) *It looks like camels are carrying books on their backs on pages 18–19.* ▪ (Q3) *On pages 14–15 children are getting books on a boat.*	

In future lessons, continue to display the Questions and Answers Chart and allow students to revisit their questions as they work with the text.

LOCATE COUNTRIES

Whole Group 15 MIN.

Remind students of how they have used a world map in this module to locate countries. Explain that *My Librarian Is a Camel* provides a great opportunity for returning to the map.

Divide all of the two-page country spreads among pairs. Pairs line up the spreads in alphabetical order.

Display the class world map.

Read each country name aloud in alphabetical order, starting with Australia. Pause after each country for students—except the pair who was assigned that country—to locate it on the map. Call on three to four students to come up to the map at the same time to point out the country.

Once the country is correctly identified, put a sticky flag on the location.

168

Copyright © 2016 Great Minds®

After all countries are located, students Think-Pair-Share: "What do you notice about all the countries on this map?" Use Equity Sticks to call on students to share their thoughts.

- *There are a lot of countries marked.*
- *The countries are all over the world.*

Display the table of contents. Ask students: "What do you notice about how the countries are listed in the table of contents?" If needed, ask students what they notice about the order of the list of countries.

- *The countries are listed in alphabetical order, just like how we lined them up.*

To help students make the connection with *Museum ABC*, ask: "What other books have a similar order that we've read?" Call on volunteers to respond.

Summarize the important learning that students accomplished in the activity. Tell students that in the next several lessons, they will continue to explore the information in this text.

ANSWER THE CONTENT FRAMING QUESTION

Wonder: *What do I notice and wonder about* My Librarian Is a Camel?

Students Mix and Mingle about what they noticed and wondered. Consider playing music as students move, and prompt them to stop and find a partner when the music stops. Circulate to listen to students.

Call on one or two volunteers to share their notices with the whole group, and one or two students to share their wonders with the whole group.

- *I notice in one photograph a woman is sitting in the wheelbarrow that transports books. She has books in her hands and looks really happy.*
- *I notice the inside of the bookbus in Pakistan looks like a real library with book shelves.*
- *I wonder how many books elephants and camels can carry.*

Celebrate the great notices and wonders. Remind students that, in the lessons to come, they will have many more chances to find answers to the wonderful questions they asked as they read the book even more closely.

Wrap 2 MIN.

ASSIGN FLUENCY HOMEWORK

Continue home reading routine. Collect Fluency Homework handouts from Lessons 7–12, and distribute Handout 13A: Fluency Homework. Remind students to share the new text with their family. Explain that the new text is an original poem based on the text *Museum ABC*.

WIT & WISDOM™   G1 > M1 > Lesson 13

Analyze

Context and Alignment

After visually exploring photographs from a section of the text *My Librarian is a Camel*, students independently formulate questions. (RI.1.1, L.1.1.j, L.1.2.b).

Check for the following success criteria:

- Formulates a question.

- Uses relevant text evidence from photographs.

- Writes a complete sentence.

Next Steps

If students do not ask questions using text evidence, meet with small groups or individuals to break the task into smaller steps. Choose a picture on the two-page spread that is the easiest one to formulate a question about. Choose one Sentence Frame to model the expectation. Generate possible questions to ask. Students choose a sentence or generate one of their own.

If students can orally formulate the question but have difficulty writing, provide support by scribing or underwriting student writing. If students experience difficulty writing words, assist them with segmenting the sounds in the word. For example: "Say the word slowly. Write a line for each sound heard. Write the letter or letters on the line."

Example:

Table

T a b l

___ ___ ___ ___

⬇ Lesson 13: Style and Conventions Deep Dive

Declarative Sentences

- **Time:** 15 min.

- **Text:** *My Librarian Is a Camel*, Margriet Ruurs

- **Style and Conventions Learning Goal:** Create a complete declarative sentence. (L.1.1.j)

- **STYLE AND CONVENTIONS CRAFT QUESTION:** Lesson 13
  Experiment: *What makes a declarative sentence complete?*

Launch

Display and read the Craft Question: *What makes a declarative sentence complete?*

Students Echo Read the question. Explain that in this lesson they will learn more about sentences and what makes them complete.

Learn

Display the following:

borrows books.

Ask students the following question and allow them to use nonverbal signals to answer the question.

- Is this a complete thought? How do you know?

Students Think-Pair-Share about why this is not a complete thought. Use Equity Sticks to choose volunteers to share their thinking.

- *I don't know who borrowed books.*
- *I don't know what borrowed the books.*
- *A noun is missing.*

Display and read the Complete Sentences Anchor Chart, affirm correct answers, and explain that complete thoughts and complete sentences have to have a noun and a verb, or a subject and what the subject is doing.

WIT & WISDOM™   G1 > M1 > Lesson 13

> **TEACHER NOTE**
>
> The goal of this Deep Dive is for students to identify and create declarative sentences. However, this is also an organic opportunity to reinforce the guidelines students have learned for developing complete sentences. Modify the instruction in this lesson (e.g., expanding or removing reminders about complete sentences) as needed in order to meet the needs of your students.

Display the Noun and Verb Charts created in earlier lessons. Review that a noun is a person, place, or thing, and that a verb is an action word.

Choose a common noun from the chart to use to add to the incomplete sentence from the Launch. For example:

- Grandpa

Add the noun to the sentence and read the sentence aloud. Students give a Nonverbal Signal to show if they think the thought or sentence is now complete.

- Grandpa borrows books.

Affirm that it is a complete sentence. Point out the noun (or subject) and the verb in the sentence by circling the subject and underlining the verb. Explain that this sentence is a declarative sentence because it is giving someone information about something. Students repeat *declarative* three times.

Ask students to select a noun from the Noun Chart and a verb from the Verb Chart to help you create a simple sentence with those words to demonstrate. Capture the sentences. For example:

- Ana writes.
- Tomás walks.
- The library lady helps.
- Camels carry.

Students Think-Pair-Share about what questions they have after reading these sentences. Refer to the Wonder Wheel if students need help with question words. Use Equity Sticks to choose volunteers to share their thinking.

- *I wonder where Ana is writing.*
- *I wonder what Ana is writing.*
- *I wonder where Tomás is walking to.*
- *I wonder who the library lady is helping.*
- *I wonder what camels carry.*

Explain that even though a sentence only needs a subject, or noun, and a verb to be complete this doesn't make the sentences very interesting. Use the questions the students generated to choose a word from the Noun Chart to help them make the sentences more interesting. Provide the articles as needed to make the sentences. For example:

173

Copyright © 2016 Great Minds®

G1 > M1 > Lesson 13　　　　　　　　　　　　　　　　　　　　WIT & WISDOM™

- Ana writes a story.
- Tomás walks home.
- The library lady helps Tomás.
- Camels carry books.

Echo Read the sentences together and circle the subject and underline the verb. Reinforce that the sentence must have these two things to be a complete sentence.

✔ Partners work together to choose words from the Nouns and Verbs Charts to create their own complete declarative sentences. Remind them to use extra words to help make their sentences more interesting.

Students Mix and Mingle to share a sentence they created with their partners. Use Equity Sticks to choose volunteers to share their sentence with everyone.

Land

Instruct students to Think-Pair-Share, and ask: "What makes a declarative sentence complete?"

Use Equity Sticks to select two pairs to share their thinking. Use their responses to reinforce that complete sentences must have a subject and a verb in order to be complete, and that a declarative sentence tells someone information about something. Explain that students will continue to learn about different kinds of sentences and how to use them in their writing.

WIT & WISDOM™

G1 > M1 > Lesson 14

■ FOCUSING QUESTION: LESSONS 13-16

How do people around the world get books?

1 2 3 4 5 6 7 8 9 10 11 12 **13 14 15 16** 17 18 19 20 21 22 23 24 25 26 27 28 29 30 31 32

Lesson 14

TEXT

▪ *My Librarian Is a Camel*, Margriet Ruurs

Copyright © 2016 Great Minds®

G1 > M1 > Lesson 14

WIT & WISDOM™

Lesson 14: At a Glance

AGENDA

Welcome (5 min.)

Launch (5 min.)

Understand the Content Framing Question

Learn (50 min.)

Listen Actively and Analyze the Introduction (40 min.)

Examine Proper Nouns (10 min.)

Land (10 min.)

Answer the Content Framing Question

Wrap (5 min.)

Homework Check-in

Vocabulary Deep Dive: Frayer Model for *Remote* (15 min.)

STANDARDS ADDRESSED

The full text of ELA Standards can be found in the Module Overview.

Reading

- RI.1.1, RI.1.4, RI.1.5

Speaking and Listening

- SL.1.1.a, SL.1.2

Language

- ⬇ L.1.6

MATERIALS

- Sticky notes
- Noun Chart
- Response Journals
- Enlarged copy of Frayer Model
- Handout 14A: Frayer Model
- Vocabulary Journals

Learning Goals

Ask and answer questions to help determine or clarify the meaning of words and phrases in *My Librarian Is a Camel*. (RI.1.4)

✔ Use the Outside-In strategy to determine the meaning of *remote* and *mobile*.

⬇ Develop vocabulary knowledge of the word *remote*. (L.1.6)

✔ Verbalize definition, characteristics, examples and non-examples of the word *remote*.

Copyright © 2016 Great Minds®

✔ Checks for Understanding

WIT & WISDOM™   G1 > M1 > Lesson 14

Prepare

FOCUSING QUESTION: Lessons 13-16

How do people around the world get books?

CONTENT FRAMING QUESTION: Lesson 14

Organize: *What is happening in* My Librarian Is a Camel?

CRAFT QUESTION: Lesson 14

Examine: *Why are proper nouns important?*

To help digest the complex, rich text *My Librarian Is a Camel*, students closely read just the introduction in this lesson. Students continue to explore the information by determining the meaning of two key words in the introduction before making connections with how the words relate to the content and their own lives. Students also experiment with proper nouns, looking at words from the text.

Welcome 5 MIN.

TEACHER NOTE

As with *Museum ABC*, the photographs in *My Librarian Is a Camel* provide an engaging way for students to interact with the visual images in the text to try to figure out more about how people get books around the world. Some students may get intrigued enough to decode some of the headings or, with very strong readers, the text to find context for the photographs, but this next step isn't essential to get students talking and thinking about the pictures and building visual literacy with the photographs from different countries. Rotate the spreads each day to ensure students have new spreads to consider.

In pairs, students visually explore a new excerpt from *My Librarian Is a Camel*. Students ask and answer questions about the photographs, identify the name of the country, and imagine what it would be like to get books there.

177

Copyright © 2016 Great Minds®

G1 > M1 > Lesson 14   WIT & WISDOM™

Launch 5 MIN.

UNDERSTAND THE CONTENT FRAMING QUESTION

Post and read the Content Framing Question and Focusing Question. Repeat the Content Framing Question, and ask: "What do we try to figure out the second time we read a book?" Volunteers respond.

Reinforce that the second time they read a text, students try to figure out what is happening. Explain that, as they reread *My Librarian is a Camel*, students will focus on important information in order to know what is happening in the text.

Learn 50 MIN.

LISTEN ACTIVELY AND ANALYZE THE INTRODUCTION

Whole Group 40 MIN.

Explain that students will continue to work with the text, *My Librarian Is a Camel*, focusing on the introduction in this lesson. Explain that this introduction includes important information that will help them determine what is happening in the text.

Read aloud the introduction on page 5 all the way through.

Display and reread the first sentence of the introduction.

Ask students: "Do you notice any familiar or interesting words in that sentence?" Call on two to three volunteers for their responses.

- *Ana's village was also remote.*

As needed, point out that students were introduced to the word *remote* in the author's note of *Waiting for the Biblioburro*. Explain that this word is important to understanding what is happening in the text, so they will use the text to find out more about the word's meaning.

Tell students they will use the Outside-In strategy to look outside *remote* for context clues, then look inside *remote*, before determining the meaning of the word.

Reread aloud the first sentence. Slowly flip through a few remote locations in the text, such as:

- Canada (pages 10–11).
- Kenya (pages 18–19).

WIT & WISDOM™   G1 > M1 > Lesson 14

- Mongolia (pages 20–21).

- Papa New Guinea (pages 24–25).

- Thailand (pages 28–29).

- Zimbabwe (pages 30–31).

On each country page spread, pause for students to look for clues and ask: "What might give you a clue about the meaning of the word *remote* on these pages?" Use Equity Sticks to call on students for their thoughts. Display two to three refined responses.

- *Canada: There are not a lot of people around and it looks very cold. A child is using a sled to get around.*

- *Kenya: Camels move books around rather than cars.*

- *Mongolia: There are no buildings or cement roads in the background. It looks like people travel by horse.*

- *Papa New Guinea: There are not many roads or houses here either.*

- *Zimbabwe: There are dirt roads, trees, and not many buildings in the background.*

Ask students to look inside the word for clues: "Do you notice anything about the word *remote*? Where else have you seen this word?" Highlight two to three refined responses.

- *It's also used to describe a remote control.*

- *A remote control can turn on the TV from far away.*

✔ Students Think-Pair-Share: "Based on the information we gathered together, what is your best guess of the meaning of the word *remote*?" Use Equity Sticks to call on students.

- *Remote might mean far away from other people and buildings.*

Use students' responses to come up with a refined definition. Display the possible definition, such as *remote* means "far away from other people, houses, and cities." Reread the first sentence substituting the definition. Students use a Nonverbal Signal, such as a thumbs-up for *yes* and a thumbs-down for *no*, to decide if the sentence makes sense. If they decide it doesn't make sense, review the sentence and the text for clues before students Think-Pair-Share another meaning.

Decide on a simple definition and sketch for *remote*. Put *remote* on the Word Wall as a module word.

Display and reread the third sentence in the introduction: "My research turned up all sorts of 'mobile libraries' . . . on legs, on wheels, and by other means."

Ask students: "Do you notice any new or interesting words?" Call on two to three volunteers for their responses.

- *Mobile is an interesting word.*

Explain that *mobile* is also important to understanding what is happening in the text, so students will use the same Outside-In strategy to look outside *mobile* for context clues and then look inside *mobile* to determine the meaning of the word.

179

Copyright © 2016 Great Minds®

G1 > M1 > Lesson 14   WIT & WISDOM™

Reread aloud the third sentence. Slowly flip through a few examples of mobile libraries in the text "on legs, on wheels, and by other means" such as:

- Australia (pages 6–7).

- England (pages 12–13).

- Finland (pages 14–15).

- Indonesia (pages 16–17).

- Pakistan (pages 22–23).

- Peru (pages 26–27).

- Thailand (pages 28–29).

On each country page spread, pause for students to look for clues and ask: "What might give you a clue about the meaning of the word *mobile* on these pages?" Use Equity Sticks to call on students for their thoughts. Highlight two to three refined responses.

- *Australia: There is a big truck that carries books inside.*

- *England: A wheelbarrow filled with books is pushed along on the beach.*

- *Finland: Books are on a boat.*

- *Pakistan: There is a bus filled with books.*

- *Peru: Children are sitting on a wagon reading books. A donkey is pulling the wagon.*

- *Thailand: There are elephants carrying boxes on their backs. Those boxes might be filled with books.*

Ask students to look inside the word for clues: "Do you notice anything about the word *mobile*? Where else have you seen this word?" Highlight two to three refined responses.

- *We make mobiles to hang up around the room.*

- *My baby brother has a mobile above his crib. It moves in circles and makes noise.*

- *My mom has a mobile phone. She can use her phone wherever she is.*

✔ Students Think-Pair-Share: "Based on the information we gathered together, what is your best guess of the meaning of the word *mobile*?" Use Equity Sticks to call on students.

- Mobile *might mean moving around.*

Use students' responses to come up with a refined definition. Display a possible definition: *mobile* means "able to move from place to place." Reread the first sentence substituting the definition. Students use a Nonverbal Signal, such as a thumbs-up for *yes* and a thumbs-down for *no*, to decide if the sentence makes sense. If they decide it doesn't make sense, review the sentence and the text for clues before students Think-Pair-Share another meaning.

Decide on a simple definition and sketch for *mobile* to add to the interactive Word Wall card.

Tell students that now that they have determined the meaning of the words *remote* and *mobile*, they will look closely at one last part of the introduction with these two words in mind.

180

Copyright © 2016 Great Minds®

WIT & WISDOM™   G1 > M1 > Lesson 14

Chorally reread the Content Framing Question aloud to remind students of the goal for this work.

Reread the second to last paragraph aloud: "Maybe you have been taking . . . as many as you wish."

Read aloud the following TDQ. Small groups of three to four students discuss possible answers based on their own experiences. Remind groups to use information they gathered when determining the meanings of the words *remote* and *mobile*.

1   How do the words *remote* and *mobile* connect with the information in this paragraph? How does your experience with books and libraries contrast with what the text describes?

   ▪ *We have local libraries that are not mobile. We are lucky that we can go visit them anytime.*

   ▪ *We have these types of libraries because we don't live in a remote place. We have buildings for libraries and roads and cars to help us get to them quickly.*

   ▪ *I wish I had a local library that I could get to. We only have mobile libraries because we live in a remote town.*

   ▪ *Some people need mobile libraries. Those people live in remote places that are harder to get to.*

   ▪ *Books and libraries are important for everyone, whether you live in a remote place or not, or have a mobile library or one that doesn't move.*

EXPERIMENT WITH PROPER NOUNS

Whole Group 10 MIN.

Students Think-Pair-Share: "What are proper nouns?" Use Equity Sticks to call on two pairs to share their responses.

Use responses to review that proper nouns name a specific person, place, or thing(s) and always begin with a capital letter no matter where they are at in a sentence. Volunteers share a few examples of proper nouns.

Remind students of their previous work with common and proper nouns in Lessons 3 and 4. Display the Nouns Anchor Chart created in Lesson 3.

Read aloud the Craft Question: "How do proper nouns work?"

Display the following sentences:

   1. The blackpool Beach library delivers books by wheelbarrow.

   2. margriet Ruurs is an author.

   3. Donkeys deliver books in peru.

Explain that students will examine each sentence for proper nouns, then determine whether the proper noun is capitalized.

181

Copyright © 2016 Great Minds®

Think Aloud and model finding the proper nouns in the first sentence. For example: Blackpool Beach Library is a specific library, so all words in the name must be capitalized. Write a large capital letter on top of the lower case letters in Blackpool and Library.

Echo Read the second and third sentences to support decoding.

Students experiment with finding the proper nouns in these sentences and writing just the proper noun with correct capitalization in their Response Journals.

Circulate to support students as they work. If some students finish quickly, they can practice writing correctly capitalized proper nouns of people and places that are meaningful to them.

Instruct students to Think-Pair-Share and ask: "What do we need to remember about proper nouns?" Select two pairs to share their answer with the class.

- *Proper nouns begin with a capital letter.*
- *Proper nouns are specific nouns.*

Remind students that they will want to be sure they have properly capitalized all proper nouns when writing about the texts they're reading.

Land 10 MIN.

ANSWER THE CONTENT FRAMING QUESTION

Organize: What is happening in *My Librarian Is a Camel*?

Students draw one thing they learned from reading the introduction in their Response Journals.

- *(Drawing of a stationary library with a child borrowing books.)*
- *(Drawing of a mobile library, such as by camel, elephant, bus, donkey, or boat, with not many people, buildings, or cities around.)*
- *(Drawing of a child holding books.)*

Students share their drawings with a partner, and describe what they learned.

- *I am lucky I can go visit my library whenever I want to and borrow books.*
- *Some people who live far away have mobile libraries that move around and come to them.*
- *Books are important to many people. That's why there are mobile libraries so more people can get books, even those people who live far away or in remote places all over the world.*

Wrap 5 MIN.

HOMEWORK CHECK-IN

Continue home reading routine. Check Fluency Homework from the previous lesson, and remind students what to do for fluency homework.

Analyze

Context and Alignment

Students engage in the study of the words *remote* and *mobile* to develop a deeper understanding of the concepts in the module (RI.1.4). Check for the following success criteria:

- Uses context clues read aloud.
- Uses illustrations to make connections to the word.
- Makes personal connections to the word.

Next Steps

If students experience difficulty understanding the meaning of words using the Outside-In Strategy, consider acting out the words.

G1 > M1 > Lesson 14   WIT & WISDOM™

⬇ Lesson 14: Vocabulary Deep Dive

Vocabulary Strategies: Frayer Model for *Remote*

- **Time:** 15 min.

- **Text:** *My Librarian Is a Camel*, Margriet Ruurs

- **Vocabulary Learning Goal:** Develop vocabulary knowledge of the word *remote*. (L.1.6)

Launch

Remind students of how they read the introduction in this lesson and studied the word *remote*.

Read the following sentence from the text to the students:

- Several years ago, I read a newspaper article about a camel in Kenya that was used to bring books to young people who lived in remote desert villages.

Students Think-Pair-Share about why these villages might be remote. Use Equity Sticks to choose two or three pairs to share their thinking. Remind the students that *remote* means "far away" and that in this lesson they will be learning more about the word.

Learn

Post a large copy of the Frayer Model for students to see. Write the word *remote* in the center circle. Read the word for the students and have them repeat it several times.

Begin to complete the chart by writing a definition in the first quadrant. Tell students that a place is *remote* if it is far away. Ensure that students understand this definition before writing it on the class chart.

As a class, generate a list of facts and characteristics for things that are remote. Use pages from the text to help students begin to generate their list. Possible responses may include:

- *Islands*
- *Mountain villages.*
- *Desert villages.*

After generating the list of characteristics, work with the class to generate examples that fit the characteristics. Encourage students to think of remote places in the text. In a similar fashion, generate a list of non-examples, such as big cities, neighborhoods, and their school.

✔ Students verbalize the definition, facts, and examples for the word *remote* with a partner.

184

Copyright © 2016 Great Minds®

Scaffold

Use the following Sentence Frames to scaffold their discussion:
- **A desert village is remote because _____.**
- **An island is _____ because _____.**
- **Our city is not remote because _____.**
- **Our school is _____ because _____.**

Land

Use Equity Sticks to choose two or three pairs to share the definition, facts, and examples for the word *remote*.

Students add the word to Handout 14A: Frayer Model from the Student Edition and fill in the information from the class chart. The students will place this in their Vocabulary Journals.

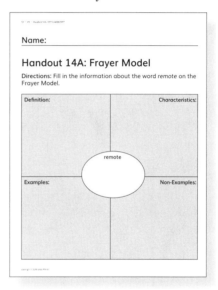

Copyright © 2016 Great Minds®

■ FOCUSING QUESTION: LESSONS 13-16

How do people around the world get books?

1 2 3 4 5 6 7 8 9 10 11 12 **13 14 15 16** 17 18 19 20 21 22 23 24 25 26 27 28 29 30 31 32

Lesson 15

TEXT

- *My Librarian Is a Camel*, Margriet Ruurs

G1 > M1 > Lesson 15   WIT & WISDOM™

Lesson 15: At a Glance

AGENDA

Welcome (5 min.)

Launch (7 min.)

Understand the Content Framing Question

Learn (55 min.)

Analyze Information (20 min.)

Record Evidence (15 min.)

Experiment with Proper Nouns (15 min.)

Land (5 min.)

Answer the Content Framing Question

Wrap (3 min.)

Assign Fluency Homework

Vocabulary Deep Dive: Frayer Model for *Mobile* (15 min.)

STANDARDS ADDRESSED

The full text of ELA Standards can be found in the Module Overview.

Reading

- RI.1.1, RI.1.2, RI.1.5

Speaking and Listening

- SL.1.1.a, SL.1.2

Language

- ↨ L.1.6

MATERIALS

- How Children Borrow Books Sentence Chart

- Handout 15A: Nouns

- Enlarged copy of Frayer Model

- Handout 15B: Frayer Model

- Vocabulary Journals

Learning Goals

Identify how pictures and captions communicate key details in *My Librarian Is a Camel*. (RI.1.7)

✔ Think-Pair-Share on how an assigned country transports books.

↨ Vocabulary Learning Goal: Develop vocabulary knowledge of the word *mobile*. (L.1.6)

✔ Verbalize the definition, facts, and examples for the word *mobile*.

✔ Checks for Understanding

Copyright © 2016 Great Minds®

WIT & WISDOM™   G1 > M1 > Lesson 15

| Prepare |

FOCUSING QUESTION: Lessons 13-16

How do people around the world get books?

CONTENT FRAMING QUESTION: Lesson 15

Reveal: *What does a deeper exploration of pictures and captions reveal in* My Librarian Is a Camel?

CRAFT QUESTION: Lesson 15

Experiment: *How do proper nouns work?*

Students look closely at the pictures and captions of select countries to gather and record evidence of how children borrow books on a sentence chart. This segues to their continued work with proper nouns using Sentence Frames.

Welcome 5 MIN.

In pairs, students visually explore a new excerpt from *My Librarian Is a Camel*. Students ask and answer questions about the photographs, identify the name of the country, and imagine what it would be like to get books there.

Launch 7 MIN.

UNDERSTAND THE CONTENT FRAMING QUESTION

Post the Content Framing Question and Focusing Question.

Ask students: "Are there any words or phrases that are new to you?"

▪ *I wonder what* captions *means.*

Point to the word *caption* and explain that a caption is a group of words that describe what a picture is about. Tell students that captions are often found in informational books, like *My Librarian is a Camel*. Flip to a page in the text and point out a caption.

Decide on a simple definition and sketch for *caption*. Put *caption* on the Word Wall as a year-long word.

189

Copyright © 2016 Great Minds®

Ask: "What does *reveal* mean?" Volunteers respond.

- *Reveal means to find something that is hidden in the text.*

Confirm that to *reveal* is to find the information that is hidden.

Ask students: "According to our Content Framing Question, what are we looking at in our book to reveal more information?" Volunteers respond.

- *We are looking at how the pictures and captions reveal more information.*

Learn 55 MIN.

ANALYZE INFORMATION

Whole Group 20 MIN.

Display and reference the Speaking and Listening Anchor Chart.

Students Think-Pair-Share: "What do you need to remember when you practice your best listening?" Choose one or two students to share their thinking.

- *Listen with your whole body.*
- *Listen with your eyes.*
- *Turn your body to the speaker.*

Prior to the lesson, select three to five of the following countries to review.

- England (pages 12–13).
- Indonesia (pages 16–17).
- Kenya (pages 18–19).
- Papua New Guinea (pages 24–25).
- Peru (pages 26–27).
- Thailand (pages 28–28).

| TEACHER NOTE | Consider choosing countries for which students have personal interests or connections, or any that connect deeply to topics students are studying in other subjects, to maximize the knowledge-building. |

WIT & WISDOM™   G1 > M1 > Lesson 15

For each country page spread, review the photographs and read aloud the headers and captions as you point to them. Remind students that headers and captions reveal deeper meaning about a text.

After displaying and reading aloud each spread, ask: "What additional information did we learn by reading the headers and captions in the text?"

- *We learned the name of the country.*
- *We learned more about what was happening in the pictures.*
- *We found out about how children get books.*

RECORD EVIDENCE

Whole Group 15 MIN.

Explain that students will figure out the type of mobile library used to transport books in each country and record this information.

Ask: "What did we learn in the previous lesson about mobile libraries?" Volunteers respond; return to the introduction as needed.

Display a three-column Sentence Chart that divides the Sentence Frame: **In _____, children borrow books from _____.**

Tell students the country name will be recorded in the first column and the way books are delivered will be recorded in the third column. The middle column will be the same for all the countries. Ask: "Which columns will change?" Students chorally respond as you point to the first and third columns.

Review each country page spread again, rereading the header and captions. Pause after each country.

✔ Students Think-Pair-Share: "What country is this? How do children get books?"

Use Equity Sticks to call on pairs to share their responses. Students use Nonverbal Signals to agree or disagree with the information. Record the information on the chart and include an illustration to show how books are transported.

191

Copyright © 2016 Great Minds®

G1 > M1 > Lesson 15   WIT & WISDOM™

HOW CHILDREN BORROW BOOKS SENTENCE CHART

In _____,	children get books from	_____.
▪ *England*	children borrow books from	▪ *a wheelbarrow (drawing of a wheelbarrow).* ▪ *a Share-a-Book library (drawing of a truck).*
▪ *Indonesia*	children borrow books from	▪ *a boat library (drawing of a boat).* ▪ *a bicycle library (drawing of a bicycle).*
▪ *Kenya*	children borrow books from	▪ *a camel (drawing of a camel).*
▪ *Papua New Guinea*	children borrow books from	▪ *volunteers who carry boxes of books (drawing of people with boxes).*
▪ *Peru*	children borrow books from	▪ *a donkey cart (drawing of a donkey).*
▪ *Thailand*	children borrow books from	▪ *an elephant library (drawing of an elephant).*

Explain that students will use this information in the next lesson as they complete the Focusing Question Task.

EXPERIMENT WITH PROPER NOUNS

Whole Group 15 MIN.

Read aloud the Craft Question.

Explain that students will experiment with proper nouns as they prepare for the Focusing Question Task in the next lesson.

Ask: "What do we already know about proper nouns?" Volunteers respond.

Reinforce that proper nouns name a specific person, place or thing(s) and always begin with a capital letter.

WIT & WISDOM™   G1 > M1 > Lesson 15

Provide pairs with word cards cut apart from
Handout 15A: Nouns. Echo Read each word card.

Write the sentences listed below on the board.
Complete the sentences one at time.

In <u>England</u>, children borrow books from a
<u>wheelbarrow</u>.

In <u>Kenya</u>, children borrow books from a <u>camel</u>.

In <u>Peru</u>, children borrow books from a <u>donkey
cart</u>.

> **Handout 15A: Nouns**
> Directions: Cut apart the word cards. Place them in front of you
> so you can read each card.
>
> | England | england | wheelbarrow |
> |---------|---------|-------------|
> | kenya | camel | Kenya |
> | donkey cart | peru | Peru |
>
> Name:

Explain to students that the word cards will fill in the blanks in the sentences. First, ask students to
sort the cards into proper nouns and common nouns. Then, students find the noun that best fits the
blank in each sentence. Pairs stand and hold up the word card. Write the proper and common nouns
in the blanks according to student responses.

Students stand and Echo Read each completed sentence.

Land 5 MIN.

ANSWER THE CONTENT FRAMING QUESTION

Reveal: *What does a deeper exploration of pictures and captions reveal in* My Librarian Is a Camel?

Students Mix and Mingle: "What information did we learn from looking at the pictures and reading
the captions?"

- *The pictures and captions in the book helped us figure out how people get books.*
- *The pictures showed how children got books. The captions gave us more information about the
  pictures.*
- *The pictures showed us how books are transported around the world.*

193

Copyright © 2016 Great Minds®

Wrap 3 MIN.

HOMEWORK CHECK-IN

Continue home reading routine. Check Fluency Homework from the previous lesson, and remind students what to do for fluency homework for this lesson.

Analyze

Context and Alignment

Students verbally express understanding of how people in remote locations get books. (RI.1.1, RI.1.2, RI.1.5). Check for the following success criterion:

- Cites evidence from the text using words and photographs.

Next Steps

If students are unable to verbalize their understanding of how people get books, work with small groups of students with one section of the text. Reread specific sections that directly tell how people in that location borrow books. Students use the Sentence Frame to share with a partner.

In _____ children borrow books from _____.

WIT & WISDOM™   G1 > M1 > Lesson 15

⬇ Lesson 15: Vocabulary Deep Dive

Vocabulary Strategies: Frayer Model for *Mobile*

- **Time:** 15 min.

- **Text:** *My Librarian Is a Camel*, Margriet Ruurs

- **Vocabulary Learning Goal:** Develop vocabulary knowledge of the word *mobile*. (L.1.6)

Launch

Ask students to close their eyes and think of a library. Use Equity Sticks to choose two volunteers to describe their visualization. Capture their answers on a T-Chart.

- *A big building.*

- *A large room in our school.*

- *Lots of books.*

- *Librarian who checks out the books.*

Ask students to close their eyes and think of the libraries mentioned in the text. Use Equity Sticks to choose two or three volunteers to describe their visualization. Capture their answers on the other side of the T-Chart.

- *Boats brought books.*

- *Animals brought books.*

- *Kids mailed the books back.*

Use their responses to reinforce that while many libraries are buildings or a room in a building, there are libraries that move from place to place. These libraries are mobile. Tell the students that in this lesson they will learn more about the word *mobile*.

Learn

Post a large copy of the Frayer Model for students to see. Write the word *mobile* in the center circle. Read the word for the students and have them repeat it several times.

Begin to complete the chart by writing a definition in the first quadrant. Students Think-Pair-Share about the definition for *mobile* they learned the previous day. Use Equity Sticks to choose volunteers to share their thinking.

- *I remember that mobile means something that moves.*

- *Things that move from place to place are mobile.*

Affirm correct answers and write a definition in the correct box.

195

Copyright © 2016 Great Minds®

As a class, generate a list of facts and characteristics for things that are mobile. Use pages from the text to help students begin to generate their list. Possible responses may include:

- *On wheels, such as cards, trucks, busses, etc.*
- *Can travel, such as boats or planes.*
- *Can be moved using a truck, such as big boxes, some machines, and mobile homes.*

After generating the list of characteristics, work with the class to generate examples that fit the characteristics. Encourage students to think of mobile objects that can easily be carried, as well as mobile objects that would have to be moved on wheels. In a similar fashion, generate a list of non-examples, such as skyscrapers, apartment buildings, and mountains.

✔ Students verbalize the definition, facts, and examples for the word *mobile* with a partner.

Scaffold

Use the following sentence starters to scaffold their discussion:
- **A phone is mobile because _____.**
- **A car is _____ because _____.**
- **A lake is not mobile because _____.**
- **Our school is _____ because _____.**

Land

Use Equity Sticks to choose two or three pairs to share the definition, facts, and examples for the word *mobile*.

Students add the word to Handout 15B: Frayer Model from the Student Edition and fill in the information from the class chart. Students will place this in their Vocabulary Journals.

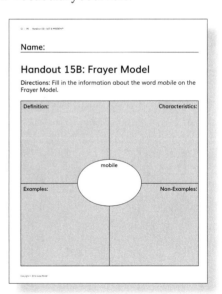

WIT & WISDOM™   G1 > M1 > Lesson 16

■ FOCUSING QUESTION: LESSONS 13-16

How do people around the world get books?

| 1 | 2 | 3 | 4 | 5 | 6 | 7 | 8 | 9 | 10 | 11 | 12 | **13** | **14** | **15** | **16** | 17 | 18 | 19 | 20 | 21 | 22 | 23 | 24 | 25 | 26 | 27 | 28 | 29 | 30 | 31 | 32 |

Lesson 16

TEXT

- *My Librarian Is a Camel*, Margriet Ruurs

Copyright © 2016 Great Minds®

G1 > M1 > Lesson 16

WIT & WISDOM™

Lesson 16: At a Glance

AGENDA

Welcome (5 min.)

Launch (5 min.)

Understand the Content Framing Question

Learn (55 min.)

Record Evidence (25 min.)

Execute and Excel Using Proper Nouns (30 min.)

Land (5 min.)

Answer the Content Framing Question

Wrap (5 min.)

Homework Check-in

Vocabulary Deep Dive: Direct Vocabulary Assessment (15 min.)

STANDARDS ADDRESSED

The full text of ELA Standards can be found in the Module Overview.

Reading

- RI.1.1, RI.1.2, RI.1.5, RI.1.7

Writing

- W.1.2, W.1.8

Speaking and Listening

- SL.1.1.a, SL.1.2

Language

- L.1.1.b, L.1.1.j, L.1.2.b
- ⬇ L.1.6

MATERIALS

- What People Say Sentence Chart
- Assessment 16A: Focusing Question Task 3
- Assessment 16B: Vocabulary Assessment
- Handout 16A: Focusing Question 3 Prompt

Learning Goals

Write, speak, and illustrate how people in different countries borrow books. (RI.1.2, RI.1.7, W.1.2, W.1.8, SL.1.1.a, L.1.1.b, L.1.1.j, L.1.2.b)

✔ Complete Focusing Question Task 3.

⬇ Demonstrate understanding of grade-level vocabulary. (L.1.6)

✔ Complete a Direct Vocabulary Assessment.

Copyright © 2016 Great Minds®

✔ Checks for Understanding

WIT & WISDOM™   G1 > M1 > Lesson 16

Prepare

FOCUSING QUESTION: Lessons 13-16

How do people around the world get books?

CONTENT FRAMING QUESTION: Lesson 16

Reveal: *What does a deeper exploration of quotations reveal in* My Librarian Is a Camel?

CRAFT QUESTION: Lesson 16

Execute: *How do I use proper nouns in my writing?*

Students study quotations from select countries to determine their meanings and record this evidence on a sentence chart. This activity gives students a sense of how real people feel about books and mobile libraries, communicating the enjoyment and appreciation in an authentic way. Students then complete Focusing Question Task 3, orally rehearsing sentences with a partner before describing how children get books in a certain country.

Welcome 5 MIN.

In pairs, students visually explore a new excerpt from *My Librarian Is a Camel*. Students ask and answer questions about the photographs, identify the name of the country, and imagine what it would be like to get books there.

Launch 5 MIN.

UNDERSTAND THE CONTENT FRAMING QUESTION

Remind students of how they looked carefully at the captions and illustrations in *My Librarian is a Camel* in the previous lesson. Explain that in this lesson they will look at a different part of the text.

Post and read the Content Framing Question and Focusing Question.

Ask students: "Are there any words or phrases that are new to you?"

- *I wonder what* quotations *means.*

Point to the word *quotation* and explain that a quotation is something a person says.

199

Copyright © 2016 Great Minds®

G1 > M1 > Lesson 16   WIT & WISDOM™

Decide on a simple definition and sketch for *quotation*. Put *quotation* on the Word Wall as a year-long word.

Point to the posted meaning of *caption* as you remind students they will pay close attention to these during this lesson.

Learn 55 MIN.

RECORD EVIDENCE

Whole Group 25 MIN.

Reread the following quotations from the text.

- Page 7: "Some stories leave children with something to think about . . . others bring laughter or tears."

- Page 9: "For us," says the librarian, "the mobile library is as important as air or water."

- Page 15: "Reading has become very important to our book-boat children . . . If the book boat didn't come, they might not be reading at all. They are always happy to see us and their supply of new books."

- Page 21: Mr. Dashdondog asks: "Which was sweeter: books or candies?" And the children always answer: "BOOKS!"

Display each quotation on a Sentence Strip.

Students Think-Pair-Share: "What additional information did we learn by reading these quotations?"

- *We learned what some people are saying about books.*
- *We found out that kids really like the books.*
- *Books are really important.*

Tell students that knowing what real people said, or their quotes, helps them better understand the text. Explain that students will record what people say about books in each country.

> **Scaffold**
>
> Teach students a Nonverbal Signal for *quotations* (e.g., making air quotes with your fingers).

Display a three-column Sentence Chart that divides the Sentence Frame: **In _____, people say ____.**

Tell students the country name will be recorded in the first column and what people say about books will be recorded in the third column. The middle column will be the same for all the countries.

200

Copyright © 2016 Great Minds®

Ask: "Which columns will change?" Students chorally respond as you point to the first and third columns.

Review the country page spreads, reading aloud the headers. When rereading the quotations, also read the sentences before and after each quotation. Pause after each country.

Ask: "What country is this?" Call on volunteers to respond before filling in the chart.

✔ Students Think-Pair-Share: "In your own words, what do you think the quotation means?"

Circulate to listen to pairs' discussions. Use Equity Sticks to call on pairs to share their thoughts.

Use student responses to come up with a refined response to record on the chart. Include Rebus-style illustrations above key words to support students' understanding of the quotations.

Alternate Activity

Begin this activity as a Think Aloud, modeling how to interpret the quotation. Gradually bring students into the process by calling on volunteers and using Equity Sticks. Then, release students to Think-Pair-Share on the above question.

WHAT PEOPLE SAY SENTENCE CHART

In _____.	people say	_____.
▪ Australia	people say	▪ stories give children things to think about and different feelings to feel (drawings of books above stories and a happy face above feelings).
▪ Azerbaijan	people say	▪ mobile libraries are as important as water or air (drawings of a truck above mobile libraries, glass of water above water, cloud above air).
▪ Finland	people say	▪ children wouldn't read without the boat library and the children are always happy to get books (drawings of a boat above boat library and books above books).
▪ Mongolia	people say	▪ books are sweeter than candy (drawings of books above books and candy above candy).

EXECUTE AND EXCEL USING PROPER NOUNS

Individuals 30 MIN.

Remind students of all that *My Librarian is a Camel* has taught them about the Focusing Question: *How do people from around the world get books?* Explain that in Focusing Question Task 3, they will answer this question with information from the text.

G1 > M1 > Lesson 16

Distribute Assessment 16A: Focusing Question Task 3.

Post Handout 16A: Focusing Question 3 Prompt. Students Echo Read:

Describe how children borrow books in your section of My Librarian Is a Camel *by answering the question: "Using evidence from the photographs, how do children in this country get books?"*

Be sure to:

- *Include details from the photographs.*

- *Write complete sentences.*

- *Capitalize proper nouns.*

- *Use end punctuation.*

Pairs visually explore the picture spread.

Post and Echo Read the What People Say Sentence Chart to support student thinking.

Students orally rehearse their sentence with a partner before independently completing the prompt.

As students finish the assessment, support them in checking their sentences for the following criteria:

- Complete sentences.

- Capitalization of proper nouns.

Call out each criterion. For each one, students use a Nonverbal Signal (thumbs-up, thumbs-down) to indicate whether they believe their writing fits that criterion. Students with a thumbs-up place a check next to the evidence of that criterion in their sentence. Students with a thumbs-down correct their papers and place a star next to corrections.

Land 5 MIN.

ANSWER THE CONTENT FRAMING QUESTION

Reveal: *What does a deeper exploration of quotations reveal in* My Librarian Is a Camel?

Instruct students to Think-Pair-Share and ask: "What information did we learn from reading the quotations?" Volunteers respond.

- *Children in different countries really enjoy books, even more than candy!*
- *The quotations tell us how important the books and libraries are for children in these countries.*
- *Kids need to get books like they need to drink water and breathe air.*

Wrap 5 MIN.

HOMEWORK CHECK-IN

Continue home reading routine. Check Fluency Homework, and remind students that their homework is the final fluency work with the passage from *My Librarian Is a Camel*.

Analyze

Context and Alignment

Students use illustrations and text evidence to answer Focusing Question Task 3. (RI.1.1, RI.1.7, W.1.2, W.1.8, SL.1.1, SL.1.2, L.1.1.b, L.1.1.j, L.1.2.b)

Check for the following success criteria:

- Include details from the photographs.
- Write complete sentences.
- Capitalize proper nouns.
- Use end punctuation.

Next Steps

If students cannot determine details from photographs, meet in a small group or individually to determine how children get books by posing questions such as, "What is happening in this photograph?" or "Where might you find the name of the country?"

If they struggle to write a complete sentence, provide the following Sentence Frame:

In _____ children borrow books from _____.

G1 > M1 > Lesson 16   WIT & WISDOM™

↓ Lesson 16: Vocabulary Deep Dive

Direct Vocabulary Assessment

- **Time:** 15 min.
- **Vocabulary Learning Goal:** Demonstrate understanding of grade-level vocabulary. (L.1.6)

Launch

Remind students that they have learned many new words in this module. Explain that they will complete an assessment where they will show their understanding of these words.

Learn

Distribute Assessment 16B: Vocabulary Assessment and pencils (as needed).

Explain to students how to fill out the response sheet. You will read a question aloud that contains the word listed beside the smiley face. If students think the answer is "yes," they should draw a circle around the smiley face. If they think the answer is "no," they should draw a circle around the frowny face.

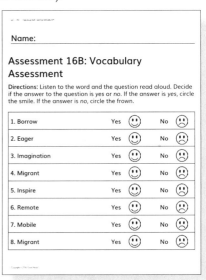

Practice with a word that is not found on the assessment.

Can you stumble while sitting?

Read students the word *stumble* and then read the sentence twice. Think aloud to demonstrate how you consider the meaning of the word and then whether the answer is "yes" or "no." Think-Pair-Share: Which answer did you pick and why?

Example: Stumble	🙂	🙁
	Yes	No

Use the teacher-facing version (with key) in Appendix C to administer the assessment.

Read each question two times before students fill out their answers. Make sure to always read the focus word before reading the question.

Can you borrow your teeth?

204

Copyright © 2016 Great Minds®

WIT & WISDOM™   G1 > M1 > Lesson 16

Monitor as students work, ensuring they are following directions and are on the correct question. Provide oral cues as necessary if students need help locating the proper row and where to mark their answers. Students will complete another assessment at the end of the module.

✔ Students begin the Direct Vocabulary Assessment.

Land

Congratulate students on their hard work.

Copyright © 2016 Great Minds®

WIT & WISDOM™   G1 > M1 > Lesson 17

■ FOCUSING QUESTION: LESSONS 17-22

How does the packhorse librarian change life for Cal?

1 2 3 4 5 6 7 8 9 10 11 12 13 14 15 16 **17** 18 19 20 21 22 23 24 25 26 27 28 29 30 31 32

Lesson 17

TEXTS

- *Museum ABC*, The Metropolitan Museum of Art
- *That Book Woman*, Heather Henson, David Small

Copyright © 2016 Great Minds®

G1 > M1 > Lesson 17   WIT & WISDOM™

Lesson 17: At a Glance

AGENDA

Welcome (10 min.)

Notice and Wonder About Museum ABC

Launch (5 min.)

Understand the Content Framing Question

Learn (50 min.)

Define the Listening Goal (10 min.)

Notice Details (20 min.)

Generate and Answer Questions (20 min.)

Land (7 min.)

Answer the Content Framing Question

Wrap (3 min.)

Assign Fluency Homework

Style and Conventions Deep Dive: Understanding Adjectives (15 min.)

STANDARDS ADDRESSED

The full text of ELA Standards can be found in the Module Overview.

Reading

- RL.1.1, RL.1.3
- RI.1.1

Speaking and Listening

- SL.1.1.a, SL.1.2

Language

- ➡ L.1.1.f

MATERIALS

- Speaking and Listening Anchor Chart
- Handout 1A: Notice and Wonder prompt cards
- Wonder Wheel
- Sticky notes
- Blank Questions and Answers Chart
- Handout 17A: Fluency Homework
- Response Journals

Learning Goals

Generate and answer questions about *That Book Woman* using key details from the text. (RL.1.1.)

✔ Contribute to Questions and Answers Chart.

➡ Generate a variety of adjectives. (L.1.1.f)

✔ Complete Sentence Frames.

Copyright © 2016 Great Minds®

✔ Checks for Understanding

WIT & WISDOM™   G1 > M1 > Lesson 17

Prepare

FOCUSING QUESTION: Lessons 17-22

How does the packhorse librarian change life for Cal?

CONTENT FRAMING QUESTION: Lesson 17

Wonder: *What do I notice and wonder about* That Book Woman?

Students learn about a new listening goal to practice before listening to the first reads of *That Book Woman*. They share notices and generate questions using different question words. The initial exploration of this challenging text is scaffolded as a whole group to support students with the complexity.

Welcome 10 MIN.

NOTICE AND WONDER ABOUT *MUSEUM ABC*

Provide each pair with a new spread of the pages in *Museum ABC*.

TEACHER NOTE	With each new opportunity to notice and wonder with *Museum ABC* spreads, be sure you give each pair a new page. By rotating pages, it keeps the content fresh.

Display the Content Framing Question.

Echo Read the Content Framing Question: *What do you notice and wonder about your page of Museum ABC?*

In pairs, students share the details they notice about the different artworks on the page by using the Sentence Frame: **I notice _____.**

- *I notice two babies playing with giant eggshells.*
- *I notice lots of colorful balls on tables.*
- *I notice a bouquet of pink roses.*
- *I notice a big star in the middle of the painting.*

Two or three students share their responses with the whole group.

209

Copyright © 2016 Great Minds®

G1 ▷ M1 ▷ Lesson 17   WIT & WISDOM™

Remind students that the things the students said they saw in the picture are called *details*, and details can help us understand more about the painting.

Ask: "When you think about the details you found, what do you wonder about the painting on your page?"

Ask a student to remind the class of what they do when they wonder about a painting.

Remind students that wonders should come in the form of a question and that they can use their question words from the Wonder Wheel to help them.

Students respond to the different artworks on the page by using the Sentence Frame **I wonder: ___?**

- ▪ *I wonder: Why are some of the eggs broken?*
- ▪ *I wonder: What is the name of the game they are playing?*
- ▪ *I wonder: How did the artist paint the roses?*
- ▪ *I wonder: What are those things around the star?*

Two or three students share their responses with the whole group.

Explain that students will try to answer a similar question about *That Book Woman* and that noticing and wondering will help them understand that story, too.

Launch 5 MIN.

UNDERSTAND THE CONTENT FRAMING QUESTION

Post the Content Framing Question and Focusing Question. Echo Read the Focusing Question.

Explain to students that over the next six lessons, they will investigate a new book, *That Book Woman*. By reading and studying the text, they will learn information to answer the Focusing Question.

Echo Read the Content Framing Question.

Ask: "What do you notice and wonder about the illustration on the cover?"

Instruct students to Think-Pair-Share.

Remind students that they will use the same process that they used with *Museum ABC* to notice and wonder about *That Book Woman*. Share that first they will learn about a strategy for listening that will help them understand what they hear.

210

Copyright © 2016 Great Minds®

Learn 50 MIN.

DEFINE THE LISTENING GOAL

Whole Group 10 MIN.

Display the Content Framing Question, circling the word *notice*.

Ask: "How do we notice something with our ears?"

Instruct students to Think-Pair-Share.

- *If I notice something with my ears, I say, "Did you hear that?"*
- *When you notice something, it means you pay attention to it.*
- *We hear with our ears, so noticing with our ears means we are listening.*

Display the Speaking and Listening Anchor Chart.

Explain that when great readers learn, they practice their best listening. Share that students will learn a strategy for noticing and listening well.

Start a new row on the Speaking and Listening Anchor chart, and write the listening goal in the appropriate column.

SPEAKING AND LISTENING ANCHOR CHART

Speaking Goals	Listening Goals
	<ul><li>Whole body listening.</li><li>Notice pauses.</li></ul>

Invite student volunteers to point to any words in the goal that are new or interesting. Provide simple definitions for any words they identify. Post any new words on the Word Wall as year-long words.

When I think about the listening goal "notice pauses," I know some important things right away. First, I know that I need to notice, or pay attention to something. Then I read the rest of the goal to find what that something is, and it says *pauses*. We just learned that a pause is a short stop or break in something. Now I know that I am paying attention to the short stops. When people speak, we can hear when they pause. Usually, it is at the end of a thought or idea.

Students Think-Pair-Share: Why might it be important to <u>notice pauses</u> when we listen?

- *If we notice pauses we can tell when someone is done speaking.*
- *Noticing pauses helps me understand what someone is saying.*
- *It might be important to know when one idea stops and another one starts.*

Choose one or two students to share with the whole group. Emphasize the importance of pauses in listening and how they help us know when a thought or idea is finished.

Explain that whenever we practice listening, including right now when listening to *That Book Woman*, they will try to use their listening goal: notice pauses.

NOTICE DETAILS

Whole Group 20 MIN.

| TEACHER NOTE | The pages of *That Book Woman* are unnumbered. In this module, pages 1–2 have text that begins with "My folks and me" and show the illustration of a house on the side of the mountain. Write small page numbers in your text for easy reference. |

Ask: "Why do we notice things as we read?" A volunteer responds. Reinforce that good readers notice as they read a text because it helps them pay attention and see details.

Students retrieve their Notice Prompt Card from Handout 1A: Notice and Wonder Prompt Cards. Tell students they will stand up with the prompt card each time they notice something.

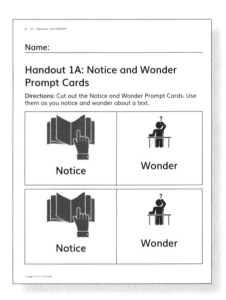

Visually explore the book by slowly, silently flipping through pages. Students stand up with the Notice Prompt Card when they notice details.

Read the text aloud, including the author's note, without interruptions.

Students Think-Pair-Share: "What do you notice in the illustrations?" Use Equity Sticks to call on students for their observations. Clarify any responses to model appropriate notices.

GENERATE AND ANSWER QUESTIONS

Whole Group 20 MIN.

Tell students that they will now focus on what they wonder by forming questions when they feel curious.

WIT & WISDOM™   G1 > M1 > Lesson 17

Ask: "Why do we wonder things as we read?" A volunteer responds. Reinforce that good readers wonder as they read because it helps them figure out questions they have and better understand the text.

Display the Wonder Wheel for reference.

Remind students of how they have focused on specific question words each time they have read a new text. Explain that their focus this time will be on: *what, how*, and *why*. Assign pairs one of the question words. Students add a star to the question word they are focusing on to generate questions.

Remind students about the purpose of each question word: *What* questions ask about specific information. *How* ask about the way something is. *Why* ask about a reason for something.

Differentiation

Students who think more concretely will be more comfortable forming questions that begin with *who, what, where*, and *when*. Students who are able to think more abstractly will be more comfortable with forming questions beginning with *why* and *how*. Introduce the more abstract question words as students are ready.

✔ Using copies of the text, pairs generate as many text-based questions as they can using their chosen word. Circulate and jot down strong text-based questions on sticky notes.

Display a blank Questions and Answers Chart to collect responses. Read the recorded questions as you place them on the chart. Pairs wave both hands above their heads if they asked a similar question to the one that is posted.

Read the text aloud again as students listen for answers to their questions.

Students stand up when they hear the answers to their questions. When they stand, flag the page in your copy of the text with a sticky note and record initials of some standing students.

After finishing the story, return to the flagged pages. Call on a student who stood up for that page to respond to a question on the Questions and Answers Chart. As needed, reread that section of the text to confirm and clarify students' thinking. Record the answer on the relevant sticky note. Each time, move sticky notes across the chart to indicate the extent to which each question has been answered. If there are any unanswered questions, explain that students will revisit the chart after they've had more time to explore the text to answer the remaining questions.

THAT BOOK WOMAN QUESTIONS AND ANSWERS CHART

Questions	Answers in progress	Complete answers
?	⟷	✓

213

Copyright © 2016 Great Minds®

▪ *(Q1) What does penny-bright mean?* ▪ *(Q2) Why does Cal become interested in reading books?* ▪ *(Q3) How does Cal learn to read?*	▪ *(Q1) Penny-bright might mean shiny like a penny (pages 9–10).* ▪ *(Q2) Cal looks interested in books when the book is in the cold snow (pages 23–24).*	▪ *(Q3) His sister Lark teaches him (pages 25–26).*

In future lessons, continue to display the Questions and Answers Chart and allow students to revisit their questions as they work with the text.

Extension

Students label one page in their Response Journals with an "N" for things they notice and another page with a "W" for things they wonder. Students draw and/or write sentences about what they notice and wonder about Cal on the pages. Encourage students to pick from different sections of the text. Students Think-Pair-Share about what they noticed and wondered.

Land 7 MIN.

ANSWER THE CONTENT FRAMING QUESTION

Wonder: *What do I notice and wonder about* That Book Woman?

Ask: "What interesting notices did you hear today? What interesting wonders did you hear?" Use Equity Sticks to choose volunteers to respond.

Celebrate the observations and wonders the students brought up. Remind students that in the lessons to come, they will have many more chances to find answers to the questions they asked as they read the book even more closely.

WIT & WISDOM™   G1 › M1 › Lesson 17

Wrap 3 MIN.

ASSIGN FLUENCY HOMEWORK

Continue home reading routine. Collect Fluency Homework handouts from Lessons 13–16, and distribute Student Handout 17A: Fluency Homework, reminding students to share the new text with their family. Explain that the new text is a passage from *That Book Woman*.

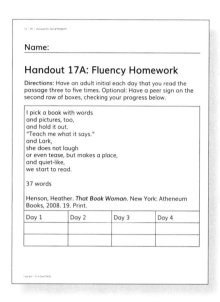

Analyze

Context and Alignment

After generating questions about the text *That Book Woman*, students listen and stand for the answers as the text is read aloud. (RL.1.1). Check students' responses for the following success criteria:

- Stands when hearing an answer to a question.
- Uses text evidence to answer the question.

Next Steps

Provide students experiencing difficulty formulating questions with a Sentence Frame beginning with *why* or *how*. Generate two to four questions in a small group setting.

If students struggle to answer a question, support them by rereading specific pages that answer the questions one at a time.

G1 > M1 > Lesson 17   WIT & WISDOM™

⤵ Lesson 17: Style and Conventions Deep Dive

Understanding Adjectives that Describe "What Kind?"

- **Time:** 15 min.

- **Text:** *Museum ABC*, The Metropolitan Museum of Art

- **Style and Conventions Learning Goal:** Generate a variety of adjectives. (L.1.1.f)

- **STYLE AND CONVENTIONS CRAFT QUESTION:** Lesson 17
  Experiment: *What are adjectives?*

Launch

Display and read the Craft Question: *What are adjectives?*

Students Echo Read the question. Explain that in this lesson they will learn about another type of word and how it functions in our texts.

Learn

Remind students of the parts of speech they have already learned in this module: nouns and verbs. Explain that in this lesson students will work with descriptive words.

Show students the "J is for Jewelry" page from *Museum ABC*. Students Think-Pair-Share to answer the following question: "What words would you use to describe the jewelry in these pictures?"

Have students share out the answers to the question. Explain that these describing words are called *adjectives* and they often tell us "what kind" of something.

As a class generate a list of their answers to the launch question that would fit into the following Sentence Frame: **I see the _____ jewelry.** As a scaffold, ask students what kind of jewelry they see represented in the paintings. Write responses in a visible place. Students' answers could include the following:

- Beautiful

- Fancy

- Expensive

- Gold

- White

- Red

216

Copyright © 2016 Great Minds®

WIT & WISDOM™   G1 ⟩ M1 ⟩ Lesson 17

- Black
- Gray

After generating the list, remind students that we call words that describe things and tell us what kind *adjectives*. Have students repeat the word several times. Students Think-Pair-Share about what they just learned about adjectives. Encourage the use of the word *adjectives* and use it in context repeatedly and purposefully. Use frames such as:

- **An adjective is a word that _____.**
- **We use adjectives to _____.**

TEACHER NOTE	Any word that does the work of an adjective is considered an adjective in that context, even if it is in the form of a noun. For example, we can use a noun as an adjective when we say: "I took my hat off and now I have hat hair." Is *hat* an adjective there, even though we know that *hat* is really a noun? Well, yes! When *hat* (or any word) is answering the question "what kind?" then we say it is an adjective in that context.

Show students the "H is for Hair" page from *Museum ABC*. As a class, generate a list of words that would fit into the following Sentence Frame: **I see the _____ hair.** Ask students "what kind" of hair they see represented in the paintings. Write responses in a visible place. Students' answers could include the following:

- White
- Black
- Brown
- Straight
- Curly
- Long
- Short

After generating a list of adjectives, ask students if anyone remembers what we call words that tell us "what kind" of something. Have students repeat the word *adjectives* several times; then Think-Pair-Share to a neighbor what they remember about adjectives. Use frames such as:

- **An adjective is a word that _____.**
- **We use adjectives to _____.**

Invite students to notice similarities and differences between the adjectives used to tell about the hair in the paintings. For example, students may notice that some of the adjectives are color words, some of the adjectives tell about the length of the hair, etc. As students notice these similarities and differences, sort the adjectives into those groups.

✓ Students work in pairs to complete the following Sentence Frames, and draw a picture in their

217

Copyright © 2016 Great Minds®

Response Journals: **I see the _____ jewelry. I see the _____ hair.**

Students Mix and Mingle to share their sentences and illustrations. Remind students that adjectives are describing words and they often tell us what kind of something.

Land

Instruct students to Think-Pair-Share, and ask: "What are adjectives?"

Use Equity Sticks to select two pairs to share their thinking. Use their responses to reinforce that adjectives are describing words and they often tell us what kind of something. Explain that students will continue to learn about adjectives and how to use them in their writing.

WIT & WISDOM™   G1 > M1 > Lesson 18

■ FOCUSING QUESTION: LESSONS 17-22

How does the packhorse librarian change life for Cal?

| 1 | 2 | 3 | 4 | 5 | 6 | 7 | 8 | 9 | 10 | 11 | 12 | 13 | 14 | 15 | 16 | **17** | **18** | **19** | **20** | **21** | **22** | 23 | 24 | 25 | 26 | 27 | 28 | 29 | 30 | 31 | 32 |

Lesson 18

TEXT

- *That Book Woman*, Heather Henson, David Small

G1 > M1 > Lesson 18

WIT & WISDOM™

Lesson 18: At a Glance

AGENDA

Welcome (5 min.)

Launch (3 min.)

Understand the Content Framing Question

Learn (50 min.)

Examine: Respond to What Others Say (10 min.)

Identify the Story Elements (20 min.)

Dramatize the Problem and Resolution (20 min.)

Retell the Story (10 min.)

Land (5 min.)

Answer the Content Framing Question

Wrap (2 min.)

Assign Fluency Homework

Style and Conventions Deep Dive: Declarative Sentences (15 min.)

STANDARDS ADDRESSED

The full text of ELA Standards can be found in the Module Overview.

Reading

- RL.1.1, RL.1.3

- RI.1.1

Speaking and Listening

- SL.1.1a, SL.1.1b, SL.1.2

Language

- ⬇ L.1.6

MATERIALS

- One set of Story Stones per student

- Speaking and Listening Anchor Chart

- *That Book Woman* Story Map

- Handout 18A: Story Map

- Response Journals

- Handout 14A: Frayer Model

- Multiple Meaning Words Chart

- Handout 18B: Multiple Meaning Words

Learning Goals

Retell *That Book Woman*, including key details about characters, settings, and major events. (RL.1.3)

✔ Create tableaux for the problem and resolution of the story.

⬇ Define multiple meanings for words *poke* and *spell*. (L.1.6)

✔ Identify the steps to finding the meaning of multiple meaning words.

✔ Checks for Understanding

Copyright © 2016 Great Minds®

WIT & WISDOM™   G1 > M1 > Lesson 18

Prepare

FOCUSING QUESTION: Lessons 17-22

How does the packhorse librarian change life for Cal?

CONTENT FRAMING QUESTION: Lesson 18

Organize: *What is happening in* That Book Woman?

CRAFT QUESTION: Lesson 18

Examine: *Why is responding to what others say important?*

Students learn a new speaking goal and practice it when they organize story elements of *That Book Woman* in small groups. Students identify the characters, setting, problem, and resolution in the same lesson. Then, students create tableaux for the problem and resolution before they orally retell the story through the lens of those story elements.

Welcome   5 MIN.

Distribute copies of *That Book Woman* and the Story Stones for character and setting to each student pair.

Pairs visually explore the illustrations in the text. One partner holds the character stone and the other holds the setting stone. Every time the illustrations show a new character or setting, the partner with the stone touches the page.

Launch   3 MIN.

UNDERSTAND THE CONTENT FRAMING QUESTION

Post the Content Framing Question and Focusing Question. Echo Read the Focusing Question.

Echo Read the Content Framing Question. Ask: "What story elements have we learned?" Volunteers respond.

Reinforce that the Content Framing Question will help students think about how the story is organized, and in this lesson they will focus on learning more about all the story elements they have learned: *character, setting, problem,* and *resolution.*

221

Copyright © 2016 Great Minds®

Learn 45 MIN.

EXAMINE: RESPOND TO WHAT OTHERS SAY

Whole Group 10 MIN.

Explain that when great readers talk about books, they practice their best speaking. Share that in this lesson, students will examine one way to speak well.

Echo Read the Craft Question: "Why is responding to what others say important?"

Display the Speaking and Listening Anchor Chart.

Start a new row on the Speaking and Listening Anchor Chart, and write the Speaking Process Goal in the Goal column: "Respond to what others say."

SPEAKING AND LISTENING ANCHOR CHART

Speaking Goals	Listening Goals
Respond to what others say.	Whole body listening.
	Notice pauses.

Invite student volunteers to point to any words in the goal that are new or interesting. Provide simple definitions for any words they identify.

> **When I think about the goal "respond to what others say," I know some important things right away. First, I know that I need to respond. *Responding* means "to answer or react." Hmm. If I have to answer or react, I must be answering or reacting to something. Then, I read the rest of the goal, which says, "to what others say." Now, I know that I am speaking with others, and when they say something, I will respond to what they say by speaking about similar things.**

Students Think-Pair-Share: "Why might it be important to respond to what others say when we speak?"

- *If we don't respond to what others say, we would just be talking to ourselves!*
- *Responding to what others say means that we are listening, too.*
- *If we don't respond to what others say, we could be talking about different things.*

Choose one or two students to share with the whole group. Emphasize the importance of people responding to one another in conversations.

Explain that whenever we practice speaking in this module and for the rest of the year, we will try to use our speaking goal: respond to what others say. In this lesson we will use our speaking goal as we identify and discuss the story elements in *That Book Woman*.

IDENTIFY THE STORY ELEMENTS

Whole Group 15 MIN.

TEACHER NOTE

By this time in the module, students should be familiar with the story elements. Based on students' understanding, review the elements, reiterating the definitions provided in previous lessons:

- Characters are who the story is about.
- The setting is where and when the story takes place.
- The problem is the main character's challenge.
- The resolution is the end of the problem.

Display a blank *That Book Woman* Story Map. Distribute Handout 18A: Story Map, Character and Setting Story Stones, and partner copies of *That Book Woman*. Explain that students will find and record the story elements in *That Book Woman* onto their own Story Maps.

Read pages 4–5 and 17 aloud as students touch pictures of characters with Story Stones.

Students Think-Pair-Share: "Who are the characters in the story? Who is the main character of the story?"

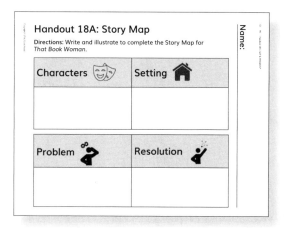

As pairs work, circulate to listen to their discussions and add refined responses to the class Story Map. Share students' good ideas you overheard and recorded on the class Story Map.

Reread pages 1, 10, and 17 aloud as students touch pictures of settings with Story Stones.

Students Think-Pair-Share: "What are the settings in the story?"

As pairs work, circulate to listen to their discussions and add refined responses to the class Story Map. Share students' good ideas you overheard and recorded on the class Story Map.

Reread page 1 and ask students: "What do you notice about where Cal lives?" Call on two to three volunteers.

- *He lives high up far away.*
- *He lives in a place where there is no one else around.*
- *There are only animals and trees nearby, no other people, buildings, or cars.*

G1 > M1 > Lesson 18   WIT & WISDOM™

Use student responses to explain that his family lives in a remote place. Connect this setting to previous discussions of remote locations in *Waiting for the Biblioburro* and *My Librarian Is a Camel*.

Extension

Instruct students to look at the illustration on pages 21–21 and imagine what it must be like for the book woman to make the journey through snow on horseback to bring the books to Cal and his family. Ask the students to mime "wrapping tip to toe," packing their books on the horse, and riding through a blizzard. Shout out some details like the "wind shrieks like a bobcat" and invite a student to provide the sound. Once the students make it once around the room, have them return to their seats to figure out the problem and resolution.

Distribute a problem Story Stone to each student. Ask: "What do we do when we hear the problem?" A volunteer responds. Reinforce that as students notice the problem changing, they shake their problem stones in the air.

Read pages 5 and 12 aloud. Students Think-Pair-Share: "What is the problem or what challenges Cal in the story?" Students discuss the problem and place the stone.

As pairs work, circulate to listen to their discussions and add refined responses to the class Story Map. Share students' good ideas you overheard and recorded on the class Story Map.

Read page 24 aloud as students shake their problem stones in the air. Explain that the problem is changing at this moment in the story when Cal starts to wonder why the book woman would travel through snow to deliver books. Record details under the arrow column.

Distribute a resolution Story Stone to each student. Explain that when they hear the resolution, they will hold their resolution stones in the air.

Read page 25 and 31–32 aloud. Students Think-Pair-Share: "What is the resolution, or the end of the problem, in the story?" Students discuss the resolution and place the stone.

As pairs work, circulate to listen to their discussions and add refined responses to the class Story Map. Share students' good ideas you overheard and recorded on the class Story Map.

TEACHER NOTE	Expect increasing detail about each story element from students.

WIT & WISDOM™   G1 > M1 > Lesson 18

THAT BOOK WOMAN STORY MAP

Characters	Setting
• Cal (drawing of Cal). • Lark (drawing of Lark). • Pap (drawing of Pap). • Mama (drawing of Mama). • Book Woman (drawing of the book woman).	• Mountains (drawing of mountains). • Outside the house (drawing of a porch). • Inside the house (drawing of a cabin). • Seasons (drawing of a sun, leaf, snowflake, and raindrop).

Problem		Resolution
• Cal doesn't want to learn how to read and doesn't understand why the book woman brings books to people (drawing of a book with an X through it).	**Cal wants to know why the book woman goes out even in bad weather to bring people books** (drawing of snow above *bad weather*, books above *books*)	• Cal asks Lark to teach him to read (drawing of books above read). • When the book woman comes again Cal reads to her (drawing of a book above reads).

DRAMATIZE THE PROBLEM AND RESOLUTION

Small Groups 15 MIN.

Ask: "In addition to identifying the story elements, what's another way for understanding what's happening in a text?" Volunteers respond.

Reinforce that creating tableaux can help students understand what is happening. Assign small groups either problem or resolution. Explain that groups will make tableaux, or pose, to show their assigned story element.

✔ Small groups create tableaux for problem or resolution.

- *(Problem: One student poses as Cal not wanting to read, with a frown. Another student poses as Lark, with hands folded together as if reading a book. Another student poses as the book woman with arms over the shoulder to represent holding a bag of books.)*

- *(Resolution: One student poses as Cal asking Lark to teach him to read. Another student poses as Lark with hands folded as if holding a book, teaching Cal to read.)*

225

Copyright © 2016 Great Minds®

G1 > M1 > Lesson 18   WIT & WISDOM™

- *(Resolution: One student poses as Cal with arms folded together as if reading a book. Another student poses as the book woman on her horse, listening to Cal read aloud. Other students pose as various family members.)*

Circulate to observe students demonstrating the problem and resolution.

Share details from the tableaux to reinforce the key ideas: stories have problems, which are things that challenge the main character. A story's resolution is when the problem is solved at the end. In this story, the problem was that Cal didn't know how to read books and didn't want to learn. The resolution was that he learned to read and enjoyed reading books.

| **TEACHER NOTE** | If possible, consider photographing students' tableaux and projecting them as you share observations and key details. |

RETELL THE STORY

Pairs 10 MIN.

Explain that now that students understand all the story elements, they will retell the story to each other with these elements in mind.

Ask: "What have you learned about retelling a story?" Volunteers respond.

Reinforce key strategies for retelling, including considering the important things that have happened, using the pictures for support, and referring to the Story Map.

Pairs take turns orally retelling the story, including key details about the characters, settings, problem, and resolution.

- *Cal lives with his family in the mountains far away from other people. In the beginning, Cal doesn't like to read. His sister Lark loves to read all the time. Then the book woman comes to Cal's house on a horse. She lets Cal's family borrow books and says she will come back later to give them more. Cal doesn't understand why the book woman would travel so far in all seasons to bring free books. She even comes during a snowstorm and Cal wonders why. So he asks his sister Lark to teach him to read. When the book woman comes back, Cal wants to give her a gift to thank her but he has nothing. He reads to her and she says that this is a gift.*

Circulate to listen as students orally retell the story to a partner.

Land 5 MIN.

ANSWER THE CONTENT FRAMING QUESTION

Organize: *What is happening in* That Book Woman?

Ask: "What is something that happened in *That Book Woman*?" Students illustrate a scene from the book in their Response Journals to answer the Content Framing Question before sharing their drawings with a partner.

Wrap 2 MIN.

HOMEWORK CHECK-IN

Continue home reading routine. Check Fluency Homework from the previous lesson, and remind students what to do for fluency homework.

> **Analyze**
>
> **Context and Alignment**
>
> Students create tableaux to illustrate the problem and the resolution in *That Book Woman* (RL.1.2). Check for the following success criteria:
>
> - Uses text and illustrations to emulate poses.
> - Accurately includes details from the text.
>
> **Next Steps**
>
> If students struggle with creating poses for the problem and resolution, support them by rereading specific sections of the book. Allow students to act out and retell what is happening on the pages rather than creating tableaux.

G1 > M1 > Lesson 18   WIT & WISDOM™

⬇ Lesson 18: Vocabulary Deep Dive

Defining Multiple Meaning Words

- **Time:** 15 min.

- **Text:** *That Book Woman*, Heather Henson, David Small

- **Vocabulary Learning Goal:** Define multiple meanings for words *poke* and *spell*. (L.1.6)

Launch

Display the word *remote* and ask students to Think-Pair-Share what they remember about this word. Use Equity Sticks to choose two to three students to share their thinking.

- *The word has been in more than one book we have read.*

- *The word has more than one meaning.*

- *I have a remote for my TV.*

- *Ana lived in a remote village in* Waiting for the Biblioburro.

- *Cal lived in a remote place in* That Book Woman.

Affirm correct answers and reinforce that *remote* has more than one meaning. Explain that in this lesson they will learn about more words that have multiple meanings from *That Book Woman*.

Learn

Display a three-column chart similar to the following and distribute Handout 18B.

Sample Multiple Meaning Words Chart

remote	1	2
poke	3	4
spell	5	6

Name: _____

Handout 18B: Multiple Meaning Words

Directions: Draw or write two different definitions for each word.

remote	1	2
poke	3	4
spell	5	6
signs	7	8
duck	9	10

228

Copyright © 2016 Great Minds®

Direct students to find the Handout 14A: Frayer Model they created for the word *remote*. Have students draw or write the definition in box 2. Remind them of the first definition they had for *remote*, which was a remote control for a television, and have them draw or write this in box 1.

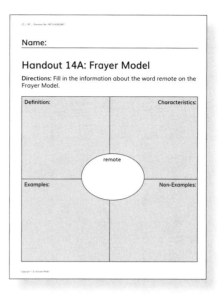

Read the second word, *poke*, for the students. Students repeat the word and then Think-Pair-Share what the word means. Most students will relate the word *poke* to poking someone else with their finger, a pencil, a stick, etc. Have students write or draw this definition for *poke* in box 3.

Read the following phrase from the text:

- A poke of berries for one book.

Ask students if the definition for *poke* from box 3 makes sense in the sentence. Guide students to determine the new meaning of *poke* by asking about the berries that Cal picked. How many berries did he pick? Because this term will be unfamiliar to many students, you may need to directly guide students to understanding that when Pap offers the book woman a poke of berries, he is giving her a set amount. Tell students that some foods are sold in set amounts. Have students Think-Pair-Share about foods they know that are sold in set amounts.

- *Loaf of bread.*
- *Dozen eggs.*
- *Gallon of milk.*

Reinforce the idea that these foods are sold in certain amounts and a poke of berries is a certain amount of berries. Have students write or draw the meaning in box 4.

Following the same procedure, read the third word, *spell*, for students. Students repeat the word and then Think-Pair-Share what the word means. Most students will relate the word *spell* to the way a word is spelled, the letters used to correctly write the word. Some may also think of a magic spell. Have students write or draw this definition for *spell* in box 5.

Read the following phrase from the text:

- I stand a spell to watch that Book Woman disappear.

Ask students if the definition for *spell* from box 5 makes sense in the sentence. Guide students to determine the new meaning of *spell* by asking students what Cal did as the book woman rode away. How long did he stand there? How long did he watch her ride away? Guide students to understand that in this case, a *spell* is an amount of time. Have students write or draw this new meaning in box 6.

✓ Students discuss the steps they learned to discover the meaning of multiple meaning words. Additionally, students talk to their partner about why multiple meaning words are hard. What can good readers do to decide which meaning to use?

Land

Students Mix and Mingle to share their thinking with other partners. Remind students that many words have multiple meanings and it is very important to ask yourself if the meaning you know makes sense in the sentence and if not the word is probably a multiple meaning word, and you will need use another strategy to figure out the meaning of the word.

WIT & WISDOM™

G1 > M1 > Lesson 19

■ FOCUSING QUESTION: LESSONS 17-22

How does the packhorse librarian change life for Cal?

| 1 | 2 | 3 | 4 | 5 | 6 | 7 | 8 | 9 | 10 | 11 | 12 | 13 | 14 | 15 | 16 | 17 | 18 | 19 | 20 | 21 | 22 | 23 | 24 | 25 | 26 | 27 | 28 | 29 | 30 | 31 | 32 |

Lesson 19

TEXT

- *That Book Woman*, Heather Henson, David Small

G1 > M1 > Lesson 19   WIT & WISDOM™

Lesson 19: At a Glance

AGENDA

Welcome (5 min.)

Launch (4 min.)

Understand the Content Framing Question

Learn (60 min.)

Experiment: Responding to What Others Say (15 min.)

Analyze the Main Character's Feelings (45 min.)

Land (3 min.)

Answer the Content Framing Question

Wrap (3 min.)

Assign Fluency Homework

Vocabulary Deep Dive: Frayer Model for *Scholar* (15 min.)

STANDARDS ADDRESSED

The full text of ELA Standards can be found in the Module Overview.

Reading

- RL.1.1, RL.1.7

Speaking and Listening

- SL.1.1a, SL.1.1b

Language

- L.1.1.f
- ⬇ L.1.6

MATERIALS

- Cal's Feelings Chart
- Response Journals
- Enlarged copy of the Frayer Model
- Handout 19A: Frayer Model

Learning Goals

Analyze the main character's feelings using key details in *That Book Woman*. (RL.1.1, RL.1.7, SL.1.1.f)

✔ Act out and identify Cal's feelings with a partner.

⬇ Develop vocabulary knowledge of the word scholar. (L.1.6)

✔ Complete a Frayer Model independently.

Copyright © 2016 Great Minds®

✔ Checks for Understanding

WIT & WISDOM™   G1 > M1 > Lesson 19

> **Prepare**

FOCUSING QUESTION: Lessons 17-22

How does the packhorse librarian change life for Cal?

CONTENT FRAMING QUESTION: Lesson 19

Reveal: *What does a deeper exploration of the main character's feelings reveal in* That Book Woman?

CRAFT QUESTION: Lesson 19

Experiment: *How does responding to what others say work?*

Students focus learning more about the main character by studying Cal's feelings in *That Book Woman*. Using key scenes from the book, they make facial expressions and come up with words to show Cal's feelings. This provides an active and meaningful way to deepen understanding of Cal's changing emotions from the beginning to the end of the story.

Welcome 5 MIN.

Distribute partner copies of *That Book Woman*. Pairs visually explore the text again, this time focusing in on people's faces in the illustration. Pairs discuss the following prompt: "What can looking at a character's face in an illustration tell us about the story?"

Launch 4 MIN.

UNDERSTAND THE CONTENT FRAMING QUESTION

Post the Content Framing Question and Focusing Question. Echo Read the Content Framing Question.

Ask: "What are we paying attention to in today's Reveal lesson?" Repeat the Content Framing Question and ask students to clap when they hear the answer. Call on a few students to explain their thinking.

- *We are exploring the main character's feelings to find out more information.*
- *Cal is the main character. We'll think more about his feelings.*

233

Copyright © 2016 Great Minds®

Learn 60 MIN.

EXPERIMENT: RESPONDING TO WHAT OTHERS SAY

Whole Group 15 MIN.

Display the Speaking and Listening Anchor Chart. Ask: "What goals have we learned so far this module?" Volunteers respond as you point to the goals on the chart.

Display the Craft Question: *How does Responding to What Others Say work?*

Echo Read the Craft Question.

Ask a student to remind the class what the speaking goal means.

Ask a different student to share one way the speaking goal helps us speak better.

Explain that students will experiment with responding to what others say as they talk about *That Book Woman*. Share that there are four steps that will help us respond to what others say.

Display the following four steps on the board.

1. Both partners listen to the question.
2. One partner shares an answer while the second partner listens carefully.
3. The second partner shares an answer that connects to what the first partner said, beginning with the words: I hear you, and _____.
4. Partners switch who goes first for the next prompt.

Explain that students will use this procedure in the next activity when they analyze the character's feelings in *That Book Woman*.

ANALYZE THE MAIN CHARACTER'S FEELINGS

Pairs 45 MIN.

Explain that students will closely read four parts of the book to learn more about Cal. As each part is read aloud, partners act out Cal's feelings using facial expressions. Explain that, as students identify Cal's feelings, you will chart them.

Display and blank chart two-column chart (see format below) and ask: "What would be a good name for a chart on Cal's Feelings?" Volunteers respond. Use responses to inform the title of the chart. Students Echo Read the title.

WIT & WISDOM™   G1 > M1 > Lesson 19

Read page 12 aloud, starting with "Now what that lady brings." Model Cal's feelings by frowning and looking down. Students Think-Pair-Share the following TDQ. Call on volunteers for responses.

1 How do you think Cal feels? What text evidence makes you think that?

- *Cal feels angry. He feels angry because he doesn't want books that the Book Woman brought. He's the only one in his family not looking at the books in the illustration.*

- *I think Cal feels upset because he thinks the Book Woman wants to sell books.*

- *Cal feels mad. In the picture, he is not looking at the Book Woman or the books she brought.*

Encourage students to go beyond common feeling words such as angry, sad, and happy. Affirm that while those are great words to describe Cal and ask if anyone knows another word that is similar. For example, instead of mad, Cal could be described as disappointed or upset.

Extension

Allow students to use a children's thesaurus to help them find additional feeling words.

Add appropriate feeling words to the Cal's Feelings Chart.

Read the following pages of the story aloud as pairs use facial expressions to show Cal's feelings to each other. After each part is read aloud, they put words to the facial expression. Students Think-Pair-Share: "What is one word that describes how Cal feels? Why do you think he feels that way?" Use Equity Sticks to call on pairs, and add refined responses to the chart.

- Read aloud page 15, starting with "To my surprise."
- ✔ Students use facial expressions to act out Cal's feelings and Think-Pair-Share to identify words to describe Cal's feelings.

  - *(Students' mouths and eyes are open wide)*
  - *I think Cal feels surprised. The text said he feels surprised.*
  - *Cal feels surprised. He can't believe the books are "free as air."*
  - *(Students frown and their brows are furrowed)*
  - *Cal is suspicious. He is looking at the Book Woman leaving on her horse and frowning.*
  - *Cal is mad. He is frowning in the picture and glaring at the Book Woman as she leaves.*

- Read page 24 aloud, starting with "I stand a spell to watch."
- ✔ Students use facial expressions to act out Cal's feelings and Think-Pair-Share to identify words to describe Cal's feelings.

  - *(Students stare into space, looking quizzical)*
  - *I think Cal feels confused. He is standing at the window just looking at the Book Woman.*
  - *Cal feels thoughtful. The text says he has thoughts going around his head.*
  - *Cal is curious. He wants to know what makes the Book Woman go out into the cold.*

235

Copyright © 2016 Great Minds®

G1 > M1 > Lesson 19   WIT & WISDOM™

- Read aloud pages 31–32, starting with "I duck my head."

- ✔ Students use facial expressions to act out Cal's feelings and Think-Pair-Share to identify words to describe Cal's feelings.

  - *(Students smile big)*

  - *I think Cal feels happy. He is smiling really big in the picture.*

  - *Cal feels excited. The Book Woman liked his gift of reading to her. He was excited to share that with her.*

  - *I think Cal feels proud. He shows the Book Woman that he can read now!*

  - *Cal is joyful. He is smiling and holding a book that he can read.*

  - *Cal is thankful. The Book Woman helped him want to learn to read.*

As students speak, circulate and celebrate pairs when they successfully respond to what others are saying. Share that the class will now take a moment to debrief the experiment with our speaking goal.

Ask: "How did practicing our Speaking Goal help you learn?"

Instruct students to Think-Pair-Share.

  - *We listened first, so what we said was connected.*

  - *I didn't just wait around for my turn to talk.*

  - *I learned something new from my friend, and he learned something new from me.*

Invite a few students to share out with the larger group.

CAL'S FEELINGS CHART

Page	Cal's Feelings
12	▪ *Mad, angry, upset*
15	▪ *Surprised, suspicious, angry*
24	▪ *Confused, thoughtful, curious*
31–32	▪ *Happy, excited, proud, joyful, thankful*

Ask: "What do you notice about the feelings we recorded on the chart?" If needed, follow up with: "How did Cal's feelings change?" Use Equity Sticks to call on students.

  - *Cal's feelings changed a lot.*

  - *Cal went from feeling angry to confused to happy.*

  - *Cal felt mad at first then he was joyful by the end.*

  - *Cal had a lot of different feelings.*

236

Copyright © 2016 Great Minds®

WIT & WISDOM™   G1 > M1 > Lesson 19

Use student responses to summarize how Cal's feelings change throughout the book: In the beginning, Cal feels angry and upset. He is mad at the Book Woman and suspicious of her bringing books to his home. Then, he feels confused and curious as he starts to wonder why the Book Woman travels so far and in bad weather to bring them new books. In the end, Cal feels excited and proud that he can read, and thankful to the Book Woman for making it possible.

> **Alternate Activity**
>
> Use prompting questions and the chart as scaffolds to bring students into creating the above summary.

Students write and illustrate a sentence in their Response Journals about Cal's feelings at the end of the story explaining why he feels that way.

At the end of the story Cal was _____ because _____.

Land 3MIN.

ANSWER THE CONTENT FRAMING QUESTION

Reveal: What does a deeper exploration of the main character's feelings reveal in *That Book Woman*?

Ask: "How did we answer this question today? What did we learn?" Volunteers respond.

- *We made a chart of Cal's feelings.*
- *We looked for changes in Cal's feelings.*
- *Cal's feelings changed.*
- *Cal had a lot of feelings.*
- *Cal's feelings changed from upset to curious to excited about books.*

237

Copyright © 2016 Great Minds®

Wrap

HOMEWORK CHECK-IN

Continue home reading routine. Check Fluency Homework from the previous lesson, and remind students what to do for fluency homework tonight.

Analyze

Context and Alignment

Pairs explore the change in Cal's feelings by acting out and identifying his emotions using the text and illustrations (RL.1.1, RL.1.7, SL.1.1.f). Check students' facial expressions and oral responses for the following success criteria:

- Accurately represents the emotions
- Uses adjectives to describe the emotions

Next Steps

If students are unable to display the appropriate facial expressions, practice the expressions in a small group. Connect the adjective to the facial expression by creating and displaying the word card to form a connection between the word and the expression.

Lesson 19: Vocabulary Deep Dive

Vocabulary Strategies: Frayer Model for Scholar

- **Time:** 15 min.
- **Text:** *That Book Woman*, Heather Henson, David Small
- **Vocabulary Learning Goal:** Develop vocabulary knowledge of the word *scholar*. (L.1.6)

Launch

Post a copy of the Frayer Model for students to see. Students Think-Pair-Share on the following questions: "What do you remember about this graphic? How was it used before?"

Circulate as students discuss and use their responses to reinforce that the Frayer Models allow us to think and talk deeply about words from the texts we're reading. Explain that in this lesson they will think and talk deeply about an important word from *That Book Woman*: *scholar*.

Learn

Write the word *scholar* in the center circle. Read the word for the students and have them repeat it several times. Students Think-Pair-Share on whether or not they have heard this word and what it might mean.

Read page 7 of the text where Cal talks about Lark playing school. Draw students' attention to the last line where Cal says, "But me, I am no scholar-boy." Students Think-Pair-Share on what they know about Cal from this page through the following questions: "What does Cal not care about? What does he mean when he says he is not a 'scholar-boy'?" Consider rereading this page of the text if students are struggling to remember the details.

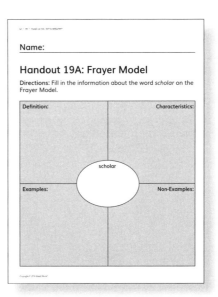

Begin to complete the chart by writing a definition in the first quadrant. Tell students that a *scholar* is someone who has great knowledge and enjoys learning and studying. As a class, use this definition to come up with a friendly definition that students can understand. Ensure students understand this definition before writing it in the box on the chart. Have students write the definition on Handout 19A: Frayer Model.

Have students work in pairs to generate a list of facts/characteristics for *scholars*. Some possible answers include liking to read, looking things up online, someone who is very smart, etc. Use Equity Sticks to choose two or three pairs to share their list and add it to the class chart, then have students add their list to their copy. Circulate and redirect as necessary.

After writing their list of characteristics, have partners work together to generate a list of examples. Choose pairs to share their lists and add to the class chart, then have students add to their individual charts. In a similar fashion, generate a list of non-examples.

✔ Students use their complete Frayer Models to verbalize the definition, facts, and examples for the word scholar.

Then, students Think-Pair-Share on the following questions:

"In the beginning of the text Cal says that he is not a 'scholar-boy.' How has Cal's attitude changed by the end of the text? Has he turned into a 'scholar-boy'?

Land

Use Equity Sticks to choose volunteers to share their thinking. Remind students that knowing words deeply helps them to better understand what they read.

WIT & WISDOM™   G1 › M1 › Lesson 20

■ FOCUSING QUESTION: LESSONS 17-22

How does the packhorse librarian change life for Cal?

1 2 3 4 5 6 7 8 9 10 11 12 13 14 15 16 **17 18 19 20 21 22** 23 24 25 26 27 28 29 30 31 32

Lesson 20

TEXT

- *That Book Woman*, Heather Henson, David Small

Copyright © 2016 Great Minds®

G1 > M1 > Lesson 20
WIT & WISDOM™

Lesson 20: At a Glance

AGENDA

Welcome (5 min.)

Launch (5 min.)

Understand the Content Framing Question

Learn (55 min.)

Analyze Character Change (35 min.)

Examine Informal Language (20 min.)

Land (5 min.)

Answer the Content Framing Question

Wrap (5 min.)

Homework Check-in

Style and Conventions Deep Dive: Adjectives are Feeling Words (15 min.)

STANDARDS ADDRESSED

The full text of ELA Standards can be found in the Module Overview.

Reading

- RL.1.1, RL.1.3, RL.1.7

Speaking and Listening

- SL.1.1.a, SL.1.2

Language

- ↓ L.1.1.f

MATERIALS

- Cal's Feelings Chart from Lesson 19
- Response Journals
- Sticky notes

Learning Goals

Analyze characters using key details in *That Book Woman*. (RL.1.3, RL.1.7)

✔ Create tableaux for beginning and ending porch scenes from the text.

↓ Use frequently occurring adjectives to describe visual images. Generate a variety of adjectives. (L.1.1.f)

✔ Complete Sentence Frames with adjectives.

✔ Checks for Understanding

Copyright © 2016 Great Minds®

WIT & WISDOM™   G1 > M1 > Lesson 20

Prepare

FOCUSING QUESTION: Lessons 17-22

How does the packhorse librarian change life for Cal?

CONTENT FRAMING QUESTION: Lesson 20

Reveal: *What does a deeper exploration of the main character's feelings reveal in* That Book Woman?

CRAFT QUESTION: Lesson 20

Examine: *What is informal language?*

Students examine the informal language used in *That Book Woman* by determining the meaning of one word using context clues. They further analyze Cal's character by comparing his feelings toward his sister Lark at the beginning and end of the story through tableaux.

Welcome 5 MIN.

Post Cal's Feelings Chart where all students can reference it.

In pairs, students take turns choosing a feeling from the chart, and using their face to silently express that feeling. The other partner tries to guess which feeling the first partner is expressing by referencing the chart.

Launch 5 MIN.

UNDERSTAND THE CONTENT FRAMING QUESTION

Post the Content Framing Question and Focusing Question. Echo Read the Content Framing Question.

Ask: "What do you notice about this Content Framing Question?" A volunteer responds.

- *It's the same question as the previous lesson.*

Share that while we analyzed Cal's feelings in the previous lesson, we noticed that Cal's feelings changed a lot from the beginning to the end of the book. Explain that when a character changes because of events that happen, it is good to try and figure out how that character changed.

243

Copyright © 2016 Great Minds®

G1 > M1 > Lesson 20   WIT & WISDOM™

Explain students will continue to look at the main character's feelings because there is more to discover in the book!

Learn 55 MIN.

ANALYZE CHARACTER CHANGE 35 MIN.

Explain students will continue to study the book to learn more about the main character, Cal. Share that this time, they will focus on how he feels about his sister, Lark, and on how those feelings change.

Display Cal's Feelings Chart from lesson 19. Ask a few students to remind the class about what they discovered in yesterday's lesson. Share that now we will look even more carefully at how Cal's feeling change about Lark from the beginning to the end of the story.

Read aloud pages 5–6, starting with "And I can bring the cow home too."

Students Think-Pair-Share: "Describe Cal and Lark in this scene."

- *Cal is annoyed at Lark.*
- *Cal looks angry while he is looking at Lark reading.*
- *Cal is doing chores like bringing the cow home.*
- *Cal looks mad at Lark.*
- *Lark is really interested in reading her book.*
- *Lark is sitting on the porch reading her book.*

Share pages 33–34. Point out that although there are no words on the page, students can use the illustrations to determine information about the characters.

Students Think-Pair-Share: "Describe Cal and Lark in this scene."

- *Cal is sitting on the porch reading a book next to Lark.*
- *Cal looks like he is enjoying reading a book.*
- *Cal looks relaxed while reading.*
- *Lark is reading a book next to Cal.*
- *Lark is sitting on the porch reading her book. She looks really interested in it.*

Assign pages 5–6 or pages 33–34 to pairs.

✔ Pairs join another pair and take turns making tableaux of the beginning or ending porch scenes. Pairs guess which scene is being created based on facial expressions and body positions.

244

Copyright © 2016 Great Minds®

WIT & WISDOM™   G1 › M1 › Lesson 20

- *(Pages 5–6: One student pretends to be Cal, frowning at Lark. The other student pretends to be Lark sitting and reading by looking at hands folded to represent a book.)*
- *(Pages 33–34: Both students sit pretend to read by looking at their hands folded to represent books.)*

Students discuss in their small groups: "What does Cal feel about Lark reading on pages 5–6? What does Cal feel about Lark reading on pages 33–34?

Circulate to listen to discussions.

Guide students to summarize how the beginning and ending porch scenes fit together, highlighting some of the following key points that students will likely surface, or making them yourself if they don't.

- *In the beginning, Cal feels annoyed at Lark. He doesn't understand why she reads all the time and he doesn't want to read. In the end, Cal's feelings toward Lark have changed. He is thankful to Lark for teaching him to read and is reading alongside her.*

Students use the following Sentence Frames to record their thoughts in their Response Journals:

- **At first Cal feels** <u>annoyed at Lark for reading so much</u>.
- **Then Cal feels** <u>thankful to Lark for teaching him to read and he joins her on the porch to read</u>.

Students then illustrate these pages with a close up portrait of Cal's face, showing clearly how he feels before and after he learns to read.

EXAMINE INFORMAL LANGUAGE

Whole Group 20 MIN.

Reread the phrase "my sister Lark would keep her nose a-twixt the pages of a book" on page 5, emphasizing Cal's dialogue, and show the picture on page 6.

Explain that the language Cal uses is not academic or formal. People use academic and formal language in classroom speaking and writing. There are some people that use words they understand that we wouldn't use in school.

Students Think-Pair-Share: "What do you think 'a-twixt' means? How would we say this word at school?" Use Equity Sticks to call on pairs for responses.

- *I think "a-twixt" means looking inside.*
- *"A-twixt" could mean between. Lark is looking between the pages of a book.*

Substitute a few refined responses into the phrase to determine if they make sense.

Ask: "What can we do if we do not know the meaning of a word?" Volunteers offer suggestions. Explain that one strategy is to look the work up in a dictionary. Look up the word *a-twixt* and reveal that it is either not in the dictionary or the dictionary says it is informal language (dialectical) for the word *between*.

245

Copyright © 2016 Great Minds®

Point out that this is one of the words in the text that Cal uses that is not in the dictionary. Though it is not a word students would normally study in the classroom, they can determine the meaning by looking at the picture and the text. Also, remind students that the dictionary is also a valuable tool.

Land 5 MIN.

ANSWER THE CONTENT FRAMING QUESTION

Reveal: What does a deeper exploration of the main character's feelings reveal in *That Book Woman*?

Echo Read the Content Framing Question. Students Think-Pair-Share: "What additional information did you learn about Cal today?"

- *Cal uses informal words when he talks.*
- *Cal's feelings toward his sister changed from the beginning to the end.*
- *Cal was annoyed at Lark at first, then he was thankful that she taught him to read.*

Wrap 5 MIN.

HOMEWORK CHECK-IN

Continue home reading routine. Check Fluency Homework from the previous lesson, and remind students what to do for Fluency Homework tonight.

Analyze

Context and Alignment

Students create tableaux for sections of text relating to two scenes between Cal and Lark on the porch (RL.1.3, RL.1.7).

Check for the following success criteria for each student:

- Uses illustrations to determine poses.
- Uses text evidence to identify characters and their actions

Next Steps

If students struggle with identifying facial expressions and positions of the characters in the scenes, support them by displaying two copies of the text side-by-side. Open the texts to pages 5–6 and pages 33–34, so students can study the differences in the two scenes.

G1 > M1 > Lesson 20   WIT & WISDOM™

⬇ Lesson 20: Style and Conventions Deep Dive

Adjectives are Feeling Words

- **Time:** 15 min.

- **Text:** *That Book Woman*, Heather Henson, David Small

- **Style and Conventions Learning Goal:** Use frequently occurring adjectives to describe visual images. (L.1.1.f)

- **STYLE AND CONVENTIONS CRAFT QUESTION:** Lesson 20
  Experiment: *How do adjectives help us create a picture in our mind?*

Launch

Display and read the Craft Question: *How do adjectives help us create a picture in our mind?*

Students Echo Read the question. Explain that in this lesson they will learn more about adjectives and how they help our reading and writing.

Learn

Display the word adjective. Remind students of how they previously studied adjectives with *Museum ABC*. Ask: "What do you remember about adjectives?" Volunteers respond.

Reinforce that adjectives are words that describe things and tell what kind.

Explain that in this lesson they will learn more about adjectives and that sometimes adjectives can tell us how someone or something is feeling. Adjectives also help us to create a picture in our mind about the person or animal it is describing.

Show students pages 5 and 6 of *That Book Woman*. Ask students to tell you the characters they see on the page. Begin making a list of the nouns on the page.

- Cal

- Lark

After listing the characters on these pages ask students if they remember what type of words these are. Confirm that these words are nouns and these nouns are people or characters.

Post and Echo Read the Cal's Feelings Chart that the class created in lesson 19.

248

Copyright © 2016 Great Minds®

WIT & WISDOM™   G1 > M1 > Lesson 20

Use Equity Sticks to choose volunteers to share the adjectives on the chart that they used to describe how the characters looked on each page.

- surprised

- busy

- bored

- excited

- disappointed

- curious

- scared

Display and read the following Sentence Frames:

- **Cal is _____.**

- **Lark is _____.**

Use Equity Sticks to choose volunteers to pick an adjective to describe each character and write it in the blank.

✔ Partners work together to complete the Sentence Frames orally. Encourage students to use the other character's names in the Sentence Frames and add an adjective for that character as well.

Use Equity Sticks to choose volunteers to share some of the sentences they created.

Land

Instruct students to Think-Pair-Share, and ask: "How do adjectives help us create a picture in our mind?"

Use Equity Sticks to select two pairs to share their thinking. Use their responses to reinforce that adjectives describe nouns, and that they help create the picture in our mind by describing what the noun is feeling or looks like. Explain that students will continue to learn about adjectives and how to use them in their writing.

249

Copyright © 2016 Great Minds®

WIT & WISDOM™   G1 > M1 > Lesson 21

■ FOCUSING QUESTION: LESSONS 17-22

How does the packhorse librarian change life for Cal?

1 2 3 4 5 6 7 8 9 10 11 12 13 14 15 16 **17 18 19 20 21 22** 23 24 25 26 27 28 29 30 31 32

Lesson 21

TEXTS

- *That Book Woman*, Heather Henson, David Small
- "Pack Horse Librarians," (**http://witeng.link/0628**)
- "ASL Sign for: same," *American Sign Language Dictionary*

Copyright © 2016 Great Minds®

G1 > M1 > Lesson 21   WIT & WISDOM™

Lesson 21: At a Glance

AGENDA

Welcome (7 min.)

Launch (3 min.)

Understand the Content Framing Question

Learn (60 min.)

Relate the Video and Author's Note to the Story (10 min.)

Participate in a Socratic Seminar (25 min.)

Execute Using Adjectives (25 min.)

Land (3 min.)

Answer the Content Framing Question

Wrap (2 min.)

Assign Fluency Homework

Vocabulary Deep Dive: Multiple Meaning Words (15 min.)

STANDARDS ADDRESSED

The full text of ELA Standards can be found in the Module Overview.

Reading

- RL.1.1, RL.1.3

Writing

- W.1.3, W1.8

Speaking and Listening

- SL.1.1a, SL.1.1b

Language

- L.1.1.b, L.1.1.f, L.1.1.j, L.1.2b
- ↓ L.1.6

MATERIALS

- Assessment 21: Focusing Question Task 4
- Handout 21A: Focusing Question Prompt 4
- Speaking and Listening Anchor Chart
- Blank word cards
- Vocabulary Chart from Deep Dive Lesson 18

Learning Goals

Write a narrative retell of *That Book Woman* that shows how the packhorse librarian changes life for Cal. (RL.1.2, RL.1.3, W.1.3, W.1.8 SL.1.1.a, L.1.1.b, L.1.1.f, L.1.1.j, L.1.2.b)

✔ Complete Focusing Question Task 4.

Respond to others and describe the connections among multiple pieces of information about packhorse librarians and cite specific details and key ideas from the *That Book Woman* in a Socratic Seminar. (RL.1.3, RI.1.3, SL.1.1.a, SL.1.1.b)

✔ Participate in a Socratic Seminar

↓ Vocabulary Learning Goal: Define multiple meanings for words *signs* and *duck*. (L.1.6)

✔ Draw pictures for a partner to guess the new word.

Copyright © 2016 Great Minds®

✔ Checks for Understanding

WIT & WISDOM™   G1 > M1 > Lesson 21

Prepare

FOCUSING QUESTION: Lessons 17-22

How does the packhorse librarian change life for Cal?

CONTENT FRAMING QUESTION: Lesson 21

Know: *How does* That Book Woman *build our knowledge of how books can change lives?*

CRAFT QUESTION: Lesson 21

Execute: *How do I use adjectives in my writing?*

Students find connections between two key pieces of information in the author's note to the story *That Book Woman*. Students then compare a short video about packhorse librarians, providing more information about the inspiration behind this story. Exploring the author's note and video provides them with additional background and the knowledge that packhorse librarians were real. They apply what they've learned to participate in their first Socratic Seminar discussing how the packhorse librarian changes live for Cal. They then apply what they've learned to Focusing Question Task 4, orally rehearsing their retelling of *That Book Woman* before writing and drawing complete the task.

Welcome 7 MIN.

Explain that students will watch an informational video to learn more facts about packhorses that deliver books to remote villages similar to how Cal and his family received books in *That Book Woman*.

Remind students that during a video, students should practice their best listening.

Display and reference the Speaking and Listening Anchor Chart.

💬 Watch the four-minute video "Pack Horse Librarians" (**http://witeng.link/0628**).

When students see a connection to the story, they make a Nonverbal Signal for *same*, such as the ASL sign for *same* (**http://witeng.link/0272**).

Remind students that they should signal briefly when they notice a similarity but then return their attention the video. Students practice signaling.

Observe as students notice similarities. Students may signal during these moments in the video:

- *"Kentucky's mountains."*
- *"They were almost totally isolated from the outside world."*

253

Copyright © 2016 Great Minds®

G1 > M1 > Lesson 21   WIT & WISDOM™

- "Since there were no paved or gravel roads, the only way in was by foot, horse, or mule."
- "The packhorse library project"
- "Librarians would deliver books and magazines to mountain families and remote schools on horseback"
- "About sixty-percent of the residents of Kentucky were without access to public libraries."
- "Were brave, determined, and dedicated members of the communities they served."
- "In all types of weather"
- "Not all were literate—able to read and write"

Launch 3 MIN.

UNDERSTAND THE CONTENT FRAMING QUESTION

Post and read the Content Framing Question and Focusing Question.

Explain that this lesson is about making connections. Students will study a video, and the author's note to connect what they learn to the story, and make connections among the story, the Focusing Question, and real life packhorse librarians in a Socratic Seminar. Share that making these connections will help students successfully complete Focusing Question Task 4.

Learn 60 MIN.

CONNECT THE VIDEO AND AUTHOR'S NOTE TO THE STORY

Whole Group 10 MIN.

Explain that students will discuss the connections they noticed between the video and *That Book Woman*.

Invite students to share the connections they noticed in the video.

Use Equity Sticks to call on students.

- *In the video, they talked about the Kentucky mountains. Cal's family lived there in the story too.*
- *The video says how some people were not in touch with the outside world. Cal's family also wasn't close to any neighbors or other cities.*

254

Copyright © 2016 Great Minds®

WIT & WISDOM™   G1 > M1 > Lesson 21

- *The Book Woman got to Cal and his family by horse. In the video, it said the only way to travel there was by foot, horse, or mule because of the roads.*
- *Both the Book Woman and the librarians in the video delivered books for free. In the video it said the books were donated.*
- *In the video, it said the librarians traveled in all types of weather. The Book Woman also traveled in all types of weather, including blizzards!*
- *The video said not everyone could read and write. Cal also couldn't read and write.*
- *The video said that the librarians did read alouds to help the people who couldn't read or write, but in the story the Book Woman didn't do this.*

Extension

Students draw one connection between the text and the video in their Response Journals.

Explain that students will read a new part of the book to build their understanding of *That Book Woman.*

Call on one to two volunteers to recall: "What does an author's note provide?" Confirm that an author's note, just like the video they watched, provides true information.

Read aloud "A Note about the Story" on page 35. Define new vocabulary from the text, such as *arduous* and *chicken scratch*. Tell students that *arduous* means "difficult" and *chicken scratch* means "messy handwriting that is hard to read." For each word, display the word on a card for the Word Wall. Explain that students will find these words helpful as they discuss the text.

Tell students you will read the note again as they listen for information that connects to, or is the same as, the story. Students indicate what is the same by using a Nonverbal Signal, such as the ASL sign for *same* (**http://witeng.link/0272**).

Use student responses to highlight important connections between the text and the Author's Note. Write and illustrate two important connections on Sentence Strips:

- A book woman would travel by horse a difficult route every two weeks carrying books in good or bad weather (drawing of a woman on a horse).
- Making readers out of people who didn't want to read "chicken scratch" (drawing of a boy reading).

Explain that now that students know the words, they will listen for more connections between the story and the Author's Note as you reread parts of the story aloud. Display the Sentence Strips in two separate areas in the room. When students notice a connected detail in the story, they will point to the appropriate posted detail written on the Sentence Strip.

Read aloud one or two key parts of the story, such as pages 7, 12, 15, 17, 21, 24, 25, 30, 31, based on the connections that students surface. After each excerpt, students point to the sign that shows the connection. If answers differ, ask a student pointing to the correct location, "What details in the text show this connection?"

255

Copyright © 2016 Great Minds®

G1 > M1 > Lesson 21　　　　　　　　　　　　　　　　　　　　　　　WIT & WISDOM™

Connections to "a book woman would travel by horse every two weeks carrying books in good or bad weather":

- *Page 12: The text says the Book Woman traveled "clear up the mountainside," and it was "a hard day's ride."*
- *Page 15: The text says the Book Woman will come back "two weeks to the day" with more books.*
- *Page 17: The illustrations show the Book Woman traveling in all kinds of weather.*
- *Page 21: The illustrations show the Book Woman traveling in a snowstorm to bring books to Cal's family.*
- *Page 24: The text says the Book Woman "risks catching cold or worse."*

Connections to "making readers out of people who didn't want to read 'chicken scratch'":

- *Page 7: The text says Cal doesn't want to "sit so stoney-still a-staring at some chicken scratch." He doesn't want to read.*
- *Page 25: Cal asks Lark to "Teach me what it says" and he learns to read.*
- *Page 30: In the text, Cal's mom thanks the Book Woman for "making two readers outta one."*
- *Page 31: Cal reads to the Book Woman. He says he used to think it was "just chicken scratch" but now he sees "what's truly there."*

Choose a few connections that students seemed especially excited about and highlight them to reinforce that making connections between the author's note and the text can help readers unlock why the author wrote the text.

PARTICIPATE IN A SOCRATIC SEMINAR

Whole Group　25 MIN.

Set Socratic Seminar expectations for students by reviewing the Speaking and Listening Goals for this module.

The goal for this Socratic Seminar is to respond to others. Students Think-Pair-Share: "How can I respond to others?" Use Equity Sticks to select two pairs to respond.

- *I can listen to what you are saying.*
- *I can say, I hear you, and add more or ask a question.*

Reminds students they can also use Sentence Frames to respond to what others are saying. Write the new Sentence Frame on a Sentence Strip and add it to the others.

Display and Chorally Read the following Sentence Frames:

- **I agree with you because _____.**
- **I disagree with you because**
- **What makes you think that?**
- **I hear you and _____.**

256

Copyright © 2016 Great Minds®

WIT & WISDOM™   G1 > M1 > Lesson 21

| TEACHER NOTE | You may wish to use a Nonverbal Signal and Talking Stick to help delineate whose turn it is to speak, and Sentence Frames to provide the structure for participating in complete sentences. |

Students form a circle. Students bring copies of *That Book Woman* for reference during the Socratic Seminar.

Alternate Activity

Place students into groups of four to six for the Socratic Seminar.

Set the purpose for the Socratic Seminar by telling students they will answer the question:

"How does the packhorse librarian change life for Cal?"

Students Think-Pair-Share to discuss the question using evidence from the text to support their answer.

Read aloud the opening question: "How does the packhorse librarian change life for Cal?"

Students support their answer with text evidence.

✔ Students follow the Socratic Seminar procedures and engage in sustained dialogue.

- *Cal learns to read*
- *Cal learns reading is important*
- *Cal learns to respect the packhorse librarian*

Record anecdotal notes on the speaking and listening observation form (see Appendix C).

Midway through the seminar, stop and call attention to the next discussion question:

"How does Cal's life change throughout the story?"

- *At the beginning of the story, Cal can't read.*
- *Cal can't figure out why Lark's nose is always in a book.*
- *Cal thinks books are dumb.*
- *Cal can't figure out why the Book Lady keeps bringing books, even in bad weather.*
- *Cal decides he wants to know what makes the Book Lady risk catching cold or worse.*
- *He asks Lark to teach him to read.*
- *Cal begins to like reading.*
- *Cal feels grateful to the Book Lady and wants to give her a gift.*
- *Cal is proud that he can read.*

257

Copyright © 2016 Great Minds®

Reread the Speaking and Listening goal from the Speaking and Listening Anchor Chart. Students use Nonverbal Signals such as thumbs up, in the middle, or down to signal their self-assessment of how well they responded to what others said. Use anecdotal notes to share notable discussion points from the group.

EXECUTE USING ADJECTIVES

Whole Group 25 MIN.

Explain to students that now that they have made connections and discussed the Focusing Question, Focusing Question Task 4 will help them show what they've learned about story elements as they write a retelling of *That Book Woman*.

Display and distribute Assessment 21: Focusing Question Task 4. Post the Handout 21A: Focusing Question 4 Prompt. Students Echo Read:

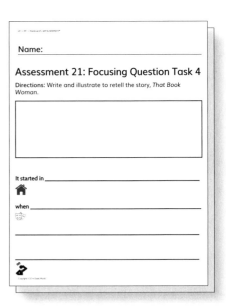

Write and draw to retell the story That Book Woman.

Be sure to include:

- *Characters (label Cal and Lark).*
- *Setting.*
- *Problem.*
- *Resolution.*
- *Complete sentences.*
- *Capitalize the first word in a sentence and proper nouns.*
- *End punctuation.*
- *Write one adjective to describe Cal below his picture on page 1.*

Ask: "What tools do we have to help us with our retelling?" Volunteers respond. Reinforce that students can use the story elements, Story Map, and Sentence Frames.

Pairs orally rehearse their retellings.

✔ Students independently complete the prompt.

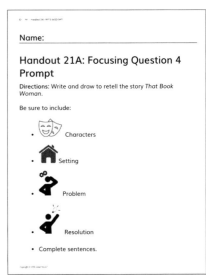

Land 3 MIN.

ANSWER THE CONTENT FRAMING QUESTION

Knowledge: *How does* That Book Woman *build our knowledge of how books can change lives?*

Ask the Content Framing Question. Encourage students to consider what they learned from the Socratic Seminar, as well as the information on the Question and Answers Chart and the Story Map, as they think about how this book builds knowledge.

Invite a student volunteer to share a response.

Wrap 2 MIN.

HOMEWORK CHECK-IN

Continue home reading routine. Check Fluency Homework and remind students that tonight is the final fluency work with the text, *That Book Woman*.

Analyze

Context and Alignment

Students write a narrative retell of *That Book Woman* (RL.1.2, RL.1.3, W.1.3, W.1.8 SL.1.1.a, L.1.1.b, L.1.1.f, L.1.1.j, L.1.2.b).

Check for the following success criteria:

- Includes story elements.
- Writes complete sentences.
- Capitalizes the first word in a sentence and proper nouns.
- Uses end punctuation.
- Uses adjectives to describe characters.

Next Steps

Review all student papers to identify error patterns the type of errors students are making. For example: Are students confused on story elements? Are they writing fragments or run-ones? Group students by similar needs and plan for small group support for these skills.

G1 > M1 > Lesson 21   WIT & WISDOM™

⬇ Lesson 21: Vocabulary Deep Dive

Defining Multiple Meaning Words

- **Time:** 15 min.

- **Text:** *That Book Woman*, Heather Henson, David Small

- **Vocabulary Learning Goal:** Define multiple meanings for words *signs* and *duck*. (L.1.6)

Launch

Congratulate students on all of the vocabulary learning they have done with *That Book Woman*, especially words with multiple, or many, meanings.

Review the three-column chart and its contents from the previous Vocabulary Deep Dive. Students Think-Pair-Share on how the class determined the new meanings for the previously discussed words. Use Equity Sticks to choose volunteers to share their thinking.

Remote	1	2
Poke	3	4
Spell	5	6
Signs	7	8
Duck	9	10

- *We thought about the meaning of the word we knew.*
- *We read the word in a sentence from the book.*
- *We asked a question about the word.*
- *We wrote a new meaning for the word.*

Explain that in this lesson they will learn two more words that have multiple meanings, and determine their meanings.

Learn

Read the fourth word, *signs*, for students. Students repeat the word and then Think-Pair-Share on what the word means. Based on their experience, students will likely relate the word signs to street signs. Have students write or draw this definition for signs in box 7.

260

Copyright © 2016 Great Minds®

WIT & WISDOM™   G1 > M1 > Lesson 21

Read the following phrase from the text:

- Pap says it's written in the signs how long or short the winter stays.

Ask students if the definition for signs from box 7 makes sense in the sentence. Guide students to determining the new meaning of signs by asking about Cal and his family. Do they live in a place that will have any signs like the ones they would see when they go down the street? What kind of signs might they have? If students are unable to give any examples of kinds of signs Cal and his family might use, consider showing students a Farmer's Almanac either in book form or at **www.almanac.com**. The almanac lists ways farmers have predicted the weather using signs from plants and animals. Using these or other questions, guide students to discovering that when used in this way, a sign is something that predicts an event, such as weather. Have students write or draw this new meaning in box 8.

Following the same procedure, read the last word, *duck*, for students. Students repeat the word and then Think-Pair-Share what the word means. Most students will relate the word duck to the type of bird that flies and says "quack." Have students write or draw this definition for duck in box 9.

Read the following phrase from the text:

- I duck my head and wait until the very last to speak my mind.

Ask students if the definition for *duck* from box 9 makes sense in the sentence. Guide students to determining the new meaning of *duck* by asking students what Cal said to the Book Woman just before she rode away. Because the illustration on this page shows Cal smiling after he reads to the Book Woman, students may need to see a dramatization of what Cal looked like as he spoke to her. Consider reading the opening lines on the page with an embarrassed or shy expression as Cal would have had on his face. Have students pay attention to what the teacher's head does as they hear Cal's words. Guide students to understanding that in this case, *duck* is a head movement where someone looks down at the ground in a shy or embarrassed way. Students write or draw this new meaning in box 10.

✔ Partners review the meanings of all the words on the chart. Partners also need to discuss the steps they need to take to discover the different meanings of words that have multiple meanings. Then each pair takes turns drawing pictures for their partner of one of the multiple meaning words and the other partner guesses the word.

Land

Students Mix and Mingle to share their thinking with other partners. Remind students that many words have multiple meanings and it is very important to ask yourself if the meaning you know makes sense in the sentence and if not the word is probably a multiple meaning word, and you will need use another strategy to figure out the meaning of the word.

Students will need multiple exposures and examples before fully comprehending and internalizing the process good readers use to decide which meaning of word to use.

261

Copyright © 2016 Great Minds®

WIT & WISDOM™   G1 > M1 > Lesson 22

■ FOCUSING QUESTION: LESSONS 17-22

How does the packhorse librarian change life for Cal?

1 2 3 4 5 6 7 8 9 10 11 12 13 14 15 16 **17 18 19 20 21 22** 23 24 25 26 27 28 29 30 31 32

Lesson 22

TEXT

- *That Book Woman*, Heather Henson, David Small

G1 > M1 > Lesson 22   WIT & WISDOM™

Lesson 22: At a Glance

AGENDA

Welcome (10 min.)

Draft a Portrait

Launch (5 min.)

Understand the Content Framing Question

Learn (55 min.)

Reflect on the Essential Question (15 min.)

Excel Using Adjectives (15 min.)

Record Knowledge (25 min.)

Land (3 min.)

Answer the Content Framing Question

Wrap (2 min.)

Assign Fluency Homework

Style and Conventions Deep Dive: Adjectives are Picture Words (15 min.)

STANDARDS ADDRESSED

The full text of ELA Standards can be found in the Module Overview.

Reading

- RL.1.2, RL.1.7

Writing

- W.1.3

Speaking and Listening

- SL.1.1a, SL.1.1b

Language

- ↓ L.1.1.f

MATERIALS

- Essential Questions Chart
- Handout 6A: Essential Questions Chart
- Sticky flags
- World map
- Handout 21A: Focusing Question Task 4
- Adjectives Anchor Chart
- Cal's Feelings Chart
- Knowledge Journal
- Handout 22A: Adding Adjectives to Nouns

Learning Goals

Write and speak about how *That Book Woman* adds to knowledge of how books change lives.

✔ Contribute to the Knowledge Journal.

↓ Use frequently occurring adjectives to describe visual images. (L.1.1.f)

✔ Complete Handout 22A.

Copyright © 2016 Great Minds®

✔ Checks for Understanding

WIT & WISDOM™ G1 › M1 › Lesson 22

Prepare

FOCUSING QUESTION: Lessons 17–22

How does the packhorse librarian change life for Cal?

CONTENT FRAMING QUESTION: Lesson 22

Know: *How does* That Book Woman *build our knowledge of how books can change lives?*

CRAFT QUESTION: Lesson 22

Execute: *How do I improve using adjectives in my writing?*

Students fill out the Essential Questions Chart with information from *That Book Woman*, before recording knowledge and learning in the Knowledge Journal. Students also revise their writing from Focusing Question Task 4, focusing on editing for descriptive words.

Welcome 10 MIN.

DRAFT A PORTRAIT

Explain that students will draft the third of four portrait illustrations to include on the cover page for their EOM project.

Distribute a blank drawing frame to each student. Students use what they know about Cal from the text to draft a portrait of Cal reading a book. Remind students to refer to the text for ideas and point out the definition of *portrait* on the Word Wall for reference.

Launch 5 MIN.

UNDERSTAND THE CONTENT FRAMING QUESTION

Read aloud the Focusing Question and Content Framing Question.

Instruct students to Think-Pair-Share and ask: "What were your favorite parts of *That Book Woman*?" Use Equity Sticks to call on students to answer.

Explain that students will discuss and write about how *That Book Woman* builds their understanding.

G1 > M1 > Lesson 22   WIT & WISDOM™

Learn 45 MIN.

REFLECT ON THE ESSENTIAL QUESTION

Whole Group 15 MIN.

Explain that now that students have built knowledge about *That Book Woman* and packhorse librarians, they will build knowledge about the module topic. Display and Echo Read the Essential Question.

Display the Essential Questions Chart and students retrieve their copies of Handout 6A: Essential Questions Chart.

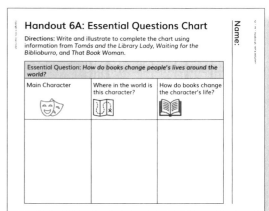

Call on volunteers to respond: "Who is the main character of the story?" Fill in Cal in the Main Character column. Students add the character to Handout 6A.

Remind students the middle column is for the place in the world where the story takes place. Ask: "Where are most of the settings in the book located?" If students struggle to come up with Kentucky, reread the first sentence of the author's note on page 35, starting with "This story was inspired by." Write Kentucky on the chart. Students add the location to their handout.

Share that Kentucky is another states in the United States of America. Add a sticky flag with the name of the location written on it to the class world map. Students add the location to their handout.

| TEACHER NOTE | Look for organic opportunities to reinforce the locations students have learned throughout this module by making connections to other content areas. |

Students Think-Pair-Share: "The Essential Question of the module is 'How do books change people's lives around the world?' How do books change Cal's life in the story?"

- *Cal goes from not being able to read and not liking books to reading and loving books.*
- *Cal learns to read and enjoys books.*

Ask students to share two to three refined responses. Record sentences and illustrations on the chart.

ESSENTIAL QUESTIONS CHART

Essential Question: *How do books change people's lives around the world?*		
Main Character	Where in the world is the character?	How do books change the character's life?
▪ Cal	▪ Kentucky	▪ Cal learns to read and begins to love books (drawing of a book with a heart around it)

EXCEL USING ADJECTIVES

Whole Group 15 MIN.

Read aloud the Craft Question.

Display a copy of Handout 21A: Focusing Question Task 4.

Congratulate students on completing Focusing Question Task 4. Explain that in this lesson students will revise Focusing Question Task 4 for adjectives. Display the charts developed in the Lesson 20 Deep Dive and Cal's Feelings Chart in Lesson 19. Students Think-Pair-Share: "What is an adjective?" Select three students to share their definition.

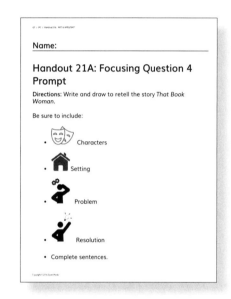

Instruct students put their finger on the adjective they wrote to describe Cal on page 1 of their Focusing Question Task paper. Ask students: "Which adjective did you use to describe Cal?" Use Equity Sticks to determine adjectives used. Point out the adjectives used on the charts. Students stand if they used the same adjective. Add any new adjectives to the list of adjectives created in lesson 20 Deep Dive. Instruct students to add a different adjective to describe Cal below the illustration. Students share both adjectives describing Cal with a partner.

RECORD KNOWLEDGE

Whole Group 25 MIN.

Congratulate students on how much they have already learned and know how to do and explain that they are now ready to add to the Knowledge Journal.

Display the Knowledge Journal. Point to the left-hand side of the Knowledge Journal, labeled "What I know." Instruct students to Think-Pair-Share and ask: "What information goes in this part of our Knowledge Journal?" Volunteers respond.

- *Something I learned.*
- *Things I learned from the book.*
- *New things we learned this week.*

Instruct students to Think-Pair-Share and ask: "What did you learn from our lessons on *That Book Woman*? What did you learn about our Essential Question?

Scaffold

Ask more concrete questions to prompt students and encourage application of key vocabulary:
- What did we learn about stories?
- What did we learn about how books change lives?

Use Equity Sticks to call on pairs to share responses. After each response, students pump their fists towards the ceiling if they believe the response is important learning and pump their fists towards the ground if they disagree or are unsure.

Use votes to choose one to three refined responses to record on the Knowledge Journal.

Display the Knowledge Journal. Point to the right-hand side of the Knowledge Journal, labeled "What I can do." Instruct students to Think-Pair-Share and ask: "What information goes in this part of our Knowledge Journal?"

- *Things I learned how to do.*
- *New things we learned how to do this week.*

Revisit artifacts from previous lessons.

Instruct students Think-Pair-Share, and ask: "What did you learn to do as a writer? What did you learn to do as a reader?"

Scaffold

Ask more concrete questions to prompt students and encourage application of key vocabulary:
- How do we make sure we are using adjectives?
- What do we do when we are speaking? Listening?

Repeat the process detailed above to engage students in a class vote and record refined responses.

What I know	What I can do
- Learning to read opens up your world to books. - You can learn to read any time. - I learned packhorse librarians traveled on bad roads through all kinds of weather just to bring people books. - I learned packhorse librarians brought books to people who couldn't get them.	- I can use adjectives to describe characters. - I can respond to what others say. - I can figure out what characters are feeling.

Land

ANSWER THE CONTENT FRAMING QUESTION

Know: *How does* That Book Woman *build our knowledge of how books can change lives?*

Choral Read the Content Framing Question.

Students Think-Pair-Share to answer the question.

Wrap 2 MIN.

HOMEWORK CHECK-IN

Continue home reading routine. Check Fluency Homework, and remind students that tonight is the final fluency work with the text *That Book Woman*.

Analyze

Context and Alignment

Write and speak about how *That Book Woman* adds to knowledge of how books change lives.

Check for the following success criteria:

- Evidence of connections to the Essential Question.
- Participation in Knowledge Journal discussion.

Next Steps

Review all student papers to ensure that students applied feedback from their revision work.

WIT & WISDOM™   G1 > M1 > Lesson 22

⬇ Lesson 22: Style and Conventions Deep Dive

Adjectives are Picture Words

- **Time:** 15 min.

- **Text:** *That Book Woman*, Heather Henson, David Small

- **Style and Conventions Learning Goal:** Use frequently occurring adjectives to describe visual images. (L.1.1.f)

- **STYLE AND CONVENTIONS CRAFT QUESTION:** Lesson 22
  Examine: *How do adjectives help us describe the setting of a text?*

Launch

Display and read the Craft Question: *How do adjectives help us describe the setting in a text?*

Students Echo Read the question. Explain that they will learn more about adjectives and how they help us describe pictures we make in our minds about the texts we are reading.

Learn

Display the words Cal, Lark, and *That Book Woman*. Ask: "What are the different types of nouns we have studied?" Volunteers respond.

Reinforce that there are common and proper nouns. Ask volunteers to identify which type of nouns these three examples are, using prompting questions as needed. Reinforce that these are proper nouns.

Students Think-Pair-Share about words that describe each character. Use Equity Sticks to choose volunteers to share their words. Capture their answers.

Students Think-Pair-ShareThink-Pair-Share about what these types of words are called. Volunteers respond.

- *They are describing words.*
- *They are feeling words.*
- *They are adjectives.*

Affirm correct answers. Explain that adjectives can also be used to describe some of the common nouns in *That Book Woman*.

271

Copyright © 2016 Great Minds®

Show students pages 7 and 8 of *That Book Woman*. Ask students to tell you the things they see on the page. Begin making a list of the common nouns on the page.

- tree
- dress
- fence
- hair
- cat

After listing the common nouns on these pages ask students if they remember what type of words these are. Confirm that these words are nouns and nouns are people, places, and things. Echo Read the words again, and ask students what adjectives could be added to these words to tell us about the common nouns. For example, ask students, "What kind of cat do you see? What size is the tree?" Write student responses next to each noun. Add any new adjectives to the Adjectives Anchor Chart.

Show students the illustration on pages 11–12 of *That Book Woman*. Ask the class to make a list of the people and things that they see on the page.

✔ As an independent task, students complete Handout 22A: Adding Adjectives to Nouns. Students choose adjectives from the Adjectives Anchor Chart to add to the common nouns on the handout.

Use Equity Sticks to choose volunteers to share some of the adjectives they added to their nouns.

Land

Instruct students to Think-Pair-Share, and ask: "How do adjectives help us describe the setting of a text?"

Use Equity Sticks to select two pairs to share their thinking. Use their responses to reinforce that adjectives describe nouns that make up the setting in the text we are reading. Explain that students will continue to learn about adjectives and how to use them in their writing.

Name:

Handout 22A: Adding Adjectives to Nouns

Directions: Choose an adjective from the Adjective Chart to add to each common noun.

the _____ checkers

the _____ dress

the _____ chickens

the _____ books

WIT & WISDOM™   G1 > M1 > Lesson 23

■ FOCUSING QUESTION: LESSONS 23-27

How can books change my life?

| 1 | 2 | 3 | 4 | 5 | 6 | 7 | 8 | 9 | 10 | 11 | 12 | 13 | 14 | 15 | 16 | 17 | 18 | 19 | 20 | 21 | 22 | **23** | **24** | **25** | **26** | **27** | 28 | 29 | 30 | 31 | 32 |

Lesson 23

TEXTS

- *Museum ABC*, The Metropolitan Museum of Art
- *Green Eggs and Ham*, Dr. Seuss

Copyright © 2016 Great Minds®

G1 > M1 > Lesson 23   WIT & WISDOM™

Lesson 23: At a Glance

AGENDA

Welcome (10 min.)

Notice and Wonder in Museum ABC

Launch (5 min.)

Understand the Content Framing Question

Learn (50 min.)

New-Read Assessment (15 min.)

Notice and Wonder (15 min.)

Generate Questions and Answers (20 min.)

Land (5 min.)

Answer the Content Framing Question

Wrap (5 min.)

Assign Fluency Homework

Style and Conventions Deep Dive: Interrogative Sentences (15 min.)

STANDARDS ADDRESSED

The full text of ELA Standards can be found in the Module Overview.

Reading

- RL.1.1, RL.1.2, RL.1.3, RL.1.7

Writing

- W.1.8

Speaking and Listening

- SL.1.1a, SL.1.1b

Language

- L.1.1b, L.1.1.j, L1.2.b
- ⬇ L.1.1.j

MATERIALS

- Handout 23A: New-Read Story Map
- Handout 1A: Notice and Wonder Prompt Cards
- Wonder Wheel
- Sticky notes
- Blank Questions and Answers Chart
- Handout 23B: Fluency Homework
- Handout 23C: Mixed Sentences

Learning Goals

Generate and answer questions about *Green Eggs and Ham* using key details from the text. (RL.1.1)

✔ Contribute to Questions and Answers Chart.

Write and draw to identify story elements in *Green Eggs and Ham*. (RL.1.2, RL.1.3, RL.1.7, W.1.8, L.1.1b, L.1.1.f, L.1.1.j, L.1.2.b)

✔ Complete a New-Read Assessment.

⬇ Recognize and define interrogative sentences. (L.1.1.j)

✔ Identify interrogative sentences.

Copyright © 2016 Great Minds®   ✔ Checks for Understanding

WIT & WISDOM™   G1 > M1 > Lesson 23

Prepare

FOCUSING QUESTION: Lessons 23–27

How can books change my life?

CONTENT FRAMING QUESTION: Lesson 23

Wonder: *What do I notice and wonder about* Green Eggs and Ham?

Continuing their work with *Museum ABC*, students notice and wonder about different artwork. They continue noticing and wondering as they listen to a new text, *Green Eggs and Ham*. Students explore *Green Eggs and Ham* with a New-Read Assessment, where they fill out a Story Map individually for the first time. They also experience partner reading as they notice and wonder about different sections of this accessible text. The purpose of using this text is to have students experience a similar transformation from a book as the characters in the previous three books experienced. Students delight in this book and begin to consider how its powerful central message can transform their lives.

Welcome 10 MIN.

Provide each pair with a new spread of the pages in *Museum ABC*.

TEACHER NOTE	With each new opportunity to notice and wonder with *Museum ABC* spreads, be sure you give each pair a new page. By rotating pages, it keeps the content fresh.

Display the Content Framing Question.

Echo Read the Content Framing Question for *Museum ABC*: "What do you notice and wonder about your page of *Museum ABC*?"

In pairs, students look at the different artworks on the page and share what they notice with the Sentence Frame: I notice _____.

- *I notice a huge, gold bug.*
- *I notice a peacock with its tail open.*
- *I notice two people trying to cut down a tree.*
- *I notice someone standing in the rain.*

Two or three students share their responses with the whole group.

275

Copyright © 2016 Great Minds®

G1 > M1 > Lesson 23   WIT & WISDOM™

Remind students that the things the students said they saw in the picture are called details, and details can help us understand more about the painting.

Ask: "When you think about the details you found, what do you wonder about the painting on your page?"

Ask a student to remind the class of what they do when they wonder about a painting.

Remind students that wonders should come in the form of a question and that they can use their question words from the Wonder Wheel to help them.

Students respond to different artworks on the page using the Sentence Frame: **I wonder: _____?**

- *I wonder: What kind of bug is it?*
- *I wonder: Where is the peacock?*
- *I wonder: Why are the trees so tall and bare?*
- *I wonder: Where is the person with the umbrella going?*

Two or three new students share their responses with the whole group.

Explain that next, students will use noticing and wondering to enjoy a new book.

Launch 5 MIN.

UNDERSTAND THE CONTENT FRAMING QUESTION

Post the Content Framing Question and Focusing Question. Echo Read the Focusing Question.

Ask: "What does it mean for something to be *famous*?" Volunteers respond.

Affirm that *famous* means "well-known," or known by a lot of people. Explain that students will now begin reading a famous book that they may be familiar with. Point out that the new Focusing Question is posed to students rather than of a character.

Students Pair-Share to recall: "What do we do ask ourselves when we read a new book?" Call on volunteers to respond.

- *We notice things about the book.*
- *We wonder and ask questions about the book.*

Affirm that students notice and wonder about a book when they first read it. Echo Read the Content Framing Question.

276

Copyright © 2016 Great Minds®

Learn 50 MIN.

NEW-READ ASSESSMENT

Individuals 15 MIN.

Students demonstrate what they've learned about story elements through a New-Read Assessment.

Distribute Handout 23A: New-Read Story Map. Students listen to *Green Eggs and Ham*, following along with the print as the story is read.

✔ Students independently write and illustrate to complete all story elements on the Story Map.

✔ Meet with students individually. Provide them with a set of Story Stones. Students recall information from *Green Eggs and Ham* for each Story Stone. Alternatively, students can also rehearse this with a partner before filling in the Story Map.

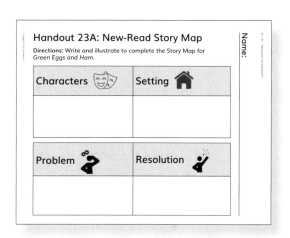

| TEACHER NOTE | This assessment may be done while students are working on independent work, or throughout the day. The assessment has two parts, one: collecting the student's Story Map, and, two: the individual conversations with each student. |

NOTICE AND WONDER

Individuals 15 MIN.

| TEACHER NOTE | Read this book with excitement and joy to demonstrate how a book comes to life. Pay special attention to the sounds of the words and the fantastical illustrations. Read the text dramatically before students respond to questions, so that students can experience the exciting nature of the text.

Students will notice and wonder about *Green Eggs and Ham* more independently than with previous texts. With its simple words and illustrations, and an initial read aloud during the New-Read Assessment, students should be able to demonstrate growing independence. |

G1 > M1 > Lesson 23

Display and reference the Speaking and Listening Anchor Chart.

💬 Students retrieve their Notice and Wonder Prompt Cards from Handout 1A: Notice and Wonder Prompt Cards.

Ask: "Why is important to Notice and Wonder when we read a text?" Volunteers respond.

Affirm that noticing and wondering help readers notice details and ask questions, and that both of these help them better understand what they are reading.

Use Equity Sticks to select a few students to demonstrate the procedure for using the Notice and Wonder Prompt Cards.

Read aloud the text without interruptions. Students stand up with the Notice Prompt Card when they notice details and stand with the Wonder Prompt Card when they wonder about the story.

Students Think-Pair-Share: "What is one thing you noticed? What is one thing you wondered?" Circulate to observe pairs sharing their notices and wonders. Explain that students will now share even more wonders about *Green Eggs and Ham.*

> **Alternate Activity**
>
> Students only use the Notice Prompt Card in the above activity, saving all questions for the next learning segment.

GENERATE AND ANSWER QUESTIONS

Pairs 20 MIN.

Explain that the class will Jigsaw the text to wonder about it. Pairs will read an assigned section of the text and come up with questions using any question word.

TEACHER NOTE	If students tend to use the same question words, you may wish to assign two to three question words to each pair to ensure variety.

Display the Wonder Wheel and call on volunteers to review how to ask questions with each word.

- Who *questions tell you about people.*
- What *questions tell you about specific information.*
- Where *questions tell you about places or locations.*

Copyright © 2016 Great Minds®

WIT & WISDOM™   G1 > M1 > Lesson 23

- When *questions tell you about a time.*
- Why *questions tell you about a reason or explanation for something.*
- How *questions tell you about the way something is.*

Remind students that using a variety of question words, especially those that they do not use that often, help them better understand the text. Encourage students to challenge themselves as they ask questions in this lesson.

Extension

Have students count, mark, or tally the various question words they use. Circulate and record anecdotal notes to inform your small group planning.

Assign pairs sections of approximately six pages each. For example:

- 3–11
- 12–17
- 18–23
- 24–29
- 30–35
- 36–41
- 42–47
- 48–57
- 58–62

✔ Students partner-read their assigned sections and generate as may text-based questions as they can.

Differentiation

In *Green Eggs and Ham*, the text changes position and is surrounded by illustrations. Students working with dyslexia, eye tracking, and other reading issues may have problems following the text. To support these students during independent reading, cover the illustrations with a sticky note but allow students to peek at the illustrations for clues about the text. Some students may benefit from a Word Window. To make a Word Window, cut a slit in a piece of paper big enough to read a few lines of text. The paper will cover the rest of the page.

Post six charts, each with a different question word: *who, what, where, when, why,* and *how.* Students Echo Read the charts.

Call on all pairs, at least twice, to share their questions with the whole group. Record questions on sticky notes and give them to students. Pairs write their names on the back of the sticky notes for assessment purposes.

Working one chart at a time, read the question word aloud. Pairs listen for the question word(s) they used, raising their hands when they hear it. Pairs place their sticky note(s) on the appropriate chart.

279

Copyright © 2016 Great Minds®

G1 > M1 > Lesson 23   WIT & WISDOM™

Repeat the process for all five charts.

Read the text aloud again, as students listen for answers to their questions.

✔ Students stand up when they hear the answers to their questions. When they stand, flag the page in your copy of the text with a sticky note and record initials of some standing students.

After finishing the story, return to the flagged pages. Call on a student who stood up for that page to respond to a question on one of the question charts. As needed, reread that section of the text to confirm and clarify students' thinking. Record the answer on the relevant sticky note and return the sticky note to the question chart.

If there are any unanswered questions, explain that students will revisit the chart after they've had more time to explore the text to answer the remaining questions.

At a later time, transfer the sticky notes to a Questions and Answers Chart, choosing strong text-based questions. Place sticky notes across the chart to indicate the extent to which each question has been answered.

GREEN EGGS AND HAM QUESTIONS AND ANSWERS CHART

Questions ?	Answers in progress ⬅➡	Complete answers ✔
▪ (Q1) Who are the characters in the book? ▪ (Q2) Why is the man angry? ▪ (Q3) When does the man decide he likes green eggs and ham? ▪ (Q4) How does Sam-I-am get the main to try green eggs and ham? ▪ (Q5) What is the man's name? ▪ (Q6) Where does the man finally try green eggs and ham?	▪ (Q1) The main characters are Sam-I-am and another man.	▪ (Q6) The man tries green eggs and ham in the ocean.

In future lessons, continue to display the Questions and Answers Chart and allow students to revisit their questions as they work with the text.

Extension

Students label one page in their Response Journals with an "N" for things they notice, and another page with a "W" for things they wonder. Students draw or write sentences about what they notice and wondered about on the pages. Students Think-Pair-Share their entries.

280

Copyright © 2016 Great Minds®

Land 10 MIN.

ANSWER THE CONTENT FRAMING QUESTION

Wonder: *What do I wonder and notice in* Green Eggs and Ham?

Students Mix and Mingle about what they noticed and wondered. Consider playing music as students move and prompt them to stop and find a partner when the music stops. Circulate to listen to students.

Call on one or two volunteers to share their notices with the whole group, and one or two students to share their wonders with the whole group.

- *I notice how Sam-I-am keeps offering the man the green eggs and ham in different ways.*
- *I wonder why the man doesn't like Sam-I-am in the beginning of the story.*
- *I wonder why the man finally changed his mind about trying green eggs and ham.*

Celebrate the great notices and wonders the students surfaced. Remind students that in the lessons to come, they will have many more chances to find answers to the wonderful questions they asked as they read the book even more closely.

Wrap 5 MIN.

ASSIGN FLUENCY HOMEWORK

Continue home reading routine. Collect Fluency Homework handouts from lessons 17–22, and distribute Handout 23B: Fluency Homework, reminding students to share the new text with their family. Explain that the new text is a passage from *Green Eggs and Ham.*

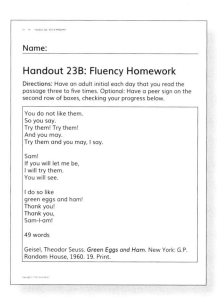

G1 > M1 > Lesson 23

Analyze

Context and Alignment

Students write and illustrate to retell key events in *Green Eggs and Ham* (RL.1.2, RL.1.3, RL.1.7, W.1.8, L.1.1b, L.1.1.f, L.1.1.j, L1.2.b). Check for the following success criteria:

- Draws and writes the setting, character(s), and event(s) from the text.
- Retells the story using Story Stones or their Story Map.

Next Steps

If students do not draw and write details about the setting, characters, and events, help them add details in just one of those categories. Provide additional support to students by underwriting, scribing or using Sentence Frames to assist with writing.

WIT & WISDOM™   G1 > M1 > Lesson 23

⬇ Lesson 23: Style and Conventions Deep Dive

Interrogative Sentences

- **Time:** 15 min.

- **Text:** *Green Eggs and Ham*, Dr. Seuss

- **Style and Conventions Learning Goal:** Recognize and define interrogative sentences. (L.1.1.j)

- **STYLE AND CONVENTIONS CRAFT QUESTION:** Lesson 23
  Experiment: *What is an interrogative sentence?*

Launch

Display and read the Craft Question: *What is an interrogative sentence?*

Students Echo Read the question. Explain that they will learn more about sentences and how to recognize different types.

Learn

Explain that one of the things that Dr. Seuss is famous for is his great writing. Explain that students will now look at a few famous Dr. Seuss lines.

Write the following sentences on the board:

- Do you like green eggs and ham?

- Would you eat them in a box?

- Could you, would you on a train?

Ask students if they notice anything about the writer's craft that the sentences have in common. List relevant observations.

TEACHER NOTE	A relevant observation would be anything that the students notice about the writer's craft, not the content. Relevant observations should focus in on what the sentences have in common that is not present in all other sentences. For example, the fact that the three sentences all begin with a capital letter and end with end punctuation would not be relevant, as these conditions apply to all sentences.

Share that this lesson's Grammar Safari focus is interrogative sentences. Explain that interrogative sentences are sentences that ask something. Interrogative sentences are sentences that interrogate, or ask questions.

283

Copyright © 2016 Great Minds®

Explain that students will work together to find "creatures that look like this."

Say: "There's a name for these creatures: we call them interrogative sentences."

Ask: "What do we notice about these interrogative sentences?"

Use Equity Sticks to choose volunteers to share their answers.

- They all have a special mark at the end.
- They are asking a question.

Students work in pairs to formulate a hypothesis about what an interrogative sentence is. Capture their answers to use for the definition later in the lesson.

Students continue to work in pairs to go on a safari through the text, collecting specimens of interrogative sentences, writing down the ones they find. After each pair has found at least one example, write the examples on chart paper.

Lead the class in an examination of the "specimens." Students Think-Pair-Share to answer the following questions: "What do all of them have in common? Do any of them not belong? Do we need to add, change, or delete anything in our hypothesis about what an interrogative sentence is?"

Use Equity Sticks to choose volunteers to share their thinking. Capture their answers and develop a definition for interrogative sentences using their thinking.

✔ Distribute Handout 23C: Mixed Sentences to each pair. Echo Read all the sentences together to ensure students know what each sentence says. Have students work together to circle the sentences that are interrogative sentences based on the class definition.

- Why does Sam-I-am always appear?
- The main character is quite grumpy.
- Just try them already!
- Green eggs and ham look delicious to me.
- Where did the fox come from?
- Use Equity Sticks to choose volunteers to share which sentences they chose as the interrogative sentences. Have students give a Nonverbal Signal to show whether they agree or disagree. If students disagree, refer back to the class definition to determine who is correct.

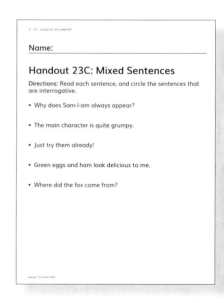

WIT & WISDOM™   G1 > M1 > Lesson 23

Land

Instruct students to Think-Pair-Share, and ask: "What is an interrogative sentence?"

Use Equity Sticks to select two pairs to share their thinking. Use their responses to reinforce that interrogative sentences ask a question. Explain that students will continue to learn about sentences and sentence types and how to use them in their writing.

WIT & WISDOM™   G1 > M1 > Lesson 24

■ FOCUSING QUESTION: LESSONS 23-27

How can books change my life?

| 1 | 2 | 3 | 4 | 5 | 6 | 7 | 8 | 9 | 10 | 11 | 12 | 13 | 14 | 15 | 16 | 17 | 18 | 19 | 20 | 21 | 22 | **23** | **24** | **25** | **26** | **27** | 28 | 29 | 30 | 31 | 32 |

Lesson 24

TEXTS

- *Museum ABC*, The Metropolitan Museum of Art
- *Green Eggs and Ham*, Dr. Seuss

Copyright © 2016 Great Minds®

G1 > M1 > Lesson 24

Lesson 24: At a Glance

AGENDA

Welcome (10 min.)

Find Details in Museum ABC

Launch (3 min.)

Understand the Content Framing Question

Learn (55 min.)

Identify the Story Elements (20 min.)

Dramatize the Problem and Resolution (15 min.)

Retell the Story (10 min.)

Examine Sequenced Events (10 min.)

Land (5 min.)

Answer the Content Framing Question

Wrap (2 min.)

Assign Fluency Homework

Vocabulary Deep Dive: Words Around Text (15 min.)

STANDARDS ADDRESSED

The full text of ELA Standards can be found in the Module Overview.

Reading

- RL.1.3

Speaking and Listening

- SL.1.1a, SL.1.1b

Language

- ⬇ L.1.6

MATERIALS

- Handout 23A: New-Read Story Map
- *Green Eggs and Ham* Story Map
- Word cards *first, next, last*
- Time Order Words Anchor Chart
- Handout 24A: Art Vocabulary

Learning Goals

Retell *Green Eggs and Ham*, including details about characters, settings, and major events. (RL.1.3)

✔ Create tableaux for the problem and resolution of the story.

⬇ Use sentence level context as a clue to the meaning of the words *portrait*, *landscape*, and *still life*. (L.1.6)

✔ Find text evidence to support vocabulary.

✔ Checks for Understanding

Copyright © 2016 Great Minds®

WIT & WISDOM™   G1 › M1 › Lesson 24

Prepare

FOCUSING QUESTION: Lessons 23-27

How can books change my life?

CONTENT FRAMING QUESTION: Lesson 24

Organize: *What is happening in* Green Eggs and Ham?

CRAFT QUESTION: Lesson 24

Examine: *Why is retelling events in sequence important?*

Students learn about subject matter to help organize what is happening in select paintings in *Museum ABC*. This segues to a review of the story elements from their New-Read Assessment to help understand the text, *Green Eggs and Ham*. Students use their bodies to create tableaux representing the problem and resolution in the text, gaining greater understanding of what is happening in the story and how the main character changes throughout the text. Then, they orally retell the story and learn about the importance of retelling events in sequence. Students learn temporal words to use in their future retellings.

Welcome 10 MIN.

FIND DETAILS IN *MUSEUM ABC*

Provide table groups with spreads of the pages C, I, O, P in *Museum ABC*. Display the Content Framing Question.

Echo Read the Content Framing Question about the art: What is happening in the artwork on your page of *Museum ABC*?

Students respond to the following TDQ in pairs or small groups.

1   **What is the same about all four pictures on your page?**

- *All the pictures have cats. (Letter C)*
- *All the pictures have bugs. (Letter I)*
- *All four pictures have cows. (Letter O)*
- *The pictures all have birds. (Letter P)*
- *Wow! All of our pictures are about animals.*

289

Copyright © 2016 Great Minds®

G1 > M1 > Lesson 24   WIT & WISDOM™

Circulate to check for understanding. If needed as a scaffold, ask students what they see in the pictures.

Choose one or two students to share their responses with the whole group. Highlight that even though different tables have different pictures, there is one thing that is true for all of the pictures: they are all about the same *subject matter*. Explain that the *subject matter* of a painting is what the painting is about. Ask: "What subject matter are all these pictures about?" Students respond in a loud whisper.

Affirm that the pictures are all about animals, so the subject matter is animals.

Share that one way to describe a painting is to discuss the *subject matter* of the painting, or what the artist chose to paint. A subject can be general, like animals, or more specific, like peacocks.

2 What details in your pictures show the subject matter of the painting?

- *This picture shows an orange cat licking its paw. (Letter C)*
- *This picture shows a really big insect walking on a plant. (Letter I)*
- *I see two oxen working in a field with a man. (Letter O)*
- *One detail is that the picture shows a blue and white pattern on the tail of a big bird. (Letter P)*

Choose one or two students to share their responses with the whole group.

Students Think-Pair-Share: "What is happening in the artwork on your page of *Museum ABC*?"

- *The subject matter of my page of* Museum ABC *is all about cats.*
- *All the artwork on my page of* Museum ABC *shows different pictures on the same subject matter: oxen.*

Choose one or two students to share their responses with the whole group.

Share that the subject matter in a work of art helps you understand what the art is all about. Explain that next, students will try to answer a similar question about *Green Eggs and Ham* (Which has animals in it, too!), and that finding details will help them understand the story.

290

Copyright © 2016 Great Minds®

Launch

UNDERSTAND THE CONTENT FRAMING QUESTION

Post the Content Framing Question and Focusing Question.

Students Echo Read the Content Framing Question.

Volunteers respond: "What are the story elements on the Story Map?"

- Characters *are the people or animals in a story.*
- Settings *are where and when the story takes place.*
- Events *are the things happening in the story.*
- Problem *is something that is a source of trouble or worry.*
- Resolution *is the answer or solution to the problem.*

Call on volunteers to respond: "According to our Content Framing Question, what will we focus on?"

- *This question will help us focus on important information in the book,* Green Eggs and Ham.

Explain that students will now show everything they have learned about how story elements help them know what is happening in a story.

Learn

IDENTIFY THE STORY ELEMENTS

Small Groups 20 MIN.

Explain students will show what they have learned by first reviewing the story elements on their handout completed during the New-Read Assessment. They will use a different colored pencil when adding or changing any information so their edits are visible.

Students retrieve Handout 23A: New-Read Story Map. Display a *Green Eggs and Ham* Story Map.

Scaffold

Use Story Stones as support for determining each story element.

Students Think-Pair-Share: "Who are the main characters in this text, and how do you know?"

- *The main characters are Sam-I-am and the man.*
- *They are the main characters because they show up the most in the story.*

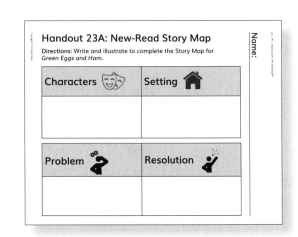

| TEACHER NOTE | There are a lot of different characters in this book, but most of them are not critical to the story. For the purposes of this text, students will only focus on the main characters. |

Call on two to three volunteers to share the main characters before adding them to the class Story Map. Other students participate with a Nonverbal Signal, such as thumbs-up/thumbs-down.

Students use a different colored pencil to add or change information on their Story Maps.

Explain that to determine the settings, small groups will Jigsaw the following assigned sections:

- Pages 18–19 (house)
- Pages 22–23 (box)
- Pages 26–27 (car)
- Pages 28–29 (tree)
- Pages 32–33 (train)
- Pages 44–45 (boat)
- Pages 50–51 (ocean)

Ask small groups: "What is the setting on your assigned pages?" Students determine the setting on their page spread.

Ask each group to share the setting they recorded before recording the final answer on the class Story Map. Students use a different colored pencil to add or change information on their Story Maps.

Explain the class will find out the problem and resolution as a whole group.

Read aloud pages 9–16. Students Think-Pair-Share: "What is the problem or what challenges the man in the story?"

WIT & WISDOM™   G1 > M1 > Lesson 24

As pairs work, circulate to listen to their discussions and add refined responses to the class Story Map. Share students' good ideas you overheard and recorded on the class Story Map.

Remind students to listen for when the problem changes, and indicate this by raising their hand and shaking it. Read pages 53–57 aloud.

Explain that the problem changes when the man finally changes his mind and decides he will try green eggs and ham if it means Sam-I-am will leave him alone. Record details under the column with an arrow between problem and resolution.

Read aloud pages 58–62. Students Think-Pair-Share: "What is the resolution or the end of the problem in the story?"

As pairs work, circulate to listen to their discussions and add refined responses to the class Story Map. Share students' good ideas you overheard and recorded on the class Story Map. Students use a different colored pencil to add or change information on their Story Maps.

GREEN EGGS AND HAM STORY MAP

Characters		Setting	
• *the man (drawing of the man)* • *Sam-I-am (drawing of Sam-I-am)*		• House *(drawing of a house)* • Box *(drawing of a box)* • Tree *(drawing of a tree)* • Train *(drawing of a train)* • Boat *(drawing of a boat)* • Ocean *(drawing of an ocean)*	
Problem			**Resolution**
• *The man doesn't like Sam-I-am and doesn't want to try green eggs and ham. (drawing of green eggs and ham with an X through it)*	**The man changes his mind and finally decides he will try green eggs and ham if it means Sam-I-am will leave him alone.** (drawing of green eggs and ham with a question mark above it)		• *The man tries green eggs and ham and likes them. He thanks Sam-I-am for encouraging him to try green eggs and ham. (drawing of a green eggs and ham with a heart around it)*

293

Copyright © 2016 Great Minds®

G1 > M1 > Lesson 24   WIT & WISDOM™

DRAMATIZE THE PROBLEM AND RESOLUTION

Small Groups 15 MIN.

A volunteer reminds the class of the Content Framing Question as you assign small groups either problem or resolution. Explain groups will make tableaux, or pose, to show their assigned story element, helping them answer the Content Framing Question.

✔ Small groups develop tableaux for problem or resolution.

  ▪ *(Problem: One student poses as the man frowning with his hand out as if refusing. The other student poses as Sam-I-am extending his arms as if offering green eggs and ham.)*

  ▪ *(Resolution: One student poses as the man smiling with one hand pretending to hold a plate and the other hand pretending to eat with a fork. The other student poses as Sam-I-am smiling at the man.)*

Circulate to observe students demonstrating the problem and resolution.

Ask students: "What do you notice about the main character from making tableaux of the problem and resolution?" If needed, follow up with: "How does the main character change?" Call on volunteers for responses.

  ▪ *The problem at the beginning of the story is that the man doesn't like Sam-I-am and doesn't want to try green eggs and ham.*

  ▪ *The resolution at the end of the story is that the man discovers he likes green eggs and ham and is thankful to Sam-I-am.*

Use student responses to reinforce how the main character changed through the problem and resolution: at first the man didn't like Sam-I-am and didn't want to try green eggs and ham. After Sam-I-am kept asking him, he finally gave in and found out he liked green eggs and ham.

Extension

Expand understanding of the main character's transformation by focusing on how his feelings toward Sam-I-am changed.

Students Think-Pair-Share: "What did you notice about how the man's feelings toward Sam-I-am changed from the beginning, middle, and end of the story? Use evidence from the text to support your answer."

  ▪ *At the beginning of the story, the man doesn't like Sam-I-am. On page 9, he says "I do not like that Sam-I-am," and he is frowning.*

  ▪ *In the middle of the story, Sam-I-am keeps bothering the man by repeatedly asking whether he likes green eggs and ham in different ways, like on page 26 he asks "Would you? Could you? In a car?" Then the man is so annoyed that he finally agrees to try green eggs and ham so Sam-I-am will leave him alone. On page 54, he says, "If you will let me be, I will try them."*

  ▪ *At the end of the story, he likes Sam-I-am and is very grateful to him. On page 62, he says "Thank you! Thank you, Sam-I-am!" and he is smiling with his arm is around Sam-I-am.*

294

Copyright © 2016 Great Minds®

WIT & WISDOM™   G1 > M1 > Lesson 24

RETELL THE STORY

Pairs 10 MIN.

Explain that now that students understand all the story elements, they will retell the story to each other with these elements in mind.

Ask: "What do we do when we retell a story?" Use probing questions to support volunteers in building on other students' responses, reinforcing that retellings are the important things that happened in a story.

Pairs take turns orally retelling the story, including key details about the characters, settings, problem, and resolution. Students flip through the text for picture support as they retell the story.

> ▪ *The man doesn't like Sam-I-am. Sam-I-am keeps trying to get him to try green eggs and ham. The man doesn't want to try green eggs and ham anywhere. He doesn't want to eat them in a house, box, tree, train, boat, or the ocean. Finally the man gets tired of Sam-I-am offering him green eggs and ham so he decides to try them so Sam-I-am will leave him alone. The man tries green eggs and ham and finds out that he likes them a lot and would eat them anywhere. The man thanks Sam-I-am for helping him try green eggs and ham.*

Circulate to listen as students orally retell the story to a partner.

EXAMINE: RETELLING EVENTS IN SEQUENCE

Whole Group 10 MIN.

Read aloud the Craft Question: "Why is retelling events in sequence important?"

Display and Echo Read the following sentences:

- Sam-I-am tried green eggs and ham.
- Sam-I-am did not like green eggs and ham.
- Sam-I-am liked green eggs and ham.

Explain that sequenced events in a story make sense. Ask: "Do these events make sense?" Students stand if the events do not make sense and stay seated if they do.

Display the word cards *first*, *next*, and *last*.

Think Aloud about what happened first in the story. Model and share finding the event in the text. Place the word *first* and the sentence at the top of the board. Repeat the procedure for the remaining sentences using Equity Sticks to call on students to select the sentences that go next and last.

295

Copyright © 2016 Great Minds®

Choral Read the sequenced sentences. Students use Nonverbal Signals to indicate if the sentences make sense.

Explain that writers use specific words to sequence events. *First*, *next* and *last* are temporal, or time order, words. Time order words are used at the beginning, middle, and end of texts. Place the word cards on the Time Order Words Anchor Chart.

TIME ORDER WORDS ANCHOR CHART

Time Order Words		
beginning	middle	end
first	next	last

Revisit the Craft Question. Students Think-Pair-Share: Why is retelling events in sequence important? Partners share their responses with the whole group, using the following Sentence Frame: **Retelling events in sequence is important because** _____. Use Equity Sticks to select three student responses.

Land 5 MIN.

ANSWER THE CONTENT FRAMING QUESTION

Organize: *What is happening in* Green Eggs and Ham?

Students Think-Pair-Share on the Content Framing Question.

Invite two or three students to share a single sentence that describes what this book is about.

Wrap 2 MIN.

HOMEWORK CHECK-IN

Continue home reading routine. Check Fluency Homework from the previous lesson and remind students what to do for fluency homework tonight.

Analyze

Context and Alignment

Students retell *Green Eggs and Ham*, including details about characters, settings, and major events. (RL.1.3)

Each student:

- Participates in a tableau scene depicting the problem or resolution of the story.
- Accurately shares events from the story with a partner.
- Retells events from the story in correct chronological order.

Next Steps

If students had difficulty retelling events from the story, return to the text with small groups of students. Model how to retell events from the first section of the story, using illustrations from the text for support. Have students take turns using illustrations to retell events from the next section of the story, providing feedback and support as needed.

↓ Lesson 24: Vocabulary Deep Dive

Words Around Text

- **Time:** 15 min.
- **Text:** *Museum ABC*, The Metropolitan Museum of Art
- **Vocabulary Learning Goal:** Use sentence level context as a clue to the meaning of the words *portrait*, *landscape*, and *still life*. (L.1.6)

Launch

Display the page H is for Hair from *Museum ABC*. Students Think-Pair-Share what they see on the page and what the pictures have in common with one another.

Use Equity Sticks to choose volunteers to share their thinking about the page.

- *They are all pictures of people.*
- *All the pictures show their head.*

Explain that students will learn new words to describe different kinds of art and that this type of picture is called a *portrait*.

Learn

Display the words *portrait*, *landscape*, and *still life*. Explain these three words are related to one another. Students Think-Pair-ShareThink-Pair-Share about how they think the words relate to one another. Choose volunteers to share their thinking. Affirm correct answers and guide students to the conclusion that they are different types of paintings.

Display a graphic organizer like the following and write different types of art in the outside circle. Write each vocabulary word in a circle coming off the main circle.

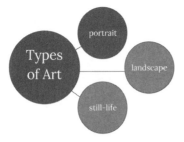

Display the page H is for Hair. Remind students of the things they decided the pictures had in common. Students Think-Pair-Share: "What do you think the word portrait means by looking at these pictures in the book?" Use Equity Sticks to choose volunteers to share their thinking.

- *People's heads*
- *A painting*
- *People's faces*

Tell students that the word *portrait* does mean a painting, drawing, or photograph of only someone's face, head and shoulders. Write this next to the circle on the graphic organizer.

Painting, drawing, or photograph of a person's face, head and shoulders

Display the page T is for Tree. Students Think-Pair-Share what these pictures all have in common. Students should recognize that all the pictures have trees and land in them. Display the page U is for Umbrella. Students Think-Pair Share what these pictures all have in common. Students should recognize that all the pictures have natural objects or scenery in them. Explain this type of art is called *landscape*.

Students Think-Pair-Share to answer the question: "Why do you think this type of art would be called *landscape*?"

- *The pictures have land in them.*
- *The pictures have things in nature in them.*

Explain that *landscape* is a type of art that has natural scenery such as mountains, valleys, trees, rivers, and forests, and it is usually a wide view of the scenery. Add the definition for landscape to the graphic organizer.

Painting, drawing, or photograph of a person's face, head and shoulders

Art that has natural scenery such as mountains, valleys, trees, rivers, and forests

Display the page V is for Vegetable. Students Think-Pair-Share what these pictures all have in common.

Students should recognize that all the pictures are of vegetables. Tell them these are *still life* pictures. Display the page E is for Egg for students to see and explain that the first three pictures are *still life* pictures as well. Display the page R is for Rose for students to see and explain that these are *still life* pictures as well. Students Think-Pair-Share what all these pictures have in common. Use Equity Sticks to choose volunteers to share their thinking.

- *All things that can't move.*
- *Things we find at our house.*

Explain that *still life* is a picture that has mostly things that don't move and are usually common things that can be from nature, such as food, plants, flowers, rocks. The pictures can also be of man-made things that don't move, such as books, jewelry, coins, and vases. Add the definition for *still life* to the graphic organizer.

Painting, drawing, or photograph of a person's face, head and shoulders

Art that has natural scenery such as mountains, valleys, trees, rivers, and forests

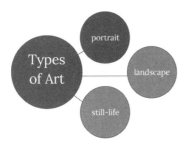

A picture that has mostly things that don't move and are usually common things such as food, or plants.

✔ Students work with a partner to go on a hunt to find at least one piece of "text evidence" for each type of art. When they find an example they write it on Handout 24A: Art Vocabulary to record their evidence.

Land

Use Equity Sticks to choose volunteers to share their favorite type of art and the example of text evidence they found for that type of art.

WIT & WISDOM™

G1 > M1 > Lesson 25

■ **FOCUSING QUESTION: LESSONS 23-27**

How can books change my life?

| 1 | 2 | 3 | 4 | 5 | 6 | 7 | 8 | 9 | 10 | 11 | 12 | 13 | 14 | 15 | 16 | 17 | 18 | 19 | 20 | 21 | 22 | 23 | 24 | 25 | 26 | 27 | 28 | 29 | 30 | 31 | 32 |

Lesson 25

TEXT

- *Green Eggs and Ham*, Dr. Seuss

Copyright © 2016 Great Minds®

G1 > M1 > Lesson 25   WIT & WISDOM™

Lesson 25: At a Glance

AGENDA

Welcome (5 min.)

Launch (5 min.)

Understand the Content Framing Question

Learn (55 min.)

Analyze the Character Speaking (25 min.)

Participate in a Reader's Theater (15 min.)

Experiment with Sequencing Events (15 min.)

Land (5 min.)

Answer the Content Framing Question

Wrap (5 min.)

Assign Fluency Homework

Style and Conventions Deep Dive: Imperative Sentences (15 min.)

STANDARDS ADDRESSED

The full text of ELA Standards can be found in the Module Overview.

Reading

- RL.1.6, RL.1.7

Writing

- W.1.3

Speaking and Listening

- SL.1.1.a, SL.1.1.b

Language

- ↓ L.1.1.j

MATERIALS

- Time Order Words Anchor Chart

- Handout 25A: Sequenced Sentences

- Handout 25B: Mixed Sentences

Learning Goals

Identify who is telling the story at key points in *Green Eggs and Ham*. (RL.1.3, RL.1.6)

✔ Participate in a Reader's Theater

↓ Style and Conventions Learning Goal: Recognize and define imperative sentences. (L.1.1.j)

✔ Determine if sentences are imperative sentences.

✔ Checks for Understanding

Copyright © 2016 Great Minds®

WIT & WISDOM™   G1 > M1 > Lesson 25

Prepare

FOCUSING QUESTION: Lessons 23-27

How can books change my life?

CONTENT FRAMING QUESTION: Lesson 25

Reveal: *What does a deeper exploration of which character is speaking reveal in* Green Eggs and Ham?

CRAFT QUESTION: Lesson 25

Experiment: *How does sequencing events work?*

Students physically indicate which character is speaking in *Green Eggs and Ham* before performing a Reader's Theater using sections of the text. They read dialogue from the two main characters with expression. Through this activity they understand the back and forth nature of the dialogue and rhythm and repetition of the language.

Welcome 5 MIN.

In their Response Journals, students practice writing the key words they remember from *Green Eggs and Ham* using phonetic spelling. Then, students check the text to find the words they wrote.

Launch 5 MIN.

UNDERSTAND THE CONTENT FRAMING QUESTION

Post the Content Framing Question and Focusing Question. Students Echo Read the Content Framing Question.

Students Think-Pair-Share: "Who are the main characters in the story? Which characters speak in the story?"

- *The characters are Sam-I-am and the man.*
- *The man and Sam-I-am speak in the story.*

Tell students that with this Content Framing Question, they will be uncovering important information by looking at who is speaking in the story.

303

Copyright © 2016 Great Minds®

Learn 55 MIN.

ANALYZE THE CHARACTER SPEAKING

Whole Group 25 MIN.

Share that students will do a choral reading to try and figure out which character is speaking at different parts of the book.

Display and reference the Speaking and Listening anchor chart.

💬 Ask: "Who are the two characters in this story?" Volunteers respond.

Affirm that there are two main characters: the man and Sam-I-am. Explain that students will indicate when each character is speaking in the story by standing up when the man is speaking and sitting down when Sam-I-am is speaking as you read aloud the story.

✔ Students follow along in their copies of the text, standing up or sitting down to identify the speaker.

Ask: "How can you tell who is speaking? What do you notice about the words?"

- *I can tell it's Sam-I-am speaking because he always asks questions to the man and says "you."*
- *I can tell it's the man speaking because he always talks about himself and says "I."*
- *I know it's Sam-I-am or the man speaking because one of the characters talks and then the other responds to him.*
- *When Sam-I-am speaks he often asks a question to the man, asking if he would try green eggs and ham a different way.*
- *When the man speaks he often replies with an exclamation, showing he's annoyed at Sam-I-am.*

Explain that students will now act out the two characters in a Reader's Theater.

PARTICIPATE IN A READER'S THEATER

Small Groups 15 MIN.

Explain that groups will Jigsaw four parts of the story, reading for the man or Sam-I-am, for a Reader's Theater.

Divide the class into four groups. Assign pairs within a group a quarter of the text, approximate 15 pages, such as the sections below:

- Pages 3–17
- Pages 18–31

WIT & WISDOM™   G1 > M1 > Lesson 25

- Pages 32–47
- Pages 48–62

Pairs take turns reading aloud with one student reading as the man, and the other student reading as Sam-I-am from their assigned section. Encourage students to express the feelings of each character to make the story sound more interesting.

Circulate the room listening for pairs who are ready to read fluently and perform for the class.

Choose one pair from each section of the text to perform the dialogue between the man and Sam-I-am for the class. Pairs should read in sequential order so the book is read aloud once through.

Ask the following TDQ to help students draw on their experience with Reader's Theater to make sense of the structure and pattern of the words in the text.

1   What did you notice about the words in the text as you and your partner read them aloud?

- *I noticed that the words rhymed.*
- *It seemed like there was a rhythm to how Sam-I-am and the man spoke to each other back and forth.*
- *The words repeated. Sam-I-am would suggest something, like on page 44 "Would you, could you, on a boat?" Then the man would respond using the same words. On page 46 he said "I could not, would not, on a boat."*
- *The words repeated. Each time the man responded to Sam-I-am, he would say all the ways he didn't want to eat green eggs and ham.*

Ask: "Who are the two characters speaking in this story? What do these characters learn?" Volunteers respond.

- *The man learned that he should have just tried green eggs and ham earlier.*
- *When the man changes his mind, we learn that he actually likes them.*
- *Sam-I-am learns that trying over and over works.*

EXPERIMENT WITH SEQUENCING EVENTS

Whole Group   15 MIN.

Read the Craft Question aloud. Explain that students will experiment with sequencing events.

Remind students that writers use temporal or time order words to sequence events. Some time order words are used at the beginning of texts, and others in the middle or end.

Display and Choral Read the Sentence Frames:

It started in _____ when _____.

305

Copyright © 2016 Great Minds®

Then _____.

Finally, _____.

Remind students that they have been using the Sentence Frames to retell sequenced events in their writing as you explain that the words *then* and *finally* are time order words.

Students Think-Pair-Share: "Where have we used the word *then* in our writing? At the beginning, middle or end?" Call on two pairs to respond. Student use Nonverbal Signals to agree or disagree. Place the card under the correct heading on the anchor chart. Repeat the question for the word *finally*.

TIME ORDER WORDS ANCHOR CHART

Time Order Words		
beginning	middle	end
first	next	last
	then	finally

Display the sequenced sentences from Lesson 24 and word cards First, Next, Last, Then, Finally, and It All Started In:

- Sam did not like green eggs and ham.
- Sam tried green eggs and ham.
- Sam liked green eggs and ham.

Distribute Handout 25A: Sequenced Sentences. Echo, then Choral Read the sentences and the word cards. Students hold up each word or phrase as they Echo Read. Model the first sentence as you Think Aloud to determine a word to place at the beginning of the sentence. Reread the sentence. Ask: "Does this sentence make sense?" Students chorally respond. Tell students to choose and place one word card at the beginning of the second sentence, and another one at the beginning of the last sentence.

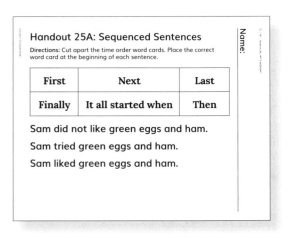

Circulate to select pairs to share their sentences. Select pairs to highlight the usage of all temporal words. Students stand if the sequenced sentences make sense. Remind students that different words can be used to sequence of events.

WIT & WISDOM™   G1 > M1 > Lesson 25

| TEACHER NOTE | Prepare the word cards on Handout 25A before the lesson.

Students may ask why the phrase "it all started in" is not on the chart. Explain that even though the words help them with writing narrative retellings, they are not considered a temporal word or phrase. Place the phrase on the outside of the chart, but in view of the students. |
| --- | --- |

Land 5 MIN.

ANSWER THE CONTENT FRAMING QUESTION

Reveal: *What does a deeper exploration of which character is speaking reveal in* Green Eggs and Ham?

- *It reveals how Sam-I-am kept trying and the man finally tried something new.*
- *Reading the voices helped us figure out which words went with which characters.*
- *It revealed how the words rhymed and repeated.*

Wrap 5 MIN.

HOMEWORK CHECK-IN

Continue home reading routine. Check Fluency Homework from the previous lesson, and remind students what to do for fluency homework tonight.

Analyze

Context and Alignment

Identify who is telling the story at key points in *Green Eggs and Ham* (RL.1.3, RL.1.6). Each student:

- Identifies the speakers.
- Participates in a Reader's Theater representing one of the voices in the text.
- Identifies the main character and what he learns.

Next Steps

If students had difficulty identifying the distinctive speakers, ask a student or colleague to conduct a Reader's Theatre of the text with you as students track the various speakers with Nonverbal Signals.

WIT & WISDOM™   G1 > M1 > Lesson 25

⬇ Lesson 25: Style and Conventions Deep Dive

Imperative Sentences

- **Time:** 15 min.

- **Text:** *Green Eggs and Ham*, Dr. Seuss

- **Style and Conventions Learning Goal:** Recognize and define imperative sentences. (L.1.1.j)

- **STYLE AND CONVENTIONS CRAFT QUESTION:** Lesson 25
  Experiment: *What is an imperative sentence?*

Launch

Display and read the Craft Question: *What is an imperative sentence?*

Students Echo Read the question. Explain that they will learn more about sentences and how to recognize different types.

Learn

Ask: "What type of sentences did we learn about already?" Volunteers respond.

Affirm that students already learned about interrogative sentences and explain that they will learn about a new type of sentence in this lesson.

Write the following sentences on the board:

- Eat them!

- Try them, and you may, I say.

Ask students if they notice anything about the writer's craft that the sentences have in common. List relevant observations.

TEACHER NOTE	A relevant observation would be anything that the students notice about the writer's craft, not the content. Relevant observations should focus in on what the sentences have in common that is not present in all other sentences. For example, the fact that the three sentences all begin with a capital letter and end with end punctuation would not be relevant, as these conditions apply to all sentences.

Share that this lesson's Grammar Safari focuses on imperative sentences. Explain that imperative sentences are sentences that demand something. Imperative sentences are often sentences that seem bossy.

309

Copyright © 2016 Great Minds®

Explain that students will work together to find "creatures that look like this."

Say: "There's a name for these creatures: we call them imperative sentences."

Ask: "What do we notice about these imperative sentences?"

Use Equity Sticks to choose volunteers to share their answers.

- They all tell someone to do something.
- One ends with an exclamation mark.

Students work in pairs to formulate a hypothesis about what an imperative sentence is. Capture their answers to use for the definition later in the lesson.

Students continue to work in pairs to go on a safari through the text, collecting specimens of imperative sentences, and writing down the ones they find. After each pair has found at least one example, write the examples on chart paper.

Lead the class in an examination of the "specimens." Students Think-Pair-Share to answer the following questions: "What do all of them have in common? Do any of them not belong? Do we need to add, change, or delete anything in our hypothesis about what an imperative sentence is?"

Use Equity Sticks to choose volunteers to share their thinking. Capture their answers and develop a definition for imperative sentences using their thinking.

✔ Distribute Handout 25B. Echo Read all the sentences together to ensure students know what each sentence says. Have students work together to circle the sentences that are interrogative sentences based on the class definition.

- Why did Sam-I-am go on the boat?
- Dr. Seuss is a great author.
- Finish your breakfast!
- The goat looks hungry.
- Don't just stand there!

Use Equity Sticks to choose volunteers to share which sentences they chose as the imperative sentences. Have students give a nonverbal signal to show whether they agree or disagree. If students disagree refer back to the class definition to determine who is correct.

WIT & WISDOM™   G1 > M1 > Lesson 25

Land

Instruct students to Think-Pair-Share, and ask: "What is an imperative sentence?"

Use Equity Sticks to select two pairs to share their thinking. Use their responses to reinforce that imperative sentences can sound bossy and sometimes have an exclamation mark at the end. Explain that students will continue to practice using the different types of sentences in their writing.

WIT & WISDOM™   G1 > M1 > Lesson 26

■ FOCUSING QUESTION: LESSONS 23-27

How can books change my life?

| 1 | 2 | 3 | 4 | 5 | 6 | 7 | 8 | 9 | 10 | 11 | 12 | 13 | 14 | 15 | 16 | 17 | 18 | 19 | 20 | 21 | 22 | 23 | 24 | 25 | 26 | 27 | 28 | 29 | 30 | 31 | 32 |

Lesson 26

TEXT

- *Green Eggs and Ham*, Dr. Seuss

Copyright © 2016 Great Minds®

G1 > M1 > Lesson 26

WIT & WISDOM™

Lesson 26: At a Glance

AGENDA

Welcome (5 min.)

Launch (5 min.)

Understand the Framing Question

Learn (55 min.)

Determine Central Message (25 min.)

Execute Sequencing Events (30 min.)

Land (5 min.)

Answer the Framing Question

Wrap (5 min.)

Homework Check-in

Style and Conventions Deep Dive: Time Order Words (15 min.)

STANDARDS ADDRESSED

The full text of ELA Standards can be found in the Module Overview.

Reading

- RL.1.2

Writing

- W.1.3, W.1.8

Speaking and Listening

- SL.1.1a, SL.1.1b

Language

- ⬇ L.1.1.i

MATERIALS

- Response Journals
- *Green Eggs and Ham* Story Map
- Time Order Words Anchor Chart
- Assessment 26: Focusing Question Task 5
- Handout 26A: Focusing Question 5 Prompt

Learning Goals

With support, determine the central message of *Green Eggs and Ham*. (RL.1.2)

✔ Write the Central Message in Response Journals.

Sequence events in a written narrative summary of *Green Eggs and Ham*. (W.1.3)

✔ Complete Focusing Question Task 5.

⬇ Identify temporal words and their use in writing. (L.1.1.i)

✔ Orally tell a story using time order words.

✔ Checks for Understanding

Copyright © 2016 Great Minds®

WIT & WISDOM™ G1 > M1 > Lesson 26

Prepare

FOCUSING QUESTION: Lessons 23-27

How can books change my life?

CONTENT FRAMING QUESTION: Lesson 26

Distill: *What is the central message of Green Eggs and Ham?*

CRAFT QUESTION: Lesson 26

Know: *How do I sequence events in writing?*

Beginning with *Green Eggs and Ham*, a text with a strong and obvious central message, students are introduced to this concept and how to determine it. They complete Assessment 26: Focusing Question Task 5 with increasing independence, using time order words to help sequence their retelling of the story.

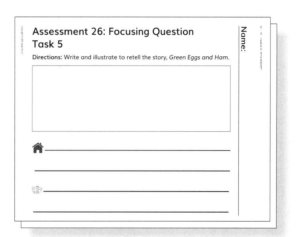

Welcome 5 MIN.

Students reread *Green Eggs and Ham* independently for enjoyment using a six-inch voice until the lesson begins.

Launch 5 MIN.

UNDERSTAND THE FRAMING QUESTION

Post the Framing Question and Focusing Question. Students Echo Read the Framing Question.

Ask students: "Are there any new words or phrases that are new to you?" Volunteers respond.

- *I wonder what "central message" means.*

G1 > M1 > Lesson 26   WIT & WISDOM™

Point to the term *central message* as you explain that students will learn a new term in this lesson. Explain that the story element of *central message* will help them describe the big idea of a text. They will find the central message of *Green Eggs and Ham* by looking closely at the words and pictures.

Learn 45 MIN.

DETERMINE CENTRAL MESSAGE

Whole Group 25 MIN.

Point again to the term *central message* and define it as "the big idea of the story." The *central message* is the lesson that the author wants us to know by reading and understanding the story, but authors don't always tell us the central message.

Tell students they will start by determining the central message starting with *Green Eggs and Ham* and will continue to explore central message in future modules.

Explain that when authors and illustrators make choices that readers really notice, or distinctive, stand-out choices, they provide clues to the central message.

Students Think-Pair-Share: "What words and illustrations stood out in *Green Eggs and Ham?*"

- *The author repeated some words. For example, the main character said he didn't like green eggs and ham.*
- *At the end, I noticed when the main character changed his words. He said the opposite—that he didn't like green eggs and ham.*
- *On page 56, the picture stood out. It doesn't have any words. It's just the main character holding the green eggs and ham.*

Record details from students' responses, placing check marks next to repeated ideas.

Read aloud the details on the chart before students Think-Pair-Share: "What idea describes all those ideas? What ties them together?"

If needed, follow up with: "What do you think the author wants us to learn from these details?"

Call on students with interesting or insightful responses to share with the class. Record the potential central messages next to the central message box in the Story Map.

- *You might think you don't like something, but just try it because you might like it!*
- *If you keep asking someone to do something, they will give in.*
- *You can change your mind after trying something.*

316

Copyright © 2016 Great Minds®

- *You have to be asked a lot of times before you want to try something.*
- *The author wants us to try new things.*
- *The author wants us to learn that you should try something before you decide about it.*

Select two to three refined options to read aloud. Students vote for the central message that best fits the text evidence by standing up for their vote. Circle the central message with the most votes on the chart.

✔ Students write the central message in their Response Journals.

- *The central message of Green Eggs and Ham is "Don't judge something until you try it."*

EXECUTE USING SEQUENCED EVENTS

Individuals 30 MIN.

Display the *Green Eggs and Ham* Story Map and the Time Order Words Anchor Chart. Explain to students they will use evidence on the charts to write a narrative retell. Remind students that their Story Map provides them with the story elements and the Time Order Words Anchor Chart helps them determine words to sequence the events.

Distribute Assessment 26: Focusing Question Task 5. Students Think-Pair-Share to discuss what story elements belong on each page. Display the booklet. Instruct students to put their finger on the icon on the first page. Ask: "What story element will you write about on the first page?" Use Equity Sticks to call on students to respond. Repeat for remaining pages.

Display and Echo Read Handout 26A: Focusing Question 5 Prompt.

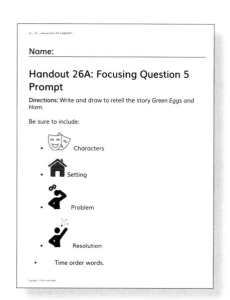

Write and draw to retell the story Green Eggs and Ham.

Be sure to include:

- *characters*
- *setting*
- *problem*
- *resolution*
- *time order words*
- *complete sentences*
- *capital letters at the beginning of a sentence and proper nouns*
- *end punctuation*
- *an adjective to describe a noun*

Pairs touch each story element icon in the booklet as they orally rehearse their retell.

G1 > M1 > Lesson 26   WIT & WISDOM™

✔ Students complete the assessment independently.

| TEACHER NOTE | Instruct students to add details to their illustrations if they finish writing before other students. |

Land 5 MIN.

ANSWER THE FRAMING QUESTION

Distill: *What is the central message of* Green Eggs and Ham?

Ask: "How did we determine the central message of *Green Eggs and Ham*?" Volunteers respond.

Affirm that students looked at ideas that stood out, or that they really noticed, in order to find the central message.

Ask: "What's one central message for this text?" Volunteers respond.

- *You should try new things because if you never tried something before you won't know if you like it or not.*
- *It is important to try something before you judge it.*

Students draw an illustration in their Response Journals to match the central message they recorded earlier. Encourage students to include details from the text in their illustrations.

318

Copyright © 2016 Great Minds®

Wrap 5 MIN.

HOMEWORK CHECK-IN

Continue home reading routine. Check Fluency Homework from the previous lesson, and remind students what to do for fluency homework tonight.

Analyze

Context and Alignment

Sequence events in a written narrative summary of *Green Eggs and Ham*. (W.1.3).

Each student:

- Retells the story in sequence.
- Uses time order words.
- Writes in complete sentences with capitalization and ending punctuation.
- Uses an adjective to describe a noun.

Next Steps

Review student writing in Focusing Question Task 5 to determine next steps for revising. Also, this module marks students' introduction to the concept of a central message. Students will continue to build this skill in Module 2 as they work with several new texts. Use the data from this assessment to determine students' miscues about identifying the central message and plan whole or small group instruction to address and correct these miscues prior to Module 2.

G1 > M1 > Lesson 26

WIT & WISDOM™

↓ Lesson 26: Style and Conventions Deep Dive

Time Order Words

- **Time:** 15 min.

- **Text:** *Green Eggs and Ham*, Dr. Seuss

- **Style and Conventions Learning Goal:** Identify temporal words and their use in writing. (L.1.1.i)

- **STYLE AND CONVENTIONS CRAFT QUESTION:** Lesson 26
  Examine: *Why are time order words important in our writing?*

Launch

Display and read the Craft Question: *Why are time order words important in our writing?*

Students Echo Read the question. Explain that they will learn more about time order words and how to use them in their writing.

Learn

Remind students of how, when they retell a story, they repeat the events in order. Display the following words:

- First

- Next

- Last

- Finally

- Then

Students Think-Pair-Share about what all these words have in common. Use Equity Sticks to choose volunteers to share their thinking. Some responses could be:

- *They are time words.*
- *They tell when things happen.*
- *They help you know when things are happening in a story.*

Explain that in this lesson students will learn more about how to use these words in a story.

Display the following events on Sentence Strips for the students:

- I put my shoes on.

- I got out of bed.

- I brushed my teeth.

320

Copyright © 2016 Great Minds®

WIT & WISDOM™   G1 > M1 > Lesson 26

Tell students that you are going to read them a short story about your morning. Read the events
in order that you have them written. Ask students the following questions and ask them to use
Nonverbal Signals, for example a thumbs-up or thumbs-down, to indicate their agreement or
disagreement with what you ask.

Does my story make sense to you?

Can you tell by my story what I did first?

Can you tell what I did last?

Students Think-Pair-Share about what they think might be missing from your story. Use Equity
Sticks to choose volunteers to share their thinking. Guide students to understand that the temporal
words, or sequence words are missing from your story.

Ask them if they remember some words from their lesson earlier that would help make the
sentences better. Have them respond using a Nonverbal Signal. Students Think-Pair-Share about
the words they remember from the craft lesson that day. Volunteers respond with words they
remember. Write student responses on a Sentence Strip or large card.

- *First*
- *Next*
- *Last*

Read the sentences again with the class and give a couple of volunteers each strip and ask them to
stand up in the order they think the story should go in. When they are in order, have students give a
Nonverbal Signal to show they agree or disagree.

- I got out of bed.

- I brushed my teeth.

- I put my shoes on.

Then, give student volunteers a card with a sequence word. Have the rest of the students direct
these students to stand in front of the sentence they think it belongs with.

- First, I got out of bed.

- Next, I brushed my teeth.

- Last, I put my shoes on.

When the students are in the correct order, reread the story to them and ask if they think it is
correct. Students give a Nonverbal Signal to show they agree or disagree.

✔ Distribute word cards with *First*, *Next*, and *Last* written on them to each pair of students. Students
work in pairs to orally tell their own story using the word cards before each event in their story.

Use Equity Sticks to choose volunteers to share a story they told their partner.

321

Copyright © 2016 Great Minds®

Land

Instruct students to Think-Pair-Share, and ask: "Why are time order words important in our writing?"

Use Equity Sticks to select two pairs to share their thinking. Use their responses to reinforce that time order words help us know when events are happening in our story. Explain that students will continue to practice using time order words in their writing.

WIT & WISDOM™   G1 > M1 > Lesson 27

■ FOCUSING QUESTION: LESSONS 23-27

How can books change my life?

1 2 3 4 5 6 7 8 9 10 11 12 13 14 15 16 17 18 19 20 21 22 **23 24 25 26 27** 28 29 30 31 32

Lesson 27

TEXTS

- *Green Eggs and Ham*, Dr. Seuss
- *Museum ABC*, The Metropolitan Museum of Art

Copyright © 2016 Great Minds®

G1 > M1 > Lesson 27

WIT & WISDOM™

Lesson 27: At a Glance

AGENDA

Welcome (10 min.)

Draft a Self Portrait

Launch (5 min.)

Understand the Content Framing Question

Learn (50 min.)

Participate in a Socratic Seminar (30 min.)

Record Knowledge (20 min.)

Land (5 min.)

Answer the Content Framing Question

Wrap (5 min.)

Assign Fluency Homework

Style and Conventions Deep Dive: Excel at Sequencing Events (15 min.)

STANDARDS ADDRESSED

The full text of ELA Standards can be found in the Module Overview.

Reading

- RL.1.1, RL.1.2

Writing

- W.1.3

Speaking and Listening

- SL.1.1a, SL.1.1b

Language

- ⬇ L.1.1.i

MATERIALS

- Speaking and Listening Anchor Chart

- Knowledge Journal

- Time Order Words Anchor Chart

- Handout 26A: Focusing Question Task 5 Booklet

Learning Goals

Respond to what others say about how books can change your lives in a Socratic Seminar. (SL.1.1.a, SL.1.1.b)

✔ Participate in a Socratic Seminar.

⬇ Identify temporal words in writing and edit writing for temporal words. (L.1.1.i)

✔ Edit writing for time order words.

✔ Checks for Understanding

Copyright © 2016 Great Minds®

WIT & WISDOM™   G1 > M1 > Lesson 27

Prepare

FOCUSING QUESTION: Lessons 23-27

How can books change my life?

CONTENT FRAMING QUESTION: Lesson 27

How can books build my knowledge?

CRAFT QUESTION: Lesson 27

How do I improve sequencing events in my writing?

Students draw the final portrait, their self-portrait, for their EOM project before they engage in a Socratic Seminar responding to the Focusing Question. Following their discussion, they record knowledge of all the new learning and knowledge they gained. They revise Focusing Question Task 5 for use of time order words in the Deep Dive.

Welcome 10 MIN.

DRAFT A SELF-PORTRAIT

Distribute blank piece of paper. Students draw a self-portrait and write a sentence answering the question: *How can books change my life?* Remind students to include details to their illustration. Collect self-portraits, or have students place it in their writing folder so it is accessible in the next lesson.

Launch 5 MIN.

UNDERSTAND THE CONTENT FRAMING QUESTION

Post the Content Framing Question and Focusing Question.

Echo Read the Content Framing Question.

Explain that students will take a closer look at how books can build their knowledge using the information they've learned about books.

325

Copyright © 2016 Great Minds®

Students Think-Pair-Share: "What was one thing you learned from the books we've read, including *Green Eggs and Ham*?"

- *I learned that books can tell you a message.*
- *Books can help your imagination.*
- *Books can inspire you to write a book.*
- *I learned that books can be really fun to read.*
- *I learned there are a lot of different kinds of books.*

Learn 50 MIN.

PARTICIPATE IN A SOCRATIC SEMINAR

Whole Group 30 MIN.

Remind students that the guidelines on the Speaking and Listening Anchor Chart will help them be successful with this lesson's discussion.

Ask: "How can noticing pauses and responding to what others say help us in a Socratic Seminar?"

Choose three or four students to share with the whole group.

- *If we notice pauses we can tell when someone is done speaking.*
- *Noticing pauses helps me understand what someone is saying.*
- *It might be important to know when one idea stops and another one starts.*
- *If we listen carefully, we can connect what we say to what others say.*

| TEACHER NOTE | You may wish to use a Nonverbal Signal, Talking Chips, or a Talking Stick to help delineate whose turn it is to speak. Similarly, Sentence Frames may be used to provide the structure for participating in complete sentences. |

Display and Echo Read the following Sentence Frames reminding students they can use the Sentence Frames to begin speaking:

- **I agree with you because _____.**
- **I disagree with you because _____.**
- **What makes you think that?**
- **I hear you and _____.**

WIT & WISDOM™   G1 > M1 > Lesson 27

Introduce vocabulary expectations. During the seminar, students should incorporate words from the assessment word list in the module overview. Set the expectation that each student should use at least two of these words during the seminar. Students should be given credit only if words are used properly and strategically to develop or enhance their ability to communicate clearly about the content (as opposed to simply thrown in a sentence in order to check off a requirement).

Review vocabulary resources with students, highlighting a few words that students might want to try using. Students set a goal by recording at least one word they want to use on a sticky note.

Students form a circle.

Write the Socratic Seminar opening question on the board: "How can books change my life?" Students Echo Read the sentence. Students Think-Pair-Share to discuss their answers.

Read aloud the opening question: "How can books change my life?"

✔ Students follow the Socratic Seminar procedures and engage in sustained dialogue.

- *I can learn to read like Cal.*
- *Books can teach me messages, like trying something new.*
- *I can learn how to do things by reading about them.*
- *I can get smarter by reading.*
- *I can learn how to understand paintings from* Museum ABC.
- *Books can make my life more fun and interesting.*

Reread the listening goal from the Speaking and Listening Anchor Chart. Students use Nonverbal signals (thumbs-up, thumbs-sideways, thumbs-down) to signal their self-assessment of how well they noticed pauses and responding to what others said.

Use anecdotal notes to share notable discussion points from the group.

RECORD KNOWLEDGE

Whole Group   20 MIN.

TEACHER NOTE	You may wish to explain to students why they are not filling out the Essential Questions Chart for *Green Eggs and Ham.* Display the chart and point out that the question in the third column, "How do books change the character's life?" doesn't work the same way for the text. Instead, they will think about the Focusing Question and include information in the Knowledge Journal.

Remind students of how much they have already learned, including information and skills, or how to do things. Explain that now they will keep track of what they have learned in a Knowledge Journal.

327

Copyright © 2016 Great Minds®

Display the Knowledge Journal. Point to the left-hand side of the Knowledge Journal, labeled "What I know." Students read the heading in a loud whisper.

Instruct students to Think-Pair-Share and ask: "What did you learn from our lessons on *Green Eggs and Ham*?"

Use Equity Sticks to call on pairs to share. Ask follow-up questions to challenge students' thinking and encourage them to use key vocabulary.

After each response, ask: "Do you think you will need to use this knowledge later?" Students stand up if they believe the response shows important learning and remain seated if they disagree or are unsure.

Use votes to choose one to three refined responses to record on the Knowledge Journal.

Display the Knowledge Journal. Point to the right-hand side of the Knowledge Journal, labeled "What I can do." Students read the heading in a loud whisper.

Revisit artifacts from previous lessons.

Instruct students Think-Pair-Share, and ask: "What did you learn to do as a writer? What did you learn to do as a reader?"

Repeat the process detailed above to engage students in a class vote and record refined responses.

What I know	What I can do
<ul><li>Books can teach me new messages.</li><li>Books can help me learn to read.</li><li>Books can help me use my imagination.</li><li>Books can be fun!</li></ul>	<ul><li>I can use temporal words in my writing.</li><li>I can fill in all the story elements on a Story Map on my own.</li><li>I can determine the central message of a story.</li></ul>

WIT & WISDOM™   G1 > M1 > Lesson 27

Land

ANSWER THE CONTENT FRAMING QUESTION

Knowledge: *How can books build my knowledge?*

Choral Read the Content Framing Question.

Students Mix and Mingle: "What did we learn about how books can build our knowledge?"

Use Equity Sticks to call on students.

- *I learned that can teach me new lessons.*
- *Books help you learn to read.*
- *Books can give you information.*

Wrap

HOMEWORK CHECK-IN

Continue home reading routine. Check Fluency Homework, and remind students that tonight is the final fluency work with the text *Green Eggs and Ham*.

Analyze

Context and Alignment

Students respond to what others say about how books can change your lives in a Socratic Seminar (SL.1.1.a, SL.1.1.b).

- Use evidence from the anecdotal record to assess students on the Speaking and Listening Process Rubric (see Appendix C).

Next Steps

Note students that have not generated enough evidence through participation in Socratic Seminars, and meet with them in advance of the final Socratic Seminar for this module to co-create a plan for how to participate. Consider pulling a small group of students that struggle with speaking skills into a small group to practice in advance.

G1 > M1 > Lesson 27

WIT & WISDOM™

⬇ Lesson 27: Style and Conventions Deep Dive

Excel at Sequencing Events

- **Time:** 15 min.

- **Text:** *Green Eggs and Ham*, Dr. Seuss

- **Style and Conventions Learning Goal:** Identify temporal words in writing and edit writing for temporal words. (L.1.1.i)

- **STYLE AND CONVENTIONS CRAFT QUESTION:** Lesson 26 Excel: *How do we edit our writing for time order words?*

Launch

Display and read the Craft Question: *How do we edit our writing for time order words?*

Students Echo Read the question. Explain that they will learn more about time order words and how to use them in their writing.

Learn

Display the Time Order Words Anchor Chart.

Students Think-Pair-Share about how they used these words this week in their writing. Use Equity Sticks to choose volunteers to share their thinking. Sample responses could be:

- *We used them to put our story in order.*
- *We used them to put events from the book in order.*
- *We used them to put pictures in order to make our own story.*
- *We used them to put the events in our narrative retell in order.*

Explain that students will use their writing to find the time order words and make sure they have used them correctly to help others understand their writing better.

Read the following to the students:

- **Sam asked the Man if he wanted green eggs and ham.**

- **The Man told Sam he didn't want green eggs and ham.**

- **The Man decided to try them, and he liked them.**

Ask students if they think your narrative retelling sounds good. Have them give a Nonverbal Signal to show their thinking. Students Think-Pair-Share about what your narrative retelling is missing. Guide students, if needed, to notice there are no time order words in your retell.

330

Copyright © 2016 Great Minds®

Display your writing and ask students to help you fix your writing. Refer to the Time Order Words Anchor Chart. Ask the students which time order word should go in front of the first sentence. Then, add it to your writing.

First Sam-I-am asked the Man if he wanted green eggs and ham.

In a similar fashion ask students which time order word should go in front of the next sentence. Then, add it to your writing.

Next the Man told Sam-I-am he didn't want green eggs and ham.

Continue until all your sentences have been edited with the time order words. Then Echo Read the retelling and ask students if the story sounds better with the time order words. Students should give a Nonverbal Signal to the question. Students Think-Pair-Share about why the story sounds better. Choose two or three volunteers to share their thinking.

Demonstrate how to underline all your time order words in yellow. Explain that, when they are reading their retellings for time order words, they should underline their words in yellow as well.

✔ Students work with their narrative retellings in Handout 26A: Focusing Question Task 5 Booklet to make sure they have included time order words to show the sequence of the events. If students do not have a time order word at the beginning of their sentence, they should put one in. Then, students switch with a partner to check their retelling for time order words.

Use Equity Sticks to choose two or three volunteers to share their retellings if time permits.

Land

Instruct students to Think-Pair-Share, and ask: "How do we edit our writing for time order words?"

Use Equity Sticks to select two pairs to share their thinking. Use their responses to reinforce that they should read their writing to look for time order words because they help the reader know when events are happening.

WIT & WISDOM™   G1 > M1 > Lesson 28

■ FOCUSING QUESTION: LESSONS 28-32

How do books change lives around the world?

1 2 3 4 5 6 7 8 9 10 11 12 13 14 15 16 17 18 19 20 21 22 23 24 25 26 27 **28** **29** **30** **31** **32**

Lesson 28

TEXTS

- *My Librarian Is a Camel*, Margriet Ruurs
- *Museum ABC*, The Metropolitan Museum of Art

Copyright © 2016 Great Minds®

G1 > M1 > Lesson 28

Lesson 28: At a Glance

AGENDA

Welcome (10 min.)

Launch (7 min.)

Understand the Content Framing Question

Learn (50 min.)

Discuss Museum ABC (15 min.)

Examine Story Elements in Narrative Writing (15 min.)

Provide Feedback in Writing (20 min.)

Land (5 min.)

Answer the Content Framing Question

Wrap (3 min.)

Assign Fluency Homework

Vocabulary Deep Dive: Direct Vocabulary Assessment (15 min.)

STANDARDS ADDRESSED

The full text of ELA Standards can be found in the Module Overview.

Reading

- RI.1.2, RL.1.3, RL.1.7

Writing

- W.1.3, W.1.8

Speaking and Listening

- SL.1.1.a, SL.1.6

Language

- L.1.1.b, L.1.1.f, L.1.1.j, L.1.2a, L.1.2.b
- ⬇ L.1.6

MATERIALS

- Handout 24A: Art Vocabulary
- Handout 28A: End-of-Module Prompt
- Handout 28B: Fluency Homework
- Assessment 28A: End-of-Module Task
- Assessment 28B: Vocabulary Assessment
- Feedback Anchor Chart

Learning Goals

Plan for giving and receiving useful peer feedback on writing. (W.1.5)

✔ Practice giving and receiving compliments using a Sentence Frame.

⬇ Demonstrate understanding of grade-level vocabulary in a direct vocabulary assessment. (L.1.6)

✔ Complete Assessment 28B

✔ Checks for Understanding

WIT & WISDOM™   G1 > M1 > Lesson 28

Prepare

FOCUSING QUESTION: Lessons 28–32

How do books change lives around the world?

CONTENT FRAMING QUESTION: Lesson 28

Distill: *What is important about* Museum ABC?

CRAFT QUESTION: Lesson 28

Examine and Experiment: *Why is using story elements to write a narrative important?*

Students begin to illustrate the cover for their book with portraits of characters before they transition to determining what makes *Museum* ABC important. This lesson is also an introduction to the EOM project that prepares students to begin writing in the next lesson.

Welcome 10 MIN.

Distribute Handout 24A: Art Vocabulary. Over the next three Welcome lessons, students elaborate on their draft sketches from earlier texts to illustrate the covers of their books about characters in the module and how books changed their lives.

Display page B from *Museum ABC*. Explain to students they will model their book covers after *Museum ABC*. Except, instead of "B is for Boat," their pages will say "B is for Book."

Think-Pair-Share: "Which characters will we draw in the boxes?"

Students draw themselves, Tomás, Ana, and Cal in each of the boxes, using their draft portrait sketches as a reference.

Name: _____

Handout 24A: Art Vocabulary

Directions: Use the graphic organizers to record text evidence of *portrait, landscape,* and *still life.*

Page: _____ is for _____

Page: _____ is for _____

Page: _____ is for _____

335

Copyright © 2016 Great Minds®

Launch

UNDERSTAND THE CONTENT FRAMING QUESTION

Post the Content Framing Question and Focusing Question.

Echo Read the Focusing Question. Ask students: "What do you notice about this Focusing Question?"

- *This Focusing Question is the same question as our Essential Question.*
- *This Focusing Question asks about people rather than a specific character.*

Point out that this Focusing Question is not focused on a specific character or person. It is a bigger question that encourages us to think about the perspective of people around the world.

Echo Read the Content Framing Question.

Explain that in this lesson we will try to put all the things we learned about *Museum* ABC together. Share that, because students have been working with many different pages and details in this text during the whole module, putting all of our learning together will help us determine why this book is important.

Learn

DISCUSS *MUSEUM ABC*

Whole Group 15 MIN.

Chorally read *Museum* ABC from A to Z, either by projecting each page on a document projector or by calling students to a rug or reading center where they can see each page as you turn it.

Distribute letter spreads so each pair has one or two letters to reference during the following discussion. For each question, students Think-Pair-Share. When student volunteers share their responses, any student who had the same or a similar response stands up to show agreement. Continue calling on new pairs until most of the class has either shared or stood up to agree.

Ask: "What do we know about how this book is organized?"

- *This is an ABC book.*
- *It is organized in alphabetical order.*

WIT & WISDOM™   G1 > M1 > Lesson 28

- *Each letter has a word it is for.*
- *All the pictures connect to the word.*
- *There are four pictures for each letter.*
- *The pictures are famous paintings from a museum.*

Ask: "What kinds of paintings are in this book?"

- *They are famous paintings from a museum!*
- *There are portraits of people.*
- *There are landscapes that show the beauty of nature.*
- *There are still lifes of fruits and veggies and flowers.*
- *Some paintings have lots of color.*
- *All of the paintings have lots of details.*

Ask: "Putting all of these ideas together, what makes this book important?"

- *It shows how art connects to the alphabet.*
- *It helps us see beautiful paintings on the same subjects.*
- *All the pictures have lots of details.*
- *It has easy words to help us read them by ourselves.*
- *It is fun to see so many different paintings in one book.*

Highlight any responses that get at the purpose of why people read this book. Celebrate the great thinking, and share that the work students did to put all of their learning together on the book is what good readers do to understand what is important about the books they read.

EXAMINE WRITING STORY ELEMENTS IN A NARRATIVE

Whole Group 15 MIN.

Share with students that over the next few lessons they will write a narrative story about a character and how books have changed their lives.

Display the Story Maps constructed for the module. Remind students they have learned about different characters around the world and how books changed their lives. Explain to students they will use their knowledge of story elements to write their story.

Students Mix and Mingle to discuss the question: "Why do authors use story elements when they write stories?" Use Equity Sticks to call on three students to share their thinking.

- *Authors use story elements to structure their stories.*
- *Authors use story elements so their stories make sense.*
- *Authors use story elements to make their stories interesting.*

337

Copyright © 2016 Great Minds®

Display and Echo Read Handout 28A: End-of-Module Prompt.

Write and illustrate a narrative about a character whose life has changed because of books.

Be sure to include:

- *Characters*
- *Setting from My Librarian Is a Camel*
- *A problem (the character doesn't have books)*
- *The resolution to the problem (using the method for getting books from that country)*

Make sure each page includes:

- *Complete sentences that begin with a capital letter and end with a punctuation mark*
- *Capitals at the beginning of proper nouns (names and countries)*
- *Illustrations to match the words on each page*

Use your best handwriting, as you will read and share your story with your classmates and teacher.

Students Think-Pair-Share: "What is the prompt asking me to do?"

Use Equity Sticks to select a few students to explain their response.

Distribute Assessment 28A: End-of-Module Task. Students examine the booklet.

Ask: "What do you notice about the booklet?' Use Equity Sticks to call on a few students to share their responses.

- *The Story Map icons are in the booklet.*
- *There is a place to write and a place to draw.*
- *There are four pages.*

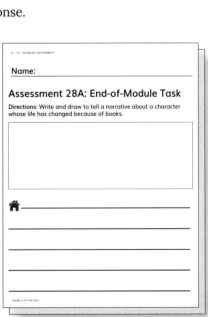

TEACHER NOTE	Students write and illustrate their story in the booklet, writing one or two story elements during a lesson. Most story element will be on separate pages.

Students begin writing in the next lesson!

PROVIDE FEEDBACK IN WRITING

Pairs 20 MIN.

Explain to students they will have the opportunity to give and receive feedback on the stories they are going to write. Feedback is part of being a writer. Feedback means, "telling someone how you feel about their writing."

One type of feedback is to give the writer a compliment.

Place two chairs side-by-side. Sit in one chair and ask a volunteer to sit in the other chair and pretend they wrote the story. Hand the student a piece of paper.

Display and Echo Read the sentences below:

- It started in Canada when James didn't have books.
- Then he ordered the books by mail.
- He read all of the books.
- Finally, James had books to read.

Display the Sentence Frame:

One thing I liked about your story was _____.

Provide a compliment to the students using the Sentence Frame. For example:

"One thing I liked about your story was that you named your character James."

Explain to students that their compliments should be about the writing. Compliments can be about the story elements, use of words, or other learning from the module.

Switch roles and ask the student to give you a compliment about the story.

Echo Read the story again. Pairs practice paying each other a compliment using the Sentence Frame.

✔ Circulate and take notes of student compliments. Create a three-column chart that you will add

339

G1 > M1 > Lesson 28   WIT & WISDOM™

to in later modules. Title the chart using the sample chart below. Write relevant student compliments on the chart for student use when providing feedback.

FEEDBACK ANCHOR CHART

Providing Feedback to Peers
Give the writer a compliment.
One thing I liked about your story was • <u>you named your character James.</u>

Explain to students that in the next lesson they will learn about a tool to help them give feedback. It is called a Narrative Checklist.

Land 5 MIN.

ANSWER THE CONTENT FRAMING QUESTION

Distill: *What is important about* Museum ABC?

Ask the Content Framing Question. Students Mix and Mingle to share their answers.

- *It makes learning the alphabet fun with art.*
- *It helps us see beautiful paintings without having to go to a museum.*
- *It makes readers want to learn more about both words and art.*

340

Copyright © 2016 Great Minds®

Wrap 5 MIN.

ASSIGN FLUENCY HOMEWORK

Continue home reading routine. Collect Fluency Homework handouts from lessons 23–27, and distribute Handout 28B: Fluency Homework, reminding students to share the new text with their family. Explain that the new text is a poem, "Museum AB–See!" Students read the first part of the poem in lessons 13–16.

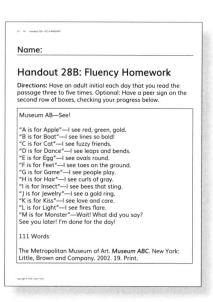

Analyze

Context and Alignment

Students plan for giving and receiving useful peer feedback on writing (W.1.5).

Check for the following success criteria:

- Compliment is related to writing goals.
- Compliment is positive.

Next Steps

Before moving on to the next part of the feedback process, give struggling students another opportunity to give and receive compliments in an earlier part of the next lesson.

⬇ Lesson 28: Vocabulary Deep Dive

Direct Vocabulary Assessment

- **Time:** 15 min.
- **Text:** [N/A]
- **Vocabulary Learning Goal:** Demonstrate understanding of grade-level vocabulary. (L.1.6)

Launch

Remind students that they have learned many new words this module. Explain that in this lesson they will complete an assessment where they will show their understanding of these words.

Learn

Distribute Assessment 28B and pencils (as needed).

Explain to students how to fill out the response sheet. You will read a question aloud that contains the word listed beside the smiley face. If students think the answer is "yes", they should draw a circle around the smiley face. If they think the answer is "no," they should draw a circle around the frowny face.

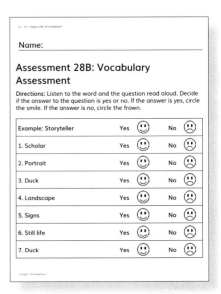

Practice with a word that is not found on the assessment, e.g., Ask: "Is a dog a storyteller?"

Read students the word *storyteller* and then read the sentence twice. Think aloud to demonstrate how you consider the meaning of the word, and then whether the answer is "yes" or "no." Think-Pair-Share: "Which answer did you pick and why?"

Use the teacher-facing version (with key) in Appendix C to administer the assessment.

Read each question two times before students fill out their answers. Make sure to always read the focus word before reading the question.

WIT & WISDOM™

G1 > M1 > Lesson 28

Ask: "Scholar: Can a pencil be a scholar?"

Monitor as students work, ensuring they are following directions and are on the correct question. Provide oral cues as necessary if students need help locating the proper row and where to mark their answers. Students will complete another assessment at the end of the module.

✔ Students begin the direct vocabulary assessment.

Land

Congratulate students on their hard work.

WIT & WISDOM™   G1 > M1 > Lesson 29

■ FOCUSING QUESTION: LESSONS 28-32

How do books change lives around the world?

1 2 3 4 5 6 7 8 9 10 11 12 13 14 15 16 17 18 19 20 21 22 23 24 25 26 27 **28** **29** **30** **31** **32**

Lesson 29

TEXTS

- *My Librarian Is a Camel*, Margriet Ruurs

- *Museum ABC*, The Metropolitan Museum of Art

- *Tomás and the Library Lady*, Pat Mora, Raul Colón

- *Waiting for the Biblioburro*, Monica Brown, John Parra

- *That Book Woman*, Heather Henson, David Small

- *Green Eggs and Ham*, Dr. Seuss

Copyright © 2016 Great Minds®

G1 > M1 > Lesson 29   WIT & WISDOM™

Lesson 29: At a Glance

AGENDA

Welcome (10 min.)

Launch (5 min.)

Understand the Content Framing Question

Learn (50 min.)

Record Knowledge (20 min.)

Execute Using Story Elements in a Narrative (30 min.)

Land (7 min.)

Answer the Content Framing Question

Wrap (3 min.)

Homework Check-in

Style and Conventions Deep Dive: Editing and Revising Sentences (15 min.)

STANDARDS ADDRESSED

The full text of ELA Standards can be found in the Module Overview.

Reading

- RL.1.2, RI.1.3, RL.1.7

Writing

- W.1.3, W.1.5, W.1.8

Speaking and Listening

- SL.1.1a, SL.1.6

Language

- ⬇ L.1.1.b, L.1.2.a

MATERIALS

- Sticky flags
- Response Journals
- Handout 28A: End-of-Module Prompt
- Enlarged End-of-Module Task Booklet
- Time Order Words Anchor Chart
- How Children Get Books Sentences Chart
- Knowledge Journal
- Handout 29A: Narrative Checklist

Learning Goals

Make connections between *My Librarian Is a Camel* and other module texts.

✔ Contribute to Knowledge Journal

Students express understanding of story elements by writing the setting and character for the first sentence in the End-of-Module Task. (RL.1.2, RL.1.3, W.1.3, W.1.8, SL.1.1.a, L.1.1.b, L.1.1.j, L.1.2.b)

✔ Continue working on the End-of-Module Task.

⬇ Edit sentences created in response to a prompt. (L.1.1.b, L.1.1.j, L.1.2.a, L.1.2.b)

✔ Edit and revise their EOM task.

✔ Checks for Understanding

Copyright © 2016 Great Minds®

WIT & WISDOM™   G1 > M1 > Lesson 29

| Prepare |

FOCUSING QUESTION: Lessons 28-32

How do books change lives around the world?

CONTENT FRAMING QUESTION: Lesson 29

Know: *How does* My Librarian Is a Camel *build my knowledge?*

CRAFT QUESTION: Lesson 29

Execute: *How do I use story elements in a narrative?*

Students return to the text *My Librarian Is a Camel* and record their knowledge and learning in the Knowledge Journal. Students apply the knowledge and demonstrate the skills they acquired over the course of the module by beginning the EOM project as they write and illustrate a setting and character to include in their narrative.

Welcome 10 MIN.

Students continue to illustrate their book cover, B is for Book.

Launch 5 MIN.

UNDERSTAND THE CONTENT FRAMING QUESTION

Post the Content Framing Question and Focusing Question. Echo Read the Content Framing Question.

Ask students: "According to our Content Framing Question, what are we finding today?"

- *We are going to think about the information we learned from* My Librarian Is a Camel.

Echo Read the Focusing Question. Ask students to consider: "How could our knowledge from the stories we read and the information from *My Librarian Is a Camel*, help us answer our Focusing Question?"

- *The stories we read tell us about children's experiences with books.*
- *My Librarian Is a Camel* gives us information about children around the world.*

347

Copyright © 2016 Great Minds®

Learn 50 MIN.

RECORD KNOWLEDGE

Whole Group 25 MIN.

Congratulate students on how much they have already learned and know how to do and explain that they are now ready to add to the Knowledge Journal.

Display the Knowledge Journal. Point to the left-hand side of the Knowledge Journal, labeled "What I know."

Remind students that this part of the Knowledge Journal is all about the new information they learned in these lessons.

Post and Echo Read the How People Get Books Anchor Chart from lesson 15.

Instruct students to Think-Pair-Share and ask: "What did you learn from our lessons on *My Librarian Is a Camel*? What did you learn about our Essential Question?"

> *Scaffold*
>
> Ask more concrete questions to prompt students and encourage application of key vocabulary:
> - What did we learn about how children get books?
> - What did we learn about mobile libraries?
> - What did we learn about how books change lives?

Use Equity Sticks to call on pairs to share responses. After each response, students reach for the sky if they believe the response is important learning and touch their toes if they disagree or are unsure.

Use votes to choose one to three refined responses to record on the Knowledge Journal.

Read each response aloud.

Point to the right-hand side of the Knowledge Journal, labeled "What I can do."

Remind students that this column is for things we can now do, whether in our heads, out loud, or on paper. Revisit artifacts from previous lessons, including anchor charts, Response Journal entries, and the Focusing Question Task.

✔ Students to Think-Pair-Share: "What did you learn to do as a writer? What did you learn to do as a reader?"

WIT & WISDOM™   G1 > M1 > Lesson 29

Scaffold

Ask more concrete questions to prompt students and encourage application of key vocabulary:
- What did we learn about the names of countries?
- What did we learn about information in pictures?

Repeat the process detailed above to engage students in a class vote and record refined responses.

What I know	What I can do
▪ Children around the world really enjoy books. ▪ Books and libraries are very important to people. ▪ Mobile libraries move around from place to place. ▪ Mobile libraries visit remote places in different countries around the world.	▪ Capitalize proper nouns. ▪ Read and spell the names of countries. ▪ Look at pictures to find clues about a topic.

EXECUTE USING STORY ELEMENTS IN A NARRATIVE

Individuals 30 MIN.

In this lesson students begin writing the End-of-Module Task.

Display and Echo Read the End-of-Module Prompt from Lesson 28.

Display an enlarged copy of the End-of-Module booklet.

Students point to and Chorally Read the icons on pages 1–2. Explain that on pages 1–2, students will write about the characters, setting and the problem.

Explain that in order to start writing, they have to think of a way to begin their stories.

Display and Echo Read the Time Order Words Anchor Chart and the phrase, "It started in."

Students Think-Pair-Share: Which words have we been using to start our narrative recalls? Choose two students to share their thinking. Share with students that they can begin their stories the same way.

Model writing "It started in" on the enlarged copy as students write the same on page 1 in their booklets.

Display and Echo Read How Children Get Books Sentence Chart from lesson 15. Explain to students that this chart will help them write parts of their story. Model selecting a setting. Write it to complete part of the sentence on page 1. Students Think-Pair-Share: "Where will my story take place?" Distribute the country page spreads across tables so students can reference them along with the anchor chart.

349

Copyright © 2016 Great Minds®

G1 > M1 > Lesson 29   WIT & WISDOM™

Students use the text spreads or anchor chart to choose and complete the first part of their sentence on page 1 by writing the name of their setting:

Page 1: It started in <u>Kenya</u>

Instruct students to turn to page 2. Students Think-Pair-Share: "Who is the main character in your story?" Create a list of student responses and write them a sheet of chart paper titled "Characters." Provide the opportunity for students to choose a character on the list, or create one on their own.

✔ Model writing the word *when* and a character's name on page 2, as students write the same in their booklets.

Page 1: It started in <u>Kenya</u>

Page 2: when <u>Amari</u>

Students illustrate pages 1–2 in their booklet using the photographs from *My Librarian Is a Camel* for inspiration for their setting. Tell students they will write and illustrate page 3 in the next lesson.

Land 7 MIN.

ANSWER THE CONTENT FRAMING QUESTION

Know: *How does* My Librarian Is a Camel *build my knowledge?*

Choral Read the Content Framing Question. Students Mix and Mingle to answer the question, referencing the Knowledge Journal for support.

- *I learned kids really enjoy books–they are sweeter than candy!*
- *I learned that mobile libraries are in countries all over the world.*
- *I know lots of different names of countries.*
- *I know new words, like mobile and remote.*

350

Copyright © 2016 Great Minds®

Wrap 3 MIN.

HOMEWORK CHECK-IN

Continue home reading routine. Check Fluency Homework from the previous lesson, and remind students what to do for fluency homework tonight.

Analyze

Context and Alignment

Students express understanding of story elements by writing the setting and character for the first sentence in the End-of-Module Task (RL.1.2, RL.1.3, W.1.3, W.1.8, SL.1.1.a, L.1.1.b, L.1.1.j, L.1.2.b).

Check for the following success criteria:

- Includes the character and setting
- Capitalizes the proper nouns

Next Steps

Review all student papers to determine the type of errors students are making.

Plan for small group support for these skills during the editing and revising process.

⬇ Lesson 29: Style and Conventions Deep Dive

Editing and Revising Sentences

- **Time:** 15 min.
- **Text:** *My Librarian is a Camel,* Margriet Ruurs
- **Style and Conventions Learning Goal:** Edit sentences created in response to a prompt. (L.1.1b, L.1.1.j, L.1.2.a, L.1.2.b)
- **STYLE AND CONVENTIONS CRAFT QUESTION:** Lesson 29
  Excel: *How do we edit our writing using a checklist?*

Launch

Display and read the Craft Question: *How do we edit our writing using a checklist?*

Students Echo Read the question. Explain that they will learn more about editing their writing to make it better.

Learn

Display the Narrative Checklist. Students Think-Pair-Share: "What is this checklist used for? How does it help me become a better writer?"

Use Equity Sticks to choose volunteers to share their thinking.

- *Things we look for when we are done writing.*
- *Things that should be in our writing when we are ready to share it.*
- *It helps us to be better writers by helping us find mistakes or things we missed.*
- *We can fix our mistakes before we share our writing.*

Affirm correct answers and explain that in this lesson they will only focus on part of the checklist to help them make their writing better.

Display Handout 29A: Narrative Checklist and highlight the following criteria in different colors:

- I have characters.
- I have a setting.

Echo Read the highlighted criteria with the students and explain that they will learn how to check their writing for these criteria.

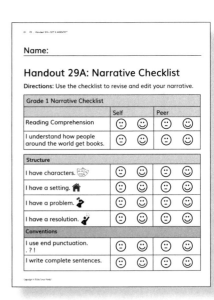

WIT & WISDOM™   G1 > M1 > Lesson 29

Display a piece of writing that you have started with the Sentence Frames. Save this to use in the next two lessons as the students work through the EOM task. The following is an example:

It started in Kenya when Amari didn't have any books.

Read your narrative. Students Think-Pair-Share about whether they hear or see any mistakes that you could fix to make your writing better. Have volunteers share their thinking.

Read the first criteria on the Narrative Checklist and ask students to give you a Nonverbal Signal if you have characters. Students Think-Pair-Share about this element of your narrative. Volunteers respond.

  ▪ *The character is Amari.*

Use the color you highlighted the chart with to identify the criteria the students noticed in your narrative. Then, put a check in the box titled *Self* and *Peer* on the checklist. Explain that since they identified the criteria in your narrative that you could check off the *Peer* box.

Read the second criteria on the Narrative Checklist and ask students to give you a nonverbal signal if you have a setting in your narrative. Students Think-Pair-Share about this element of your narrative. Volunteers respond.

  ▪ *The setting is Kenya.*

Use the color you highlighted the chart with to identify the criteria students noticed in your narrative. Then put a check in the box titled *Self* and *Peer* on the checklist.

✔ Distribute the Narrative Checklist to each student. Students work with the checklist and their writing, making any changes they find that they need to make. After a sufficient amount of independent work time, students work with their partner to check their narrative. Encourage students to provide positive feedback to their partner using the Sentence Frame: **One thing I liked about your story was** _____. Students make any necessary changes.

Use Equity Sticks to choose two or three volunteers to share their writing for the day. Model providing positive feedback to two of the students after they read. Choose two or three students to give positive feedback on the last writer's story using the Sentence Frame: **One thing I liked about your story was** _____.

Land

Instruct students to Think-Pair-Share, and ask: "How do we edit our writing using a checklist?"

Use Equity Sticks to select two pairs to share their thinking. Use their responses to reinforce that a checklist helps us to know what we are looking for as we read through our story to make sure we have all the elements of a story. Explain that they will practice using the Narrative Checklist to help them make their writing better.

353

Copyright © 2016 Great Minds®

WIT & WISDOM™   G1 > M1 > Lesson 30

▨ FOCUSING QUESTION: LESSONS 28-32

How do books change lives around the world?

1 2 3 4 5 6 7 8 9 10 11 12 13 14 15 16 17 18 19 20 21 22 23 24 25 26 27 **28 29 30 31 32**

Lesson 30

TEXTS

- *My Librarian Is a Camel*, Margriet Ruurs
- *Museum ABC*, The Metropolitan Museum of Art
- *Tomás and the Library Lady*, Pat Mora, Raul Colón
- *Waiting for the Biblioburro*, Monica Brown, John Parra
- *That Book Woman*, Heather Henson, David Small
- *Green Eggs and Ham*, Dr. Seuss

Copyright © 2016 Great Minds®

G1 > M1 > Lesson 30

WIT & WISDOM™

Lesson 30: At a Glance

AGENDA

Welcome (5 min.)

Organize for the EOM

Launch (5 min.)

Understand the Content Framing Question

Learn (55 min.)

Revisit Module Texts (20 min.)

Execute Using Story Elements in a Narrative (30 min.)

Land (5 min.)

Answer the Content Framing Question

Wrap (5 min.)

Homework Check-in

Style and Conventions Deep Dive: Editing and Revising Sentences (15 min.)

STANDARDS ADDRESSED

The full text of ELA Standards can be found in the Module Overview.

Reading

- RI.1.2, RI.1.3

Writing

- W.1.3, W.1.5, W.1.8

Speaking and Listening

- SL.1.1.a

Language

- L.1.1.b, L.1.1.j, L.1.2.a, L.1.2.b
- ⬇ L.1.1.j

MATERIALS

- Enlarged End-of-Module Task Booklet
- Time Order Words Anchor Chart
- How Children Get Books Sentences Chart
- Handout 29A: Narrative Checklist

Learning Goals

Write a sequenced event in a narrative. (W.1.3, W.1.8)

✔ Continue working on the End-of-Module Task.

⬇ Edit and revise sentences created in response to a prompt. (L.1.1.j, W.1.5)

✔ Use the Narrative Checklist to edit and revise writing.

✔ Checks for Understanding

Copyright © 2016 Great Minds®

WIT & WISDOM™   G1 > M1 > Lesson 30

Prepare

FOCUSING QUESTION: Lessons 28-32

How do books change lives around the world?

CONTENT FRAMING QUESTION: Lesson 30

Know: *How do all the Module 1 texts build our knowledge of how books can change lives around the world?*

CRAFT QUESTION: Lesson 30

Execute: *How do I use story elements in a narrative?*

Students revisit module texts and discuss with a partner how each builds knowledge of how books change lives. They continue work on the EOM project, writing and illustrating the problem for their narratives.

Welcome 5 MIN.

Students compile and order their responses to Focusing Question Tasks 1–4 and finalize the B is for Book cover.

Pairs share their favorite response.

Launch 5 MIN.

UNDERSTAND THE CONTENT FRAMING QUESTION

Post the Content Framing Question and Focusing Question. Echo Read the Content Framing Question and the Focusing Question.

Ask students: "What do you notice about the Content Framing Question and The Focusing Question?

- *I notice that they both ask how books change lives around the world.*
- *I notice that the Content Framing Question asks us specifically about the books we've read in this module.*

357

Copyright © 2016 Great Minds®

G1 > M1 > Lesson 30   WIT & WISDOM™

Explain that students will use the same Content Framing Question for the next three lessons as they write their narratives, to help them think about the texts they've studied and how they add to their knowledge of how books can change lives.

Learn 50 MIN.

REVISIT MODULE TEXTS

Small Groups 20 MIN.

Divide the class into six table groups, and provide each table with one of the following six texts: *Museum ABC*, *My Librarian Is a Camel*, *Tomás and the Library Lady*, *Waiting for the Biblioburro*, *That Book Woman*, and *Green Eggs and Ham*.

At each table, students Think-Pair-Share for two minutes on the following prompt related to the Content Framing Question: "How does this book build my knowledge of how books change lives?"

At the end of two minutes, students pass their book clockwise to the next table, and repeat the process until all tables have had all books.

Two to three students share out something important they heard.

EXECUTE USING STORY ELEMENTS IN A NARRATIVE

Individuals 30 MIN.

Display the enlarged copy of the End-of-Module Task, How Children Get Books Sentences Chart, and the Time Order Words Anchor Chart.

Students share their writing with a partner. Reread enables students to remember where they stopped writing the previous lesson.

Share with students that they will write and illustrate the problem and the moment of change in their stories.

Instruct students to turn to page 2 in their booklets.

Explain that everyone will have the same problem—the character doesn't have books. Point to the problem icon on page 2, and model completing the sentence as students follow your direction.

Page 1: It started in Kenya

358

Copyright © 2016 Great Minds®

Page 2: when Amari did not have books.

Instruct students to turn to page 3. Explain that on page 3, the moment of change happens.

TEACHER NOTE Students are not expected to have internalized the moment of change. If you feel the students need a review, display and review the Story Map for *Green Eggs and Ham*. Ask "When was the moment of change in *Green Eggs and Ham*?" Use Equity Sticks to call on students to respond.

Display the Sentences Chart from lesson 15. Explain that students can use the Sentences Chart to write the moment of change. Refer to the chart and explain that children get books from a camel in Kenya, so that means the moment of change in the story is when Amari gets books from the camel library. Turn to an enlarged copy of page 3 and model writing the moment of change using a word from the Time Order Words Anchor Chart.

Page 1: It started in Kenya

Page 2: when Amari did not have books.

Page 3. Then the camel came to the village with books.

Share with students that their moment of change may be different depending on the setting of their story. Echo Read the Sentences Chart. Students orally process the moment of change with a partner using evidence from the Sentences Chart.

Students turn to page 3 and write the moment of change.

Students illustrate pages 2–3 when they are finished writing.

Land 5 MIN.

ANSWER THE CONTENT FRAMING QUESTION

Know: *How do all the Module 1 texts build our knowledge of how books can change lives around the world?*

Students Mix and Mingle to answer the Content Framing Question, continuing their earlier discussion when reviewing each module text.

- *Museum ABC* can make the lives of people learning the alphabet more colorful.
- *That Book Woman* built my knowledge about packhorse librarians.

- *Tomás and the Library Lady built my knowledge of how books helped Tomás become someone important.*
- *Green Eggs and Ham built my knowledge of how books have messages that inspire people to try new things.*
- *My Librarian Is a Camel built my knowledge of mobile libraries in different countries.*
- *Waiting for the Biblioburro built my knowledge of how important books are to children in remote villages.*

Wrap 5 MIN.

HOMEWORK CHECK-IN

Continue home reading routine. Check Fluency Homework from the previous lesson, and remind students what to do for fluency homework tonight.

Analyze

Context and Alignment

Students express understanding of story elements by writing the problem and moment of change in the End-of-Module Task (RL.1.2, RL.1.3, W.1.3, W.1.5, W.1.8, SL.1.1.a, L.1.1.b, L.1.1.j, L.1.2.a, L.1.2.b).

Check for the following success criteria:

- Includes the problem, and moment of change
- Writes complete sentences
- Uses end punctuation
- Capitalizes the proper nouns

Next Steps

Review all student papers to determine the type of errors students are making. Group student papers by needs, to revise and edit the sentences. Support students experiencing difficulty writing sentences by providing them with Sentence Frames.

WIT & WISDOM™   G1 › M1 › Lesson 30

↓ Lesson 30: Style and Conventions Deep Dive

Editing and Revising Sentences

- **Time:** 15 min.

- **Text:** *My Librarian is a Camel*, Margriet Ruurs

- **Style and Conventions Learning Goal:** Edit and revise sentences created in response to a prompt. (L.1.1.j)

- **STYLE AND CONVENTIONS CRAFT QUESTION:** Lesson 30
  Excel: *Why is it important to revise our writing?*

Launch

Display and read the Craft Question: *Why is it important to revise our writing?*

Students Echo Read the question. Explain that they will learn more about revising their writing to make it better.

Learn

Display the following words:

- First

- Next

- Then

- Last

- Finally

Students Think-Pair-Share about what these words have in common. Use Equity Sticks to choose volunteers to share their thinking. Students should recognize these as time words, sequence words, or temporal words.

Students Mix and Mingle to use each word in a sentence. Call out each word and have students find a partner they haven't talked to and share a sentence using the word.

Explain that in this lesson they will use the Narrative Checklist to edit and revise the writing they have done for the EOM Task so far.

Display the Narrative Checklist and highlight the following criteria in a different color:

- I have a problem.

361

Copyright © 2016 Great Minds®

Echo Read the highlighted criteria with the students and explain that students will learn how to check their writing for these criteria.

Display the piece of writing you used from the previous day with the two sentences added to the end of the narrative. Save this to use in the next lesson as the students work through the EOM Task. The following is an example:

It started in Kenya when Amari didn't have any books. Then the camel came to the village with some books.

Read your narrative. Students Think-Pair-Share about whether they hear or see any mistakes that you could fix to make your writing better. Have volunteers share their thinking.

Read the criteria on the Narrative Checklist and ask students to give you a nonverbal signal if you have a problem and a moment of change. Students Think-Pair-Share about these elements of your narrative. Use Equity Sticks to choose volunteers to share their thinking.

- *The problem is that Amari didn't have any books.*
- *The moment of change was when the camel came to the village with books.*

Use the color you highlighted the chart with to identify the criteria the students noticed in your narrative. Then put a check in the box titled *Self* and *Peer* on the checklist.

✔️ Distribute the Narrative Checklist to each student. Students work with the checklist and their writing, making any changes they find that they need to make. After a sufficient amount of independent work time, students work with their partners to check their narratives. Encourage students to provide positive feedback to their partners using the Sentence Frame: **One thing I liked about your story was _____.** Students make any necessary changes.

Use Equity Sticks to choose two or three volunteers to share their writing for the day. Model positive feedback for the first two students using the Sentence Frame: **One thing I liked about your story was _____.** Then, allow one or two students to provide positive feedback using the Sentence Frame.

Land

Instruct students to Think-Pair-Share, and ask: Why is it important to revise our writing?

Use Equity Sticks to select two pairs to share their thinking. Use their responses to reinforce that revising our writing makes it better. Explain that they will practice using the Narrative Checklist to help them make their writing better.

WIT & WISDOM™   G1 > M1 > Lesson 31

■ FOCUSING QUESTION: LESSONS 28-32

How do books change lives around the world?

1 2 3 4 5 6 7 8 9 10 11 12 13 14 15 16 17 18 19 20 21 22 23 24 25 26 27 **28 29 30 31 32**

Lesson 31

TEXTS

- *My Librarian Is a Camel*, Margriet Ruurs
- *Museum ABC*, The Metropolitan Museum of Art
- *Tomás and the Library Lady*, Pat Mora, Raul Colón
- *Waiting for the Biblioburro*, Monica Brown, John Parra
- *That Book Woman*, Heather Henson, David Small
- *Green Eggs and Ham*, Dr. Seuss

Copyright © 2016 Great Minds®

G1 > M1 > Lesson 31   WIT & WISDOM™

Lesson 31: At a Glance

AGENDA

Welcome (5 min.)

Read Aloud Original Narratives

Launch (5 min.)

Understand the Content Framing Question

Learn (55 min.)

Create Tableaux (25 min.)

Execute Using Story Elements in a Narrative (30 min.)

Land (7 min.)

Answer the Content Framing Question

Wrap (3 min.)

Homework Check-in

Style and Conventions Deep Dive: Editing and Revising Sentences (15 min.)

STANDARDS ADDRESSED

The full text of ELA Standards can be found in the Module Overview.

Reading

- RL.1.2, RL.1.3

Writing

- W.1.3, W.1.5, W.1.8

Speaking and Listening

- SL.1.1.a, SL.1.1.b

Language

- L.1.1.b, L.1.1.j, L.1.2.a, L.1.2.b
- ⬇ L.1.1.j

MATERIALS

- Enlarged End-of-Module Task Booklet
- Assessment 28A: End-of-Module Task
- Time Order Words Anchor Chart
- Handout 29A: Narrative Checklist

Learning Goals

Write the resolution to a narrative (W.1.3).

✔ Complete the End-of-Module Task.

⬇ Edit sentences created in response to a prompt. (L.1.1.j)

✔ Complete Narrative Checklist.

Copyright © 2016 Great Minds⁺   ✔ Checks for Understanding

WIT & WISDOM™   G1 > M1 > Lesson 31

Prepare

ESSENTIAL QUESTION: Lessons 28-32

How do books change lives around the world?

CONTENT FRAMING QUESTION: Lesson 31

Know: *How do all the Module 1 texts build our knowledge of how books can change lives around the world?*

CRAFT QUESTION: Lesson 31

Execute: *How do I use story elements in a narrative?*

In this lesson, students continue to express understanding gained by reading the Module 1 texts. They create tableaux to demonstrate "before and after books" using the module texts. They write and illustrate the resolution of their narrative to complete their work on the EOM Task.

Welcome 5 MIN.

READ ALOUD ORIGINAL NARRATIVES

Pairs take turns reading the first few pages of their original narratives to each other with fluency and expression and practice giving each other feedback on their delivery.

Launch 5 MIN.

UNDERSTAND THE CONTENT FRAMING QUESTION

Post the Content Framing Question and Focusing Question. Echo Read the Content Framing Question.

Ask students: "What do you notice about the Content Framing Question?"

- *It's the same Content Framing Question that we had in yesterday's lesson.*

Explain that this is an important question for the module and students will have several lessons for students to have the time to have understand and answer it.

365

Copyright © 2016 Great Minds®

Learn 55 MIN.

CREATE TABLEAUX

Small Groups 25 MIN.

Divide the class into six table groups, and provide each table with one of the following six texts: *Museum ABC*, *My Librarian Is a Camel*, *Tomás and the Library Lady*, *Waiting for the Biblioburro*, *That Book Woman*, and *Green Eggs and Ham*.

At each table, students plan and practice a "Before and After" Tableau that shows either the main character's life before and after they had books (Tomás, Ana, Cal) or a reader's life before and after they read the book (*Green Eggs and Ham*, *Museum ABC*, *My Librarian Is a Camel*)

When ready, each small group performs their tableau for the whole class.

EXECUTE USING STORY ELEMENTS IN A NARRATIVE

Individuals 30 MIN.

Display the enlarged copy of the End-of-Module Task and the Time Order Words Anchor Chart.

Explain that students will draft and illustrate the resolution to the problem in their story.

Remind students that the resolution is how the problem ends.

Have students stand and share their writing with a partner. Instruct students to turn to page 4 in their booklets, and put their fingers on the resolution icon.

- Page 1: *It started in Kenya*
- Page 2: *when Amari did not have books.*
- Page 3. *Then the camel came to the village with books.*

Pairs orally process by retelling the resolution before writing it in their story booklets. Students illustrate page 4 when they finish the writing. Encourage students to return to their illustrations in their booklets and add additional details.

WIT & WISDOM™   G1 > M1 > Lesson 31

Land 7 MIN.

ANSWER THE CONTENT FRAMING QUESTION

Know: *How do all the Module 1 texts build our knowledge of how books can change lives around the world?*

Student Think-Pair-Share on the Content Framing Question.

Ask: "Which text built your knowledge the most?"

Conduct a Whip Around for student responses.

Wrap 3 MIN.

HOMEWORK CHECK-IN

Continue home reading routine. Check Fluency Homework from the previous lesson, and remind students what to do for fluency homework tonight.

Analyze

Context and Alignment

Students express understanding of story elements by writing the resolution to the problem in their story to complete the End-of-Module Task (RL.1.2, RL.1.3, W.1.3, W.1.5, W.1.8, SL.1.1.a, L.1.1.b, L.1.1.j, L.1.2.a, L.1.2.b).

Check for the following success criteria:

- Includes the resolution
- Writes complete sentences
- Uses end punctuation
- Capitalizes the proper nouns

Next Steps

Review all student papers to determine the type of errors students are making. Group student papers by needs, to revise and edit the sentences. Support students experiencing difficulty writing sentences by providing them with Sentence Frames.

G1 > M1 > Lesson 31   WIT & WISDOM™

⬇ Lesson 31: Style and Conventions Deep Dive

Editing and Revising Sentences

- **Time:** 15 min.

- **Text:** *My Librarian is a Camel*, Margriet Ruurs

- **Style and Conventions Learning Goal:** Edit sentences created in response to a prompt. (L.1.1.j)

- **STYLE AND CONVENTIONS CRAFT QUESTION:** Lesson 31
  Excel: *Why is it important to edit our writing?*

Launch

Display and read the Craft Question: *Why is it important to edit our writing?*

Students Echo Read the question. Explain that they will learn more about editing their writing to make it better.

Learn

Display the following end marks:

- .

- ?

- !

Students Think-Pair-Share what they know about these end marks. Use Equity Sticks to choose volunteers to share their thinking. Students should recognize these are punctuation marks that we use at the end of sentences.

Students Mix and Mingle to use each word in a sentence. Call out one of the end marks while students find a partner they have not shared with yet to share a sentence using the correct end mark. Remind them of their work with declarative, interrogative, and imperative sentences.

Explain that they will continue editing their writing using the Narrative Checklist to get ready for sharing their writing the next day.

Display the Narrative Checklist and highlight the following criteria in different colors:

- I have a resolution.

- I use end punctuation.

- I write complete sentences.

368

Copyright © 2016 Great Minds®

WIT & WISDOM™   G1 > M1 > Lesson 31

Echo Read the highlighted criteria with the students and explain that they will learn how to check their writing for these criteria.

Display the piece of writing you used from the previous day with a sentence added to the end of the narrative. Save this to use in the next lesson as the students work through the EOM Task. The following is an example:

It started in Kenya when Amani didn't have any books. Then the camel came to the village with some books. Now Amani has books to read.

Read your narrative. Students Think-Pair-Share about whether they hear or see any mistakes that you could fix to make your writing better. Have volunteers share their thinking.

Read the first criteria on the Narrative Checklist and ask students to give you a Nonverbal Signal if you have a resolution to the problem. Students Think-Pair-Share about this element of your narrative. Use Equity Sticks to choose volunteers to share their thinking.

- *There is a resolution to the problem.*
- *The resolution is that now Amani has books to read.*

Read the second criteria on the Narrative Checklist and ask students to give you a Nonverbal Signal if you have punctuation. Students Think-Pair-Share about this element of your narrative. Use Equity Sticks to choose volunteers to share their thinking.

- *There are periods at the end of each sentence.*
- *All the sentences are declarative sentences giving information.*

Use the color you highlighted the chart with to identify the ending punctuation for all the sentences. Place a check in the column titled *Self* and *Peer*.

Read the last criteria on the Narrative Checklist. Students Think-Pair-Share about what makes a sentence complete. Use Equity Sticks to choose volunteers to share their thinking.

- *A subject or noun.*
- *Who or what the sentence is about.*
- *A verb or action word.*
- *What the subject is doing.*
- *Any extra words to make the sentence interesting.*

Ask students to give you a nonverbal signal if they think you have complete sentences. Students Think-Pair-Share about this element of your narrative. Use Equity Sticks to choose volunteers to share their thinking.

- *I see started in sentence that is a verb.*
- *I see Amani in the sentence that is a noun or subject.*

369

Copyright © 2016 Great Minds®

G1 > M1 > Lesson 31   WIT & WISDOM™

> **TEACHER NOTE**
>
> Students may have difficulty understanding that *It* is the subject of the first sentence since it is a pronoun. Help students understand that sometimes, when we don't want to use the name of something, we use other words. Do not spend time discussing the fact that it is a pronoun, that will be covered later in the year.

Underline the nouns and circle the verbs in the sentences in the color you used to highlight the criteria on the Narrative Checklist.

✔ Distribute the Narrative Checklist to each student. Students work with the checklist and their writing, fixing any mistakes they find or adding any elements that are missing. After a sufficient amount of independent work time, students work with their partners to check their narratives. Encourage students to use the Sentence Frame they have learned to provide positive feedback to their partner. Students make any necessary changes.

Use Equity Sticks to choose two or three volunteers to share their writing for the day. Model positive feedback for the first student using the Sentence Frame the students have learned. Then allow one or two students to provide positive feedback using the Sentence Frame for the last two students.

Land

Instruct students to Think-Pair-Share, and ask: "Why is it important to edit our writing?"

Use Equity Sticks to select two pairs to share their thinking. Use their responses to reinforce that editing our writing makes it better. Explain that tomorrow they will share their finished writing with their friends.

370

Copyright © 2016 Great Minds®

WIT & WISDOM™   G1 > M1 > Lesson 32

■ FOCUSING QUESTION: LESSONS 28-32

How do books change lives around the world?

1 2 3 4 5 6 7 8 9 10 11 12 13 14 15 16 17 18 19 20 21 22 23 24 25 26 27 **28 29 30 31 32**

Lesson 32

TEXTS

- *My Librarian Is a Camel*, Margriet Ruurs
- *Museum ABC*, The Metropolitan Museum of Art
- *Tomás and the Library Lady*, Pat Mora, Raul Colón
- *Waiting for the Biblioburro*, Monica Brown, John Parra
- *That Book Woman*, Heather Henson, David Small
- *Green Eggs and Ham*, Dr. Seuss

Copyright © 2016 Great Minds®

G1 > M1 > Lesson 32　　　　　　　　　　　　　　　　　　　　WIT & WISDOM™

Lesson 32: At a Glance

AGENDA

Welcome (5 min.)

Read aloud original narratives

Launch (10 min.)

Understand the Content Framing Question

Learn (40 min.)

Participate in a Socratic Seminar (25 min.)

Excel at Using Story Elements in a Narrative (15 min.)

Land (15 min.)

Answer the Content Framing Question

Wrap (5 min.)

Assign Fluency Homework

STANDARDS ADDRESSED

The full text of ELA Standards can be found in the Module Overview.

Writing

- W.1.3

Speaking and Listening

- SL.1.1.a, SL.1.1.b

MATERIALS

- Socratic Seminar Checklist (Appendix C)

- Module 1 Story Maps

- Speaking and Listening Anchor Chart

- Handout 32A: Socratic Seminar Self-Reflection

Learning Goals

Write and speak to show understanding of the Module Learning Goals.

✔ Read completed EOM Task in small groups.

✔ Checks for Understanding

Copyright © 2016 Great Minds®

WIT & WISDOM™   G1 > M1 > Lesson 32

Prepare

FOCUSING QUESTION: Lessons 28-32

How do books change lives around the world?

FRAMING QUESTION: Lesson 32

Know: *How do all the Module 1 texts build our knowledge of how books can change lives around the world?*

CRAFT QUESTION: Lesson 32

Excel: *How can I respond to what others are saying in a Socratic Seminar?*

In the final lesson of Module 1, students express understanding of the knowledge gained through reading the Module 1 texts in a Socratic Seminar to discuss the Essential Question. They share their EOM narratives to celebrate their hard work and quality writing and learn to give positive feedback to one another.

Welcome 5 MIN.

Display the Speaking and Listening Anchor Chart. In pairs, students practice reading their original narratives aloud, using their speaking and listening strategies.

Launch 10 MIN.

UNDERSTAND THE CONTENT FRAMING QUESTION

Post the Content Framing Question and Focusing Question. Echo Read the Content Framing Question.

Explain that students will use this Content Framing Question to help guide their discussion in this lesson's Socratic Seminar.

Students Think-Pair-Share: "What's something you've notice about the way people get and use books?"

- *People get books in many different ways.*
- *People enjoy reading books.*

373

Copyright © 2016 Great Minds®

Learn 40 MIN.

PARTICIPATE IN A SOCRATIC SEMINAR

Whole Group 25 MIN.

> **TEACHER NOTE**
>
> Use the Socratic Seminar Checklist in Appendix C to assess students' participation and record anecdotal notes in the last Socratic Seminar in Module 1.
>
> For the Socratic Seminar, all texts and story elements charts need to be present. Place all charts on the board or in an area where students can view them when sitting in the Socratic Seminar circle. Lay all texts out on the floor in the middle of the circle for students to use for citing evidence. During a mini-lesson, establish a protocol for students to understand the appropriate way to access these texts.

Students form a circle. Display the Speaking and Listening Anchor Chart. Remind students that the guidelines on the Speaking and Listening Anchor Chart will help them be successful with the day's discussion.

Display and Echo Read the Craft Question: "How can I respond to what others are saying in a Socratic Seminar?"

Think-Pair-Share: "How can I to respond to what others are saying in a Socratic Seminar?"

- *I can notice pauses to let me know it's my turn to talk.*
- *I can use my whole body to listen so I know what is being discussed.*
- *I can use a Sentence Frame to begin my sentence.*
- *I can use complete sentences when I speak.*
- *I can speak loud enough to be heard.*
- *I can use a talking stick.*

Explain that everyone should respond at least once during the Socratic Seminar.

Review additional guidelines and procedures from the previous seminars and introduce new Sentence Frames and vocabulary expectations.

- Nonverbal Signals, pass the talking stick, one student at a time talks while others sit silently.
- Cite text: Model how to signal when a book needs to be used for citing a text and how to access the book from middle of the circle.

- Introduce Sentence Frames posted on Sentence Frames from past lessons and incorporate new.
  - I agree with you because _____.
  - I disagree with you because _____.
  - What makes you think that?
  - I think _____ because.
- New:
  - I like that idea because _____.

Teacher reviews Story Maps and each text briefly.

Post and Echo Read the opening question.

Students Think-Pair-Share the opening question: "How do books change lives around the world?"

Students participate in sustained dialogue using evidence from the texts read during the module.

Students discuss how the class is doing with following Socratic Seminar roles; use a physically active procedure like lining up on a spectrum for strongly agree/ disagree and folding the line to discuss with a partner.

Continue with sustained dialogue around the essential question.

Close the Socratic seminar with a self-reflection using Handout 32A: Socratic Seminar Self-Reflection.

Read each expectation aloud, providing clarity where needed, while students place an A (I always did that), S (I sometimes did that), or N (I'll do that next time) in the second column to rate their participation. Pause after students complete each row so they may Pair-Share on the following question: "Which letter did I give myself, and why?" Collect students' self-assessments and retain them to reference prior to the next Socratic Seminar. Use students' N ratings to guide class and individual goal setting.

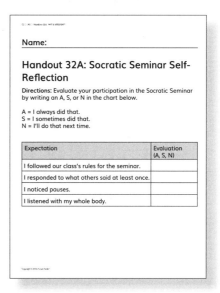

EXCEL AT USING STORY ELEMENTS IN A NARRATIVE

Small Groups 15 MIN.

Over the past few lessons, students have written, edited, and revised their original narratives about how books changed a character's life. Today is a celebration of learning. Students have the opportunity to read their narratives to others.

G1 > M1 > Lesson 32   WIT & WISDOM™

TEACHER NOTE

The oral presentations and celebration can be done in a multitude of ways. The lesson below is just one example of how to go about it. The main goal is to make this a celebration about the completion of the module and how well students have learned about the impact books have on peoples' lives. To make this sharing a special time, invite guests into the classroom, visit another classroom to read the stories, or record each student's presentation to share digitally. Planning ahead and involving the students in deciding some components of the event will help them anticipate what to expect and increase their investment in the writing.

Congratulate students on completing their stories. Share that they have the opportunity to read their stories to peers. Part of being a writer is sharing your writing.

Remind students that providing feedback is also part of being a writer.

In this lesson, students will compliment the writer using the Sentence Frame:

One thing I liked about your story was _____.

Provide a structure for students to give feedback to each other. For example, use a talking stick to take turns providing feedback one at a time.

✔ Students read their stories to each other in small groups. Remind students to practice their best speaking and listening skills.

376

Copyright © 2016 Great Minds®

WIT & WISDOM™   G1 > M1 > Lesson 32

Land 15 MIN.

ANSWER THE CONTENT FRAMING QUESTION

Know: *How do all the Module 1 texts build our knowledge of how books can change lives around the world?*

Tell students to imagine that they are a character in a book whose life was change by the books in this module. Ask: "What is your story?"

Instruct students to Think-Pair-Share.

Provide the Sentence Frame structure below and call on student volunteers to fill in the blanks.

Hold up a setting Story Stone.

It all started in . . .

▪ *Wit Elementary School*
▪ *Mrs. Wise's classroom*

Hold up a character Story Stone.

When . . .

▪ *Addison*
▪ *Alejandro*
▪ *KeShawn*

Hold up the problem Story Stone.

▪ *Didn't have books!*

Hold up the resolution Story Stone.

So . . .

▪ *Mrs. Wise gave them books about books.*
▪ *They read and read until they understood them.*
▪ *They learned all about how children around the world get books.*
▪ *They wrote their own books about books.*
▪ *They celebrated how many books they read.*

Celebrate the wonderful learning from the module.

377

Copyright © 2016 Great Minds®

Wrap

HOMEWORK CHECK-IN

Continue home reading routine. Check Fluency Homework, and remind students that their homework is the final fluency work with the poem "AB–See!"

Analyze

Context and Alignment

Students write and speak to evidence understanding of the Module Learning Goals.

Check the following artifacts holistically:

- Socratic Seminar anecdotal record.
- Revised EOM Task.

Next Steps

Review the EOM writing and assess it on the Grade 1 Writing Rubric using the criteria for narrative writing along with the module specific checklist. Use the data you generate to plan differentiated supports and interventions for students as they begin the new module.

* Note that there is no Deep Dive in this lesson. Use any additional time to support practice of the vocabulary and/or style and conventions skills introduced in the module.

Appendix A: Text Complexity

Methodology: Great Minds carefully selects module texts that are both content-rich and complex. Module texts, especially the core texts, must be appropriately challenging so that students develop their literacy skills and make progress toward Anchor Standard for Reading 10 by the end of the year. Each core module text is evaluated using quantitative and qualitative criteria as outlined in both Appendix A and the Supplement to Appendix A in the CCSS.

Core Texts:

Title and Author	*Green Eggs and Ham*, Dr. Seuss	
Description of Text	A classic Dr. Seuss story with signature rhyming, Sam-I-am insists on another character trying his green eggs and ham in different ways and in different locations.	
Complexity Ratings	Quantitative: 30Lexile	Qualitative: Meaning/Purpose: This classic narrative is a fantastical, silly story with a clear central message. It has an accessible conflict and a joyful resolution. Structure: Picture cues highlight the alternating dialogue between two speakers while rhythm and meter add structure to the narrative. Language: This book is composed of simple words and short sentences organized in rhyming and repeated lines. Knowledge Demands: The knowledge demands are minimal, as the illustrations make what is happening apparent.

Title and Author	*Museum ABC*, Metropolitan Museum of Art	
Description of Text	This stunning text is a unique ABC book that uses four different masterful works of art to describe a word for each letter of the alphabet.	
Complexity Ratings	Quantitative: Not applicable	Qualitative: Meaning/Purpose: This text provides a new twist on a traditional ABC book, with visually rich, detailed works of art from different cultures and time periods. Structure: The organization is straightforward. Language: Simple words are supported by a variety of illustrations in this text. The index offers additional information about the art. Knowledge Demands: Familiarity with the alphabet is needed.

Title and Author	*My Librarian Is a Camel: How Books Are Brought to Children Around the World*, Margriet Ruurs
Description of Text	This text is an informational book filled with interesting facts and real photographs that explore the different ways people get books through mobile libraries in thirteen countries around the world.

Complexity Ratings	Quantitative:	Qualitative:
	700Lexile	Meaning/Purpose: This information book provides a world perspective of how people access books. It also includes a small map and basic information for each country.
		Structure: The organization is straightforward. Each country has a dedicated page spread, including pictures with captions, and a sidebar with a small map and basic information such as the capital, population, and language.
		Language: There is some challenging vocabulary and country-related terms. The overall density of text is challenging.
		Knowledge Demands: The book demands knowledge of geography of certain countries and characteristics of library systems.

Title and Author	*That Book Woman*, Heather Henson, David Small
Description of Text	This picture book is the story of a young boy living in the rural Appalachian mountains who initially says he does not like books, but a curiosity about why a persistent packhorse librarian continues to deliver books leads him to decide to learn to read and discover a love for books.

Complexity Ratings	Quantitative:	Qualitative:
	920Lexile	Meaning/Purpose: Theme is clear throughout the text but is conveyed subtly over time.
		Structure: Organization of storyline is clear and easy to predict. The illustrations support and assist in interpreting the text, and the author's note provides additional background on packhorse librarians.
		Language: Many unfamiliar words with a heavy use of vocabulary in an Appalachian dialect (*a-twixt, britches, 'course*), where spelling and diction indicate geographical and economic factors; dense and complex ideas from a first person perspective. There is also some figurative language that is not supported through illustration.
		Knowledge Demands: Understanding of life in the 1930s, including living in rural areas not close to a town, no vehicles, and one-room homes, is needed.

Title and Author	*Tomás and the Library Lady*, Pat Mora, Raul Colón
Description of Text	An inspiring, true story of a young migrant worker and a kind librarian who introduces him to books–encouraging a love for learning and opening his imagination.

Complexity Ratings	Quantitative:	Qualitative:
	440L	**Meaning/Purpose:** While the narrative has a straightforward story with a clear theme, it also has more than one level of meaning, including the view outside (reality) and inside (imagination) books.
		Structure: The structure is conventional with a straightforward storyline and illustrations that support the text. The author's note provides additional background on Tomás Rivera.
		Language: Most of the language in the text is explicit and easy to understand, though there is some unfamiliar vocabulary and some Spanish terms. Sentence structure is mainly simple and compound sentences, with a few complex sentences.
		Knowledge Demands: The book includes slightly complex references to migrant experiences wherein Tomás's family has to move regularly so his parents can work. Other knowledge demands include other cultural elements of a Spanish migrant family.

Title and Author	*Waiting for the Biblioburro*, Monica Brown, John Parra
Description of Text	A story of a young girl who loves books, whose small village is visited by a traveling library. Inspired by a real-life librarian's efforts to bring books to people in rural Colombia.

Complexity Ratings	Quantitative:	Qualitative:
	880L	**Meaning/Purpose:** The narrative is a slightly complex story with multiple levels of meaning, including Ana's love for books, the struggle to get books to Ana's village, and her growth from a reader to a writer.
		Structure: The organization of the storyline is predictable. The illustrations directly support the written text, though some illustrations leave room for interpretation of the character's feelings. The author's note provides additional cultural background on the story.
		Language: The text includes simple and compound sentences, with some Spanish vocabulary that is supported with English context clues and the illustrations.
		Knowledge Demands: Understanding of the cultural elements of a Spanish family and some understanding of experiences with the library system to compare with a mobile library system are needed.

Appendix B: Vocabulary

Wit & Wisdom focuses on teaching and learning words from texts. Students develop an awareness of how words are built, how they function within sentences, and how word choice affects meaning and reveals an author's purpose.

The purpose of vocabulary study in Wit & Wisdom is to achieve the following three key student outcomes:

- Improve comprehension of complex texts.

- Increase students' knowledge of words and word parts (including affixes, Latin or Greek roots, etc.).

- Increase students' ability to solve for unknown words on their own.

In order to achieve these outcomes, vocabulary study in Wit & Wisdom emphasizes the following three categories of vocabulary words:

- **Content Vocabulary:** Necessary for understanding a central idea of the domain-specific text and/or module topic).

- **Academic Vocabulary:** High-priority words that can be used across disciplines and are likely to be encountered in other texts. Often abstract and with multiple meanings, these words are unlikely to be known by students with limited vocabularies.

- **Text-Critical Vocabulary:** Words and phrases that are essential to students' understanding of a particular text or excerpt.

Vocabulary study in Wit & Wisdom will occur within the following types of instruction:

- **Core 75-min. daily lessons:** Vocabulary study that is essential to understanding the text at hand. Instructional strategies are explicitly introduced and practiced during vocabulary instruction and put into practice during a reading of a text.

- **Vocabulary Deep Dives:** Vocabulary instruction and practice that advances students' knowledge of high-value words and word-solving strategies, focusing on aspects such as abstract or multiple meanings, connotation, relationships across words, and morphology.

Vocabulary learning is assessed indirectly through application, and directly through two-question assessments (Grades K-2) and sentence assessments (Grades 3–8). Assessment words are selected because of their importance to the module's content as well as their relevance and transferability to other texts and subject areas.

- **Indirect Assessment*:** Students are expected to use and incorporate words from the below list into their academic discourse, through speaking and listening (during Socratic Seminars) and writing (during formal writing tasks, such as the EOM Task).

- **Direct Assessment:** Teachers should make this list available to students through the Assessed Vocabulary Study Guide. (Words appear on two Assessed Vocabulary Study Guides for those grades that provide a mid- and end-of-module vocabulary assessment.)

G1 > M1 > Appendix B: Vocabulary

WIT & WISDOM™

* You will note that Indirect Assessments are not specified in Module 1; rather, there are reminders about referencing the Word Wall and bringing previously studied vocabulary into the lessons when appropriate. This is an instructional decision to reduce the cognitive load required of students, allowing them to focus on acclimating to classroom procedures and expectations. Indirect Assessments will begin in Module 2.

The following is a complete list of all words taught and practiced in the module. Those that are assessed, directly or indirectly, are indicated.

Tomás and the Library Lady

Lesson Number	Word	Content-Specific	Academic	Text Critical	Teaching Strategy	Assessment
2	character		✓		Teacher-provided definition	
2 DD	storyteller			✓	Ask questions about unknown words	
2 DD	borrow		✓		Ask questions about unknown words	Direct Vocabulary Assessment
2 DD	eager			✓	Ask questions about unknown words	Direct Vocabulary Assessment
3	setting		✓		Teacher-provided definition	
4	problem		✓		Teacher-provided definition	
4	resolution		✓		Teacher-provided definition	

384

Copyright © 2016 Great Minds®

		Content-Specific	Academic	Text Critical	Teaching Strategy	Assessment
5 DD	imagination	✓			Teacher-provided definition; Frayer Model	Direct Vocabulary Assessment
6	migrant			✓	Teacher-provided definition	Direct Vocabulary Assessment
6 DD	value			✓	Teacher-provided definition; Frayer Model	
6	encouraged			✓	Teacher-provided definition	

Waiting for the Biblioburro

Lesson Number	Word	Content-Specific	Academic	Text Critical	Teaching Strategy	Assessment
8	landscape		✓		Teacher-provided definition	
8 DD	village			✓	Ask questions about unknown words	
8 DD	burros			✓	Ask questions about unknown words	
8 DD	market			✓	Ask questions about unknown words	
8 DD	collect			✓	Ask questions about unknown words	
11 DD	inspire			✓	Teacher-provided definition; Frayer Model	Direct Vocabulary Assessment

G1 > M1 > Appendix B: Vocabulary

My Librarian Is a Camel

Lesson Number	Word	Content-Specific	Academic	Text Critical	Teaching Strategy	Assessment
13	granted			✓	Ask questions about unknown words	
13	passionate			✓	Ask questions about unknown words	
14 DD	remote			✓	Teacher-provided definition; Frayer Model	Direct Vocabulary Assessment
14, 15 DD	mobile			✓	Teacher-provided definition; Frayer Model	Direct Vocabulary Assessment

That Book Woman

Lesson Number	Word	Content-Specific	Academic	Text Critical	Teaching Strategy	Assessment
18 DD	poke			✓	Categorization	
18 DD	spell			✓	Categorization	
19 DD	scholar			✓	Frayer Model	Direct Vocabulary Assessment
21 DD	signs			✓	Categorization	Direct Vocabulary Assessment
21 DD	duck			✓	Categorization	Direct Vocabulary Assessment

Museum ABC

Lesson Number	Word	Content-Specific	Academic	Text Critical	Teaching Strategy	Assessment
24 DD	landscape	✓			Relationship mapping	Direct Vocabulary Assessment
24 DD	portrait	✓			Relationship mapping	Direct Vocabulary Assessment
24 DD	still-life	✓			Relationship mapping	Direct Vocabulary Assessment

WORDS TO KNOW

Understanding vocabulary and building background knowledge are essential for students' comprehension of complex text. Wit & Wisdom students study topics for an extended period of time, building background knowledge. However, students may need additional support with unfamiliar vocabulary as they access complex text.

The words listed here may pose a challenge to student comprehension. Provide definitions or a glossary for these challenging words so that students will comprehend complex text. Use a free resource such as Wordsmyth (**http://witeng.link/glossary**) to generate glossaries for students.

Tomás and the Library Lady, Pat Mora, Raul Colón

- migrant
- eager
- borrow
- dump
- valued

Waiting for the Biblioburro, Monica Brown, John Parra

- collects
- village
- market
- creatures

My Librarian Is a Camel, Margriet Ruurs

- remote
- mobile
- contact
- inspire

G1 > M1 > Appendix B: Vocabulary

That Book Woman, Heather Henson and David Small

- fancy
- scholar
- britches
- reckon
- yearn

Appendix C:
Answer Keys, Rubrics, and Sample Responses

TABLE OF CONTENTS

- Lessons 1–6: Focusing Question Task 1

- Lesson 7: New-Read Assessment

- Lessons 7–12: Focusing Question Task 2

- Lessons 13–16: Focusing Question Task 3

- Lesson 13: New-Read Assessment

- Lesson 16: Vocabulary Assessment 1

- Lessons 17–22: Focusing Question Task 4

- Lessons 21, 27, and 32: Socratic Seminar Grade 1 Speaking and Listening Process Rubric

- Lesson 23: New-Read Assessment

- Lessons 23–27: Focusing Question Task 5

- Lesson 28: Vocabulary Assessment 2

- Lesson 28–32: EOM Task

- Lesson 32: EOM Rubric

G1 > M1 > Appendix C: Sample Student Responses

Lessons 1–6: Focusing Question Task 1

Text: *Tomás and the Library Lady*, Pat Mora, Raul Colón

Focusing Question: *How do library books change life for Tomás?*

Prompt: Write and draw to retell the story *Tomás and the Library Lady*

Include key details about:

- Characters
- Setting
- Problem
- Resolution

(RL.1.2, RL.1.3, W.1.3, W.1.8, SL.1.1.a)

Sample Response:

It started in <u>Iowa</u> when <u>Tomás knew all of Papa Grande's stories.</u>

Then, Tomás read books from the library.

Finally, <u>he was a storyteller.</u>

Lessons 7–12: Focusing Question Task 2

Text: *Waiting for the Biblioburro*, Monica Brown, John Parra

Focusing Question: How does the Biblioburro change Ana's life?

Prompt: Write and draw to retell the story *Waiting for the Biblioburro*.

Be sure to include:

- Characters
- Setting
- Problem
- Resolution
- Complete sentences.
- End punctuation.

(RL.1.2, RL.1.3, W.1.3, W.1.8, SL.1.1.a, L.1.1.j, L.1.2.b)

Sample Response:

It started in a village when Ana had one book.

Then the Biblioburro came to the village.

Finally, Ana writes a book.

G1 > M1 > Appendix C: Sample Student Responses

Lesson 7: New-Read Assessment

Text: *Waiting for the Biblioburro*, Monica Brown, John Parra

Individually, students write and draw to formulate a question. After the Read Aloud, students write and draw to answer their question.

Answer	Relevant Standards
Questions will vary but should directly relate to the text. ▪ *Who is the man with the donkeys?* ▪ *The man is a librarian bringing books to the village.*	RL.1.1, L.1.1.j, L.1.2.b

WIT & WISDOM™   G1 > M1 > Appendix C: Sample Student Responses

Lessons 13–16: Focusing Question Task 3

Text: *My Librarian Is a Camel*, Margriet Ruurs

Focusing Question: How do people from around the world get books?

Prompt: Describe how people get books in your section of *My Librarian Is a Camel* by answering the question: "Using evidence from the photographs, how do people in this country get books?"

Be sure to:

- Include details from the photographs.
- Write complete sentences.
- Capitalize proper nouns.
- Use end punctuation.

(RI.1.1, RI.1.7, W.1.8, SL.1.1.a, SL.1.2, L.1.1.b, L.1.1.j, L.1.2.b)

Sample Student Response:

In Peru, children get books from a donkey cart.

G1 > M1 > Appendix C: Sample Student Responses

Lesson 13: New-Read Assessment

Text: *My Librarian Is a Camel*, Margriet Ruurs

In this New-Read Assessment students visually explore photographs and illustrations to formulate a question about the text *My Librarian Is a Camel*.

Individually, students write and draw to formulate a question.

Answer	Relevant Standards
Questions will vary but should directly relate to the text. 　■　*Why is the woman showing a book to a donkey?*	RI.1.1, L.1.1.j, L.1.2.b

Lesson 16: Vocabulary Assessment 1

1. *Borrow*: Can you borrow your teeth? (No)

2. *Eager*: If a girl is eager, is she sad? (No)

3. *Imagination*: Can you picture things in your imagination? (Yes)

4. *Migrant*: Is a migrant someone who moves around for work? (Yes)

5. *Inspire*: Can you inspire people with kind acts? (Yes)

6. *Remote*: Is a city a remote place? (No)

7. *Mobile*: Is a mountain mobile? (No)

8. *Migrant*: Do migrants stay in the same place? (No)

9. *Imagination*: Can you find your imagination on a map? (No)

10. *Inspire*: Can you inspire people by hiding from them? (No)

11. *Eager*: Is an eager boy ready for anything? (Yes)

12. *Mobile*: Does something that is mobile move around? (Yes)

13. *Borrow*: Can someone borrow a hammer? (Yes)

14. *Remote*: Are remote places hard to reach? (Yes)

This material is based on research from the following study and on materials based on the study created by Gail Kearns:

Kearns, Gail, & Andrew Biemiller (2010). Two-Questions vocabulary assessment: Developing a new method for group testing in kindergarten through second grade. Journal of Education, 190 (1/2), 31–41.

Lessons 17–22: Focusing Question Task 4

Text: *That Book Woman*, Heather Henson, David Small

Focusing Question: How does the packhorse librarian change life for Cal?

Prompt: Write and draw to retell the story *That Book Woman*.

Be sure to include:

- Characters
- Setting
- Problem
- Resolution
- Complete sentences.
- Capitalize the first word in a sentence and proper nouns.
- End punctuation.
- A drawing of Cal and one adjective to describe him.

(RL.1.2, RL.1.3, W.1.3, W.1.8 SL.1.1.a, L.1.1.b, L.1.1.f, L.1.1.j, L.1.2.b)

Sample Response:

It started in <u>the mountains</u> when <u>Cal did not know how to read.</u>

The Book Woman brought books to the family.

Finally, <u>Cal learns to read.</u>

WIT & WISDOM™   G1 > M1 > Appendix C: Sample Student Responses

Lessons 21, 27, and 32: Socratic Seminar Grade 1 Speaking and Listening Process Rubric

Grade 1 – Speaking and Listening Process Rubric

	4 (Exceeds expectations)	3 (Meets expectations)	2 (Partially meets expectations)	1 (Does not yet meet expectations)
Process	▪ Alternates speaking and listening in conversations through multiple exchanges. ▪ Follows all agreed-upon rules for conversations. ▪ Responds directly to what others say.	▪ Speaks in conversations through multiple exchanges. ▪ Follows most agreed-upon rules for conversations. ▪ Responds to what others say.	▪ Speaks in conversations. ▪ Follows some agreed-upon rules for conversations. ▪ Sometimes responds to what others say.	▪ Does not speak in conversations. ▪ Follows few, if any, agreed-upon rules for conversations. ▪ Rarely, if ever, responds to what others say.
Listening	▪ Eye contact and body language demonstrate interest. ▪ Can repeat back what is heard in sequence from memory.	▪ Eye contact and body language demonstrate attention. ▪ Can repeat back what is heard in sequence.	▪ Tracks speakers. ▪ Can repeat back what is heard.	▪ Sometimes tracks speakers. ▪ Doesn't remember what is heard.

397

Copyright © 2016 Great Minds®

G1 > M1 > Appendix C: Sample Student Responses

Lesson 23: New-Read Assessment

Text: *Green Eggs and Ham*, Dr. Seuss

Focusing Question: How can books change my life?

Characters	Setting	Relevant Standards
▪ *The man* ▪ *Sam*	▪ *In a house* ▪ *A box* ▪ *A car* ▪ *A tree* ▪ *A train* ▪ *A boat* ▪ *In the water*	RL.1.2, RL.1.3, RL.1.7, W.1.8, L.1.1.b, L.1.1.j, L.1.2.b
Problem	**Resolution**	
▪ *Sam wants the man to try green eggs and ham. The man doesn't want to try them.*	▪ *The man eats green eggs and ham and likes them.*	

WIT & WISDOM™   G1 > M1 > Appendix C: Sample Student Responses

Lessons 23–27: Focusing on Task 5

Text: *Green Eggs and Ham*, Dr. Seuss

Prompt: Write and draw to retell the story *Green Eggs and Ham*.

Be sure to include:

- Characters
- Setting
- Problem
- Resolution
- Temporal words.
- Complete sentences.
- Capitalize the first word in a sentence and proper nouns.
- End punctuation.
- An adjective to describe a noun.

(RL.1.2, RL.1.3, W.1.3, W.1.8, SL.1.1.a, L.1.1.b, L.1.1.f, L.1.1.j, L.1.2.b)

Sample Response

> It started in a house when the man would not eat green eggs and ham.
>
> Sam wanted the yellow man to eat the green eggs and ham.
>
> Then, the man ate the eggs and ham.
>
> Finally, the man liked the green eggs and ham.

Copyright © 2016 Great Minds®

Lesson 28: Vocabulary Assessment 2

1. *Scholar*: Can a pencil be a scholar? (No)

2. *Portrait*: Are there vegetables in a portrait painting? (No)

3. *Duck*: Can you duck your head when going under something? (Yes)

4. *Landscape*: Does a landscape painting show the beauty of nature? (Yes)

5. *Signs*: Can signs in nature predict the weather? (Yes)

6. *Still Life*: Can a still life painting show a sunset? (No)

7. *Duck*: Can you duck your new coat? (No)

8. *Landscape*: Do landscape paintings have people in them? (No)

9. *Scholar*: Do scholars study hard to learn? (Yes)

10. *Portrait*: Does a portrait painting show something important about a person? (Yes)

11. *Still Life*: Can a still life painting show objects on a table? (Yes)

12. *Signs*: Can you use signs to eat your breakfast? (No)

This material is based on research from the following study and on materials based on the study created by Gail Kearns:

Kearns, Gail, & Andrew Biemiller (2010). Two-Questions vocabulary assessment: Developing a new method for group testing in kindergarten through second grade. Journal of Education, 190 (1/2), 31–41.

WIT & WISDOM™   G1 > M1 > Appendix C: Sample Student Responses

Lesson 28–32: EOM Task

Write and illustrate a narrative about a character whose life has changed because of books.

Be sure to include:

- Characters.

- Setting from *My Librarian Is a Camel*.

- A problem (the character doesn't have books).

- The resolution to the problem (using the method for getting books from that country).

Make sure each page includes:

- Complete sentences that begin with a capital letter and end with a punctuation mark.

- Capitals at the beginning of proper nouns (names and countries).

- Illustrations to match the words on each page.

Use your best handwriting, as you will read and share your story with your classmates and teacher.

(RL.1.2, RL.1.3, W.1.3, W.1.8, SL.1.1.a, L.1.1.b, L.1.1.j, L.1.2.b)

EOM Annotated Sample Response:

It started in Pakistan when Lee did not have books. Then a white van with books came to the city. Finally, Lee went to the book van and got more books.	RL.1.3: Story elements are evident, including key details. W.1.3: The narrative includes a beginning, middle and end. It includes more than two sequenced events and includes the use of temporal words (*then, finally*).
Content knowledge: The story tells about a boy from Pakistan who doesn't have books. This demonstrates the student's knowledge of places in the world where children don't have easy access to books and get books in unconventional ways. The student demonstrates control of story elements and story sequence.	

401

Copyright © 2016 Great Minds®

Lesson 32: EOM Rubric

Grade 1 – Narrative Writing

	4 (Exceeds expectations)	3 (Meets expectations)	2 (Partially meets expectations)	1 (Does not yet meet expectations)
Structure	▪ Responds thoroughly to all elements of prompt. ▪ Recounts three or more appropriately sequenced events. ▪ Provides a more thorough sense of closure. ▪ Uses a variety of temporal words to signal event order.	▪ Responds to all elements of prompt. ▪ Recounts two or more appropriately sequenced events. ▪ Provides a sense of closure. ▪ Uses temporal words to signal event order.	▪ Responds to some elements of prompt. ▪ Recounts only one event or recounts two or more events in a confusing or unclear sequence. ▪ Attempts to provide a sense of closure but ending is unclear. ▪ Inconsistently or incorrectly uses temporal words to signal event order.	▪ Does not respond to prompt; off-topic. ▪ Does not recount any events. ▪ Does not provide closure. ▪ Does not use temporal words.
Development	With guidance and support such as collaborative planning: ▪ Includes several precise or well-chosen details to describe what happened.	With guidance and support such as collaborative planning: ▪ Includes two or more details to describe what happened.	With guidance and support such as collaborative planning: ▪ Includes one or two general details.	With guidance and support such as collaborative planning: ▪ Does not include details to describe what happened.
Style	▪ Uses a variety of adjectives effectively. ▪ Uses several words and phrases specific to the text and topic.	▪ Uses frequently occurring adjectives. ▪ Uses several words and phrases relevant to the text and topic.	▪ Attempts to use adjectives but may be improperly used. ▪ Uses 1–2 words and phrases related to the topic.	▪ Does not use adjectives. ▪ Uses limited vocabulary inappropriate to the content.
Conventions	▪ Shows consistent command of end-of-grade-level language standards for conventional written English, including mechanics, usage, and spelling; occasional errors may interfere with meaning but main points are intelligible to reader.	▪ Shows general command of end-of-grade-level language standards for conventional written English, including mechanics, usage, and spelling; some errors interfere with meaning.	▪ Shows partial command of end-of-grade-level language standards for conventional written English, including mechanics, usage, and spelling; errors interfere with meaning and some main points are not intelligible to reader.	▪ Does not show command of end-of-grade-level language standards for conventional written English, including mechanics, usage, and spelling; errors significantly interfere with overall meaning and writing is difficult to follow.

WIT & WISDOM™   G1 > M1 > Appendix C: Sample Student Responses

Socratic Seminar Checklist

Name	Speaking				Listening		Reading	Notes
	Number of Comments (tally)	Responds to What Others Say (tally)	Initiates New Idea (+)	Insightful (+)	Uses Vocabulary (tally)	Notices Pauses (+)	Whole Body Listening (+)	Cites Text (+)	
1									
2									
3									
4									
5									
6									
7									
8									
9									
10									
11									
12									
13									
14									
15									
16									
17									
18									

403

Copyright © 2016 Great Minds®

Appendix D: Volume of Reading

Students may select from these recommended titles that support the module content or themes. These texts can be used as part of small-group instruction or as part of an independent and/or choice reading program. In addition, the Volume of Reading Reflection handout located in the back of the Student Edition provides response questions for these texts.

Lexile measures are listed below when available. The Lexile code AD (Adult Directed) refers to a book that is usually read aloud to a child and includes difficult language or text elements. A text labeled with NP (Non-Prose) Lexile indicates a book with more than 50% non-standard or non-conforming prose that cannot be measured using the Lexile measurement.

Picture Books

- (340L) *Poppleton*, Cynthia Rylant
- (420L) *Rain School*, James Rumford
- (470L) *Library Lion*, Michelle Knudsen
- (480L) *Abe Lincoln: The Boy Who Loved Books*, Kay Winters
- (AD580L) *Biblioburro: A True Story from Colombia*, Jeanette Winter
- (AD650L) *Thank You, Mr. Falker*, Patricia Polacco
- (680L) *The Stone Lion*, Margaret Wild
- (NP) *Wild about Books*, Judy Sierra
- (NP) *The Library*, Sarah Stewart
- (N/A) *You Wouldn't Want to Live Without Books!* Alex Woolf

Copyright © 2016 Great Minds®

Appendix E: Works Cited

American Sign Language Dictionary, Handspeak, Web. Accessed 2016.

Brown, Monica. *Waiting for the Biblioburro*. Illus. John Parra. Berkeley: Tricycle, 2011. Print.

Henson, Heather. *That Book Woman*. Illus. David Small. New York: Atheneum Books for Young
    Readers, 2008. Print.

Mora, Pat. *Tomás and the Library Lady*. Illus. Raul Colón. New York: Dragonfly, 2000. Print.

NY Metropolitan Museum of Art. *Museum ABC*. Little, Brown for Young Readers, 2002. Print.

The Old Farmer's Almanac, Yankee Publishing, Web. Accessed 2016.

"Pack Horse Librarians." *YouTube*. SLIS Storytelling, 9 May 2013. Web. 10 Apr. 2016.

Ruffins, Ebonne. "Teaching kids to read from the back of a burro." Online video. CNN. CNN Heroes,
    26 Feb. 2010. Web. 10 Apr. 2016.

Ruurs, Margriet. *My Librarian Is a Camel: How Books Are Brought to Children around the World*.
    Honesdale: Boyds Mills, 2005. Print.

Seuss, Dr. *Green Eggs and Ham*. New York: Random House, 1960. Print.

CREDITS

Great Minds® has made every effort to obtain permission for the reprinting of all copyrighted material. If any owner of copyrighted material is not acknowledged herein, please contact Great Minds® for proper acknowledgment in all future editions and reprints of this module.

- All material from the *Common Core State Standards for English Language Arts & Literacy in History/Social Studies, Science, and Technical Subjects* © Copyright 2010 National Governors Association Center for Best Practices and Council of Chief State School Officers. All rights reserved.

- All images are used under license from Shutterstock.com unless otherwise noted.

- For updated credit information, please visit **http://witeng.link/credits**.

G1 > Module 1   WIT & WISDOM™

ACKNOWLEDGMENTS

Great Minds® Staff

The following writers, editors, reviewers, and support staff contributed to the development of this curriculum.

Ann Brigham, Lauren Chapalee, Sara Clarke, Emily Climer, Lorraine Griffith, Emily Gula, Sarah Henchey, Trish Huerster, Stephanie Kane-Mainier, Lior Klirs, Liz Manolis, Andrea Minich, Lynne Munson, Marya Myers, Rachel Rooney, Aaron Schifrin, Danielle Shylit, Rachel Stack, Sarah Turnage, Michelle Warner, Amy Wierzbicki, Margaret Wilson, and Sarah Woodard.

Colleagues and Contributors

We are grateful for the many educators, writers, and subject-matter experts who made this program possible.

David Abel, Robin Agurkis, Elizabeth Bailey, Julianne Barto, Amy Benjamin, Andrew Biemiller, Charlotte Boucher, Sheila Byrd-Carmichael, Jessica Carloni, Eric Carey, Janine Cody, Rebecca Cohen, Elaine Collins, Tequila Cornelious, Beverly Davis, Matt Davis, Thomas Easterling, Jeanette Edelstein, Kristy Ellis, Moira Clarkin Evans, Charles Fischer, Marty Gephart, Kath Gibbs, Natalie Goldstein, Christina Gonzalez, Mamie Goodson, Nora Graham, Lindsay Griffith, Brenna Haffner, Joanna Hawkins, Elizabeth Haydel, Steve Hettleman, Cara Hoppe, Ashley Hymel, Carol Jago, Jennifer Johnson, Mason Judy, Gail Kearns, Shelly Knupp, Sarah Kushner, Shannon Last, Suzanne Lauchaire, Diana Leddy, David Liben, Farren Liben, Jennifer Marin, Susannah Maynard, Cathy McGath, Emily McKean, Jane Miller, Rebecca Moore, Cathy Newton, Turi Nilsson, Julie Norris, Galemarie Ola, Michelle Palmieri, Meredith Phillips, Shilpa Raman, Tonya Romayne, Emmet Rosenfeld, Jennifer Ruppel, Mike Russoniello, Deborah Samley, Casey Schultz, Renee Simpson, Rebecca Sklepovich, Amelia Swabb, Kim Taylor, Vicki Taylor, Melissa Thomson, Lindsay Tomlinson, Melissa Vail, Keenan Walsh, Julia Wasson, Lynn Welch, Yvonne Guerrero Welch, Emily Whyte, Lynn Woods, and Rachel Zindler.

Early Adopters

The following early adopters provided invaluable insight and guidance for Wit & Wisdom:

- Bourbonnais School District 53 • Bourbonnais, IL
- Coney Island Prep Middle School • Brooklyn, NY
- Gate City Charter School for the Arts • Merrimack, NH
- Hebrew Academy for Special Children • Brooklyn, NY
- Paris Independent Schools • Paris, KY
- Saydel Community School District • Saydel, IA
- Strive Collegiate Academy • Nashville, TN
- Valiente College Preparatory Charter School • South Gate, CA
- Voyageur Academy • Detroit, MI

Design Direction provided by Alton Creative, Inc.

Project management support, production design, and copyediting services provided by **ScribeConcepts.com**

Copyediting services provided by Fine Lines Editing

Product management support provided by Sandhill Consulting